# TIPTOEING THROUGH THE COLD WAR

## A veteran correspondent looks back

# By Colin McIntyre

Tiptoeing Through the Cold War
Colin McIntyre

*To Sigi, Stefanie and Alex.*

# Contents

1. REUTERS ...............................................................1

2. GOING ABROAD.................................................9

3. STEPPING INTO THE COLD WAR .........................12

4. BERLIN ...............................................................19

5. LIFE IN THE GDR................................................26

6. THE TWO GERMANIES START TALKS ....................41

7. COLD WAR IN A HOT CLIMATE ...........................57

8. TIMOR.................................................................60

9. VIETNAM, LAOS, CAMBODIA................................63

10. TIMOR REVISITED ............................................74

11. RETURN TO THE "COLD" COLD WAR .................78

12. CZECHOSLOVAKIA.............................................81

13. ROMANIA .........................................................93

14. ALBANIA............................................................99

15. BULGARIA .......................................................106

16. POLAND ..........................................................109

17. IRELAND...........................................................117

18. GOING NORTH .................................................127

19. THE STATE TAKES ON THE CHURCH...................140

20. NEW ANGLO-IRISH AGREEMENT IN TROUBLE................144

21. THE MOTHER OF PARLIAMENTS.............................149

22. THATCHER GOES TO MOSCOW ................................155

23. THE EAST BLOC CRACKS ..........................................160

24. 1989, REVOLUTION YEAR .........................................173

25. IRON CURTAIN BREACHED ......................................177

26. THE WALL COMES DOWN ........................................180

27. CEAUSESCU FALLS ....................................................187

28. ALBANIA JOINS THE FUN .........................................193

29. FREE ELECTIONS .......................................................198

30. GOODBYE IVAN .........................................................206

31. YUGOSLAVIA...............................................................210

32. BOSNIA .......................................................................217

33. KOSOVO......................................................................225

34. BELGRADE HIT ...........................................................236

35. OVERTHROW OF MILOŠEVIĆ....................................248

EPILOGUE ........................................................................251

Acknowledgments...........................................................254

# 1. REUTERS

If you walked into the 4$^{th}$ floor of Reuters news agency in the 1960s, you could visit most of the world in a few minutes. The World Desk, as it was then called, sucked in news from Europe, Africa and the Middle East, knocked it into shape and sent it back out again. With regional desks packed together on a single floor of a building spanning just one small block of central London, it was noisy, chaotic, and, for the dozen graduate trainees joining in 1967, quite terrifying.

Entering the imposing headquarters at 85 Fleet St, one had a strong sense of British Empire, or, since that was long gone, British Commonwealth. This was hardly surprising as the iconic building was designed by Edwin Lutyens, who played a major part in the design of New Delhi. It also reflected the current owners of Reuters, the world's second oldest news agency at the time we were starting our careers: the British, Australian and New Zealand press.

The agency was founded in 1851 by Paul Julius Reuter, a German who made his name and fortune using carrier pigeons to fly stock market prices to cover a gap in the telegraph line between Brussels and Aachen, giving French and German investors who subscribed to his service a handy time advantage. Shortly afterwards Reuter moved his operation to London, the financial centre of the Victorian world, and began adding major items of general news, of the kind that move financial markets in a big way. This gave Reuters an advantage over a small group of other agencies specialising in economic and financial news, including Havas, the world's oldest founded in Paris in 1835, which became Agence France Press. An early Reuters scoop was news of a major British victory in the Crimean war in 1855.

But the news break that sealed the company's reputation was the assassination off Abraham Lincoln on April 14, 1865. The news took 12 days to reach Europe by sea, but Reuters' subscribers got it hours ahead of anyone else. The company's American agent was too late for the departure of the British mail steamer from New York, but pursued the ship in a hired tugboat, threw his report aboard, and it was dropped into the sea in a sealed container off the Irish coast, picked up by nets and relayed on a private line to Cork, and on to London. While news scoops back then could be measured in days, or even weeks, by the time we were starting at Reuters they were in hours, rarely, or minutes. By the end of the 20th century, with advances in electronic communication, they were measured in seconds, or nanoseconds, particularly for top financial news.

By the time Reuters was taken over by the British national and regional press, along with those of Australia and New Zealand, early in the 20th century, it was handling both financial and general news from all over the world. It was charging newspapers and broadcasters for access to foreign news that only a few big papers could afford to cover through their own correspondents. It competed on the world stage with three other major players – the Associated Press and the United Press of America, which were backed by U.S. newspapers, and Agence France Press, funded by the French government.

Fleet Street, where we were based, had been the centre of Britain's newspaper industry for over 300 years. Located on a direct route between the City of London financial centre and the government at Westminster, and with the main law courts within walking distance, it was the ideal place to pick up the latest gossip.

With history weighing heavily on our shoulders, the class of '67 began their training. Most of us had foreign languages, a major requirement for graduates coming in with no journalistic experience. We were expected to pick up the craft of journalism and head off into the world, hitting the ground running with whatever language was required.

Our initial training could only be described as rudimentary. It involved a couple of days of lectures by a former Australian naval commander, covering various wider aspects of journalism without mentioning any of its techniques. In fairness to Reuters, within a few years the training was expanded to an intensive five-week course centred on writing and editing.

We were divided into two groups, covering either general news or economic news. We were strongly advised that if we wanted to get on, and particularly abroad, the second group was the one to go for. Three years previously Reuters' specialist financial reporters and technicians had come up with an electronic desk-top box that enabled stockbrokers around the world to get the latest prices at the touch of a button. The device was taking off, and Reuters was starting to earn serious money, for the first time in its history.

Ignoring the advice, I headed for the World Desk on the fourth floor, which was divided into a multitude of different units. There was the chief sub-editor's desk, handling the day's main stories from correspondents abroad, the lead subs' desk, looking at other important incoming stories, and the down-table subs, who handled the rest. Then came the Africa and Middle East desks, compiling Reuters' outgoing services to the two regions, and Regional Unit, which mainly took copy coming in from Francophone and Portuguese-run Africa, where we did not have our own correspondents but relied mainly on part-time "stringers", often civil servants or government employees. There was also a features desk and a French desk, which translated the file for Francophone clients. It was a resoundingly male environment, the imbalance not helped by our intake of 11 graduates, all men. Many of the staff had seen war service, at least one had taken part in the Allied D-Day landings in France in 1944. One taciturn senior journalist, when asked if he had ever been to Germany, would reply "only at night".

It was a fully paper-led operation. All these desks sent their copy, thrashed out on typewriters, to rows of teleprinter operators who punched out the stories onto tape which was then fed out to the world. A hard copy of the outgoing stories was printed on a long roll which was cut up into individual reports by messengers and stored on appropriate clips.

If you needed some background material while editing a story, a messenger brought you the clip.

Speaking French, I was called to the Regional Unit, which turned out to be a useful place to learn some of the basics of journalism. Reports from Francophone Africa came trickling in, often long rambling speeches by a government official, unedited, and it was then a case of "find the story". Some had a surprise in the tail, such as "at the end of the speech there was a disturbance in which an unknown number of people are thought to have died". After a couple of months it was moving on to the Africa desk, which transmitted the main world stories and added items of regional or local commercial interest. In the absence of any electronic means of editing, it was a true cut-and-paste operation, sticking the items together to be sent back to the punchers. The guidance for story selection, given by an elderly journalist who was unlikely to have spent much time in Africa, was simple: "They are interested in three things – "Gold, diamonds, and sex." Similar advice was given when I moved on to the Middle East desk a month later. This time it was "Oil, gold, and sex."

By the time I returned to London from abroad five years later all three operations had been transformed, and within a few years the editing had moved to the regions, with many more correspondents, and a lot more local knowledge.

The desk the trainees aspired to was the London Reporting bureau, the only place for general news journalists to get to do real reporting. The bureau was not even in the Reuters building but located a few blocks away after being forced to move for lack of space in 85 Fleet Street. There we were sharing space with the Press Association, the domestic British news agency, which owned the building. The move out was also aimed at encouraging the London desk to act as a true foreign bureau. Reinforcing this, the bureau chief refused to take telephone calls from the World Desk, apart from true emergencies, and insisted on electronic messages in the same way as other bureaus were contacted. I happened to be working in the bureau when it was involved in the devaluation of the British pound in 1967, a huge story for the financial desks but also for general news, as it affected everyone from tourists to shoppers and pensioners. I remember being sent to 10 Downing Street, the Prime Minister's official office and residence, in anticipation of possible public demonstrations. Unbelievably in these security-conscious times I was able to walk into the street, close to the Houses of Parliament, and up to the famous door, like any other member of the public. The heavy iron gates blocking the entrance to the street were not erected until 1989, following an increase in violence by Irish Republic Army guerrillas, and only after a heated debate over whether public access should be barred at all.

One other desk where all trainees had to spend time was involved in handling messages to and from the foreign bureaus, and other parts of Reuters. My month coincided with the killing of two young Reuter journalists in Vietnam during the 1968 communist Tet offensive, and involved sending condolence messages to family members in the UK and Australia, their home countries. An early reality check.

For meals during lunchtime and evening breaks, depending on which shift one was on, there was a canteen for the ordinary staff, and a top-floor dining room for the executives. But many journalists were drawn, hardly kicking and screaming, towards the more traditional Fleet Street lunch, a couple of pints of beer and conversation in one of the dozens of pubs that littered the street. At one time there were reported to be one every 100 metres. Many had been around for centuries and had been frequented by historic figures such as the novelist Charles Dickens, the 17th century essayist Samuel Pepys and Dr Samuel Johnson, who compiled the first English dictionary in the 18th century. One pub on the street was designed by Sir Christopher Wren, who rebuilt St Paul's Cathedral after it was damaged in the Great Fire of London in 1666, for the stone masons working on another of his reconstructions, St Brides Church, which was also destroyed by the fire. Each news organisation tended to keep to one pub, but there was plenty of mingling. One pub was locally known as the "Stab in the Back", another was notorious for being the place where journalists were fired by their editors. There was even a pub at the back of the Reuters building, The Cogers, which could be accessed through a series of corridors and stairways without leaving the building, if you knew how. One popular pub around the corner was known to be owned by the former driver of London gangster Jack Spot, a gift from a grateful boss for his contribution to crime. From time to time the entrance would be filled by a number of large men with hard faces who would disappear silently into a back room. A favourite with Reuters journalists was a dingy cellar with no formal name, once the dive bar of a pub that became a pizzeria. The pub was known locally as Mrs Moon's, after its formidable landlady who ran it like a private club. The slightest wobble coming down the steep staircase from the street, clear signs of drunkenness for her, and you were barred, sometimes for days, even if you were a regular. One good reason for its popularity, apart from its proximity to our office, was that it served "real ale", from the Young's brewery across the river, traditional beer which was naturally fizzy while still fermenting in the barrel. This was at a time when real ale was hard to find as the big breweries had gone over to producing filtered and pasteurised beer with the bubbles added by carbon dioxide, easier to produce in bulk. After one of the most successful consumer campaigns in history in the 1970s, the brewers were forced to give in to public taste and reinstate the old methods.

Many in the UK tended to automatically associate journalism with excessive drinking, prompting one critic to remark: "Fleet Street is not run on printing ink, it is run on alcohol."

Others took a more charitable view of a profession whose members often worked irregular hours with one eye constantly on the competition. Journalist Peter Corrigan, looking back over the past decades as his paper the Observer joined others moving out of the street in the 1980s, wrote: "But this fine industry, which for so long has served the entire nation with some of the world's great newspapers – and others – from this tiny patch of London, has received more help than hiccup from the many licensed premises so close to hand." He noted that the office pub often served as "oasis, intensive care unit, ego massage parlour, moneylender, bureau de change and job centre". A reporter could get the sack in the morning and know exactly in which pub to start trawling for a new job.

Apart from the pubs, there were some private drinking clubs, mostly open in the afternoon, offering refreshment outside the restrictive pub opening hours at the time, 10.30am to 2.30pm and 6.30pm to 10.30pm. The restrictions were eventually relaxed in the 1980s and abolished in 2005. A favourite drinking haunt was the City Golf Club, located just off Fleet St, where golfers could hit against screens before moving to the bar. Gradually the screens disappeared, but the bar remained. For a £1 fee, you could join for life. The club eventually morphed into the City Snooker Club, which started out with several tables that gradually disappeared to leave more room for drinkers. It was not as though people needed a drink all the time. It was more a rebellion against pub-opening times, particularly by the many journalists and print-workers forced to work odd, "unsocial" hours. The opening and closing times had remained unchanged since they were introduced during the First World War because of government fears that munitions workers were spending too much time drinking. A glorious bid by Reuters' journalists to beat the system came during a fire drill, when we had to leave the building in an orderly fashion and return half an hour later. The time had been carefully selected by World Desk's senior editors to ensure we could not get a drink. As we milled outside, a voice yelled "Wolsey's Wine Bar", and indeed it was open. Bottles of wine were ordered and drunk at speed and we returned to work, feeling happy to have outsmarted our bosses, who, not surprisingly, were furious.

One curious drinking place was the Print-Workers' Club, which was open during the night for printers working the newspaper presses, and journalists working an overnight shift. Again, entry was £1 at the door for lifetime membership. The printers had plenty of free time as their unions had succeeded over the years in negotiating deals including over-generous manning levels and other restrictive practices which made them among the wealthiest workers in the country. They eventually became an embarrassment to the rest of the union movement, and there were few tears shed when the national papers left the street to introduce much-needed new technology to the industry with different unions. Another spot for night-owls was Smithfield wholesale meat market, an easy walk away, whose pubs served the men who worked from the early hours setting up their stalls.

## 2. GOING ABROAD

Nine months after joining, aged 24 with little practical journalism under my belt, I was told I was being sent to Brussels for an estimated two-week assignment because the correspondent destined for the post had a temporary health problem. I was told I would have a language test by the head of the French desk, which was staffed by experienced French nationals who rarely got posted abroad and watched with gloomy resignation as youthful and undertrained graduate trainees headed off to the far corners of the world. My spoken French was not great, despite a recent boost through close proximity to a French au pair. The verdict was "it's not very good, but probably good enough for Reuters", and I was sent home to pack.

Walking through the door of our office in Brussels, I was greeted with: "Hi, ring the station to ask about trains to Spa tomorrow, you're covering the Belgian Formula One Grand Prix." The next day I headed for the town in the Ardennes forest that gave the name to spas around the world, and was known to the Romans, to report a sport about which I knew nothing. As the race began I tried to catch sight of the drivers as they flashed past, feeling increasingly nervous. After about three laps a man from the London Daily Telegraph, who had been watching me, commented: "You've never done this before, have you." It was pointless to deny it, and he went on to explain that I needed only to enter the number on the side of each car in the position it passed on each lap. As cars were overtaken or dropped out, this gave an instant read-out at the end of the race. It was won eventually by New Zealander Bruce McLaren in one of his own cars, after Britain's Jackie Stewart was well ahead but ran out of fuel in the penultimate lap. Having phoned through my story, I headed home, after gratefully accepting a lift to the station from one of the Belgian journalists. This proved to be a mistake, as he and three other large colleagues who piled in insisted on taking a spin around the circuit at full speed in a flabbily sprung family car. Belgium had the worst record for traffic deaths in Europe, unsurprising as they only introduced a driving test in 1977.

Back in the office the expected two weeks stretched to three months. There was not a lot going on in the summer months, known in Fleet Street as the "silly season". The French equivalent, apparently, was "return of the sea serpents". While three or four economic news reporters crunched the financial and commodity data coming from the EU's various bodies, the general news was scarce. One of the few regular items was reporting serious car accidents involving British nationals on Belgian roads (see above), reflecting Reuters' policy at the time giving prominence to home-interest stories that lasted well into the 1980s. Covering these stories threw up one of the constant problems for foreign reporters in Belgium, the language divide. The country of just over 11 million people is split between Dutch-speaking Flanders and French-speaking Wallonia, with Brussels officially bi-lingual. A large wall map of Belgium was essential for any Brussels-based reporter to locate an accident or other item of news, and establish which part of the country it was in. To call the local police in Flemish territory and begin talking French would be greeted with silence, or an abrupt end to the call. The accepted drill was to open the conversation in English, ask if they spoke the language, and if not, ask whether the conversation could be in French. In almost all cases this was accepted by local officials, aware that Flemish, a local version of Dutch, was not widely spoken outside the region. In Brussels Flemish nationalists regularly insisted that the dual-language status of the capital, though in practice French dominated, be reinforced. On a few occasions I was heading for the door after a long routine news conference in French when a Flemish journalist would leap up from the back and ask for everything to be translated.

Occasionally I would be on my own in the general news section of the bureau when the bureau chief visited Strasbourg in France, where the European Parliament was located. It was during one of these periods that

I woke on August 21 to the news that 250,000 Warsaw Pact troops had invaded Czechoslovakia to crush the "Prague Spring" of reformist Communist leader Alexander Dubček and his dreams of "Socialism with a human face". The move sent shockwaves around the world, and immediate calls for a response from NATO – which was based in Brussels. My calls to NATO HQ were met with no comment. It was not until the first week in November that the 15 member states of the Western alliance at the time came up with a response, which was, basically, to do nothing.

While the invasion prompted our bureau chief to race back to Brussels, it sent me in another direction, to Vienna, and an introduction to the Cold War that would remain the background to most of my 34 years in journalism.

# 3. STEPPING INTO THE COLD WAR

In 1946, a year after the end of the Second World War in Europe, Britain's wartime leader Winston Churchill declared: "From Stettin in the Baltic to Trieste in the Adriatic, an iron curtain has descended across the Continent." The remark, made during a visit to the United States, is widely seen as signalling the start of the Cold War as the British leader recognised that the Soviet Union, his wartime ally, was quietly transforming the political face of Europe by forcing countries under its occupation to turn communist.

Austria, in the heart of Europe, became the geographic centre of the Cold War as the curtain fell on neighbouring Czechoslovakia and Hungary and near-neighbours Poland and Romania, which remained under Moscow's control for the next 45 years. Austria itself was partly occupied by Soviet forces at the end of the war, along with those of the other three victorious allies Britain, France and the USA. Like Germany and Berlin, the country and capital were divided into four sectors each occupied by one of the Allies, but the occupation ended in 1955 after Austria agreed to become a neutral country. Evidence of a Soviet presence was everywhere, particularly a huge Soviet war memorial in the square directly in front of the Reuters office in a building in central Vienna with an ornate lift dating back to the heyday of the Austrian empire.

Though there was little evidence of war damage in the Austrian capital when I arrived, in 1945 U.S. and British planes dropped over 80,000 tonnes of bombs on the city, destroying 12,000 buildings and leaving some 270,000 people homeless. Over 300 bombs fell on the world's oldest zoo at Schönbrunn, the Imperial summer palace, killing two thirds of the 3,000 animals.

I recalled watching the classic 1949 film "The Third Man", shot in war-damaged Vienna, about a notorious American black marketeer hiding out in the Soviet sector, with its haunting musical theme. During a later spell in Vienna I heard an interview on the car radio with Anton Karas, the local zither player who performed the theme tune. Karas described how he auditioned for British director Carol Reed but failed to impress him with his virtuoso pieces. He finally gave up, disconsolately plucking out his routine warm-up exercise, at which point Reed shouted "That's it!", and history was made as the theme went on to top international music charts.

Its geographic position and history made Vienna the obvious choice for Reuters as the main bureau to cover what was widely referred to as Eastern Europe, even though much of the Soviet Bloc was located in central Europe. Vienna also covered Yugoslavia, officially communist but outside Moscow's influence after its long-time leader Josip Broz Tito quit the Communist International in 1948 and introduced wide-ranging reforms to the system.

It was against this background that I headed to Vienna, knowing little of the history of the region. My job was to look after the bureau while our correspondents were covering the invasion fall-out in Prague. But my first move on arrival in the city was to head to the Hungarian embassy for a visa to allow me to cover a football match, the final of what was then known as the Inter-Cities Fairs Cup in Budapest, where we lacked a full-time London-based correspondent, relying on a locally based "stringer".

The next day I headed for Hungary with no time to read up on the country and its history. Two main facts stood out in my mind – it was on Hitler's side during World War Two, and a popular uprising against the Communist rule in 1956 was brutally crushed by Soviet tanks. Neither offered great encouragement to a young Australian on his first visit behind the Iron Curtain.

Arriving in Budapest, I went straight to the office of the national news agency MTI to organise someone to take down and transmit to Vienna my report of the match between Leeds United and Hungarian champions Ferencváros. Since a leading British club was involved, Reuters wanted a virtual running report of the game, particularly for the British regional press which could not afford to send their own reporters. I met my copytaker, a delightful young female journalist who spoke perfect English, and the next day the match passed without a hitch, with Leeds winning 1-0 on aggregate after finishing 0-0. I left Budapest having enjoyed the city, food, wine and people, giving me a rather too rosy picture of life in the East Bloc. Over my the next 30-odd years mainly reporting this part of the world, Hungary pursued a relatively relaxed and liberal form of communism, and the country was destined to play a key role in the overthrow of communist rule in Europe.

Back in Vienna, I handled routine reports from other East Bloc countries where we had no full correspondent, Romania, Bulgaria and Albania, and relied on their national news agencies.

Communication was largely through telex, a system of sending written messages using teleprinters rather than phones. It involved punching out a tickertape which was then fed through a telegraph line. Sometimes the stories were tapped out on a "blind puncher", which showed no hard copy of the article as it was being typed. To use this required some expertise in reading punched tape, which I was forced to pick up after having to rewrite several stories from the beginning interrupted by a telephone call or a knock at the door. The main advantages of the telex system were that most post offices across the world in the 1970s and 80s, however remote, had a telex machine, transmission was cheap, and interference by state security services less likely provided you could punch out your own tape. The system was eventually phased out in the 1980s with the development of the fax machine.

The main focus of my work however was to handle reports coming from our correspondents in Prague, my first experience of Czechoslovakia, checking them before passing them on to London.

Like many in the West expecting ordinary Czechs to reflect the drabness of life as portrayed in the Soviet Union and elsewhere in East Europe, pictures and TV footage showed they were pretty much like us.

Fashionably dressed, many speaking foreign languages, those interviewed by Western media constantly reminded everyone that their country was situated geographically to the west of Vienna, and therefore hardly the East. Between the World Wars Czechoslovakia, created in 1918 from the ruins of the Austro-Hungarian empire, enjoyed one of the strongest democracies and most developed economies in Europe. But after the communist takeover in 1948 there was little tourist travel to a country that staged Stalinist show trials and executed 10 leading officials in the 1950s and was ruled by hard-line communists through most of the 60s.

The invasion itself was a relatively bloodless event, with 137 killed and 500 seriously wounded after Dubček called on people not to resist, and they themselves decided armed resistance against such massive force was futile. People opted instead for a country-wide policy of non-violent resistance, with road signs painted over or turned around to confuse the invading troops.

A first-hand account of the invasion came from a journalist working at the national news agency CTK as they reported the invasion to the world. Speaking to Prague radio on the anniversary of the invasion, Jan Krčmář said he was woken by a neighbour, turned on his radio and heard someone speaking bad Czech announce the Warsaw Pact armies had "come to the assistance of Czechoslovak patriots".

Rushing to the office, the journalists worked until late "because the Russians couldn't find us, people had taken down road signs. They had maps, but when they asked for directions they were sent in the opposite direction". After preparing two reports, that Russians were entering the building and that this was the final report from "free CTK", the door opened "and a small figure with a helmet right down to his eyes and with a coat down to his feet brandishing an automatic rifle, came in and just stood there, probably as scared as we were". They sent out the first message, but another man in civilian clothes yelled "Stop! Stop!" and tore off the tape before all of the second was transmitted.

Three years later Jan, known to all as Johnny, was Reuters local correspondent in Prague, and later still a much-travelled reporter based in Vienna.

There were sporadic acts of violence in Czechoslovakia over the next few months, and a handful of self-immolations, including that of Jan Palach, a 20-year-old student, in January 1969. His funeral turned into a major protest against the invasion, and the 20th anniversary of his death in 1989 sparked a week of demonstrations considered one of the catalyst protests leading up to the fall of communism in Czechoslovakia 10 months later.

Many Czechs tried to engage with the ordinary soldiers, speaking Russian which was a compulsory subject in schools. Many of the soldiers were drawn from distant Soviet central Asian republics, and some were clearly confused at being met with hostility rather than welcomed with open arms. The official justification for the invasion was the so-called Brezhnev doctrine which obliged communist countries to go to the aid of another where the system was under threat. The invasion, according to the Soviet version, was in response to an appeal for help from the Czechoslovak Communist Party.

Among the combined Warsaw Pact troops called up for the invasion were units from East Germany, but they were held at the border, indicating Soviet awareness of the sensitivity of a German military presence in Czechoslovakia 30 years after the brutal Nazi occupation of the country.

For foreign journalists covering the event, particularly those used to battling against East Bloc officialdom and security, it was a welcome change to be greeted as friends by Czech authorities. With borders closed, many journalists were queuing at crossing points trying to talk their way in. One British reporter, using a ballpoint pen, changed "journalist" to "pharmacist" in his passport – back then listing occupations was obligatory – and got in. I saw the passport later, even someone half-blind could see the fakery. An American journalist well known in the region had taken the opportunity on a previous visit to drop by a leading Czech glass crystal manufacturer and held a letter inviting him back to discuss a major sales contract. He was waved through by guards who almost certainly knew his true profession. A decade later I had a similar experience while covering a short-lived revolution in Poland sparked by the independent trade union Solidarity.

Reuters had another correspondent in the country unbeknown to them, a London-based sports journalist who was visiting a small town away from Prague with a local youth football team when the invasion happened, and immediately left the country to return home. When he finally checked in with head office he was hauled in and grilled by a senior editor. The result was a story beginning "The chamber-maid ran across my hotel room and handed me a red rose, saying 'take this and remember Czechoslovakia'."

The invasion caused an estimated 300,000 largely qualified people to emigrate to a variety of Western countries, where they were accepted with few formalities and open arms. It also led to the stationing of 75,000 Soviet troops in Czechoslovakia, with 30,000 family members, an ever-present threat until the overthrow of the Communist Party in 1989 when they began leaving to the sound of wild cheering.

As the situation in Prague began to settle into the "normalisation" that was to follow a year or two later as the last traces of the reform movement were snuffed out, our correspondents returned to Vienna, and I received my next orders. Proceed to London, then to Bonn, the capital of West Germany, for a thorough briefing, and then on to East Berlin, the capital of Communist East Germany, formed in 1949 as the German Democratic Republic (GDR) but not recognised by the West until 1974, to take over the bureau. It transpired that Reuters had picked another young correspondent for the East Berlin job but got cold feet at the last minute when it dawned on them that he was the son of a former British ambassador to Prague who had been frequently quoted on British media loudly condemning the Soviet invasion. Thus, for the second time in my brief journalistic career, I was taking over a job after the original choice had dropped out. And I would be the only accredited correspondent working for a Western media organisation in my new home.

On a flying visit to London I had a brief meeting with Reuters' intimidating General Manager Gerald Long, a senior news executive whispered "try and keep your f***ing to the West" and handed me a card with his home number "if you are in trouble", and I was headed for Bonn.

# 4. BERLIN

If Vienna was the geographic centre of the Cold War, Berlin was its symbolic heart, if for nothing else because of the infamous Wall that divided the city into communist and capitalist halves, blocking escape from the communist East.

I flew into West Berlin, landing at Tempelhof airport in the centre, a perfect introduction to the troubled history of the divided city. The airport's main terminal, rebuilt by the Nazis, was once one of the largest structures in Europe. It had been used to test some of the world's first aircraft, housed prisoners-of-war in World War Two, provided a vital lifeline to West Berliners during the Cold War, and was later to become temporary home to thousands of refugees from the Middle East and Africa

Berlin during the Cold War was a surreal place. Like Germany itself, it was divided into four sectors between the victorious World War Two allies Britain, France, the USA and the Soviet Union. The three Western allies took control of newly-created West Germany but the former German capital Berlin, located in the east of the country, ended up stuck in the Soviet zone, which became East Germany, officially the German Democratic Republic. West Germany was thus forced to move its capital to Bonn, a small town on the River Rhine.

West Berlin ended up marooned 160 kilometres inside communist East Germany, with a few designated road, rail and canal links to the west and three air corridors, which were used by planes of USA, France and Britain. In one of the many anomalies in the confused situation surrounding the city's status, communist Poland's state airline LOT was also allowed to use the corridors to fly to London and Paris from East Berlin's Schönefeld airport. This was in recognition of the contribution Polish airmen made to the Allied cause during World War Two, with 145 joining the Royal Air Force in the Battle of Britain in 1940. One of them,

Antoni Glowacki, shot down five German planes in one day, becoming one of only four pilots to achieve this during the battle.

In 1948 the Soviet Union tried to force the Allies out of West Berlin by blocking the road and rail links. Using the air corridors, which were guaranteed by treaty, the Allies organised The Berlin Airlift which kept the city alive for a whole year, flying in 400,000 tonnes of supplies, two-thirds of it coal. At the height of the airlift an Allied aircraft landed in Berlin every minute, unloaded in 20-30 minutes.

But the structure in Berlin that imprinted the city in public consciousness was the Wall, Die Mauer, the single most potent symbol of the Cold War. It started going up overnight on August 13, 1961, ordered by East German leader Walter Ulbricht to stop East Germans fleeing to the west -- though officially as a protective barrier against Western "fascism" from the Nazi era. People woke the next day to find themselves separated from family, friends, work and even homes. Up until then there was a massive border fence between the two Germanies, but nothing between the two parts of Berlin. While the city remained open it provided a permanent escape route. An estimated three million East Germans had made use of it since the country was formed in 1949.

Reuters East Berlin, which opened in 1959, was first to report the Wall to the world. Our correspondent Adam Kellett-Long had cited rumours circulating in both parts of the city that drastic action was imminent, but there was no hard evidence. At about 1 a.m. on August 13 he received an anonymous phone call in German saying simply: "I strongly advise you not to go to bed tonight." Soon afterwards the office teleprinter sprang into life with a report from the ADN news agency citing a Warsaw Pact communique urging "effective control" around Berlin. Hurrying to the border, Adam found that the main Brandenburg Gate crossing-point to the west was closed. The Wall was about to go up.

Within a few days a wall 140 kilometres long and 3.6 metres high had gone up across the city. It was in fact two walls, with another some 100 metres inside the East enclosing "the death strip", patrolled by hundreds of guard dogs. For the next three decades the wall was a continuous source of stories as desperate easterners climbed over it or tunnelled under it to escape. An estimated 5,000 succeeded, including over a thousand border guards. Around 200 people died in the attempt. Among the more spectacular escapes was the railway worker who drove a steam engine across the border, a soldier who took a tank through the barricades, and a man who sailed across on a zip-wire, then flew an ultralight plane back to pick up his brother. In the most successful mass escape, 57 people crawled through a tunnel built by students in the West over two days.

Berlin was not just divided by a wall across the city centre but encircled by another barrier cutting the city off from surrounding East Germany. At some point, driving in West Berlin, you came up against a wall. There was even an invisible border across the middle of the Wannsee, one of the most popular lakes on the edge of West Berlin. On one shore westerners sailed and swam, taking care not to stray too far, while the other side was a restricted area closed to easterners, as a police boat patrolled the middle. West Berliners in boats or even inflatable rafts often floated over to the wrong side, where they were immediately arrested. The western part of the underground railway at one point passed through a section of East Berlin, speeding through dark tunnels guarded by soldiers to prevent escapes. The overhead S-Bahn railway which ran through both parts of the city was controlled and staffed, inexplicably, by East Germans. At Friedrichstrasse S-Bahn station in East Berlin, a large waiting room where western visitors bid farewell to relatives and friends in the east was nicknamed the "Palace of Tears". There were several crossing points in the wall, including Checkpoint Charlie for foreigners, one for West Germans (West Berliners were not allowed to visit the eastern part), and one specifically for coffins. Allied personnel in uniform could cross at any time, with no controls.

To add to the confusion, there were Allied military missions in Potsdam, East Germany bordering West Berlin, staffed by intelligence officers authorised to travel the country apart from a few areas off-limits, particularly those housing the estimated 380,000 Soviet troops stationed in East Germany. In practice these limitations were often ignored, leading to clashes and deaths in the East German countryside that were never officially reported. I was told by a young British soldier of an incident where an unmarked Porsche sports car tried to cut off their armour-plated limousine, was rammed amidships, flew over a hedge and burst into flames. Travelling on the motorways one often saw large American cars with curtained windows, mud-splattered tyres and bits of branches hanging off, indicating some adventurous cross-country travel.

On a visit to the twice-yearly International Trade Fair in Leipzig, south of Berlin, a major focus for East-West commerce, I once watched as two U.S. intelligence officers in full uniform, with radio equipment and earphones, tried to climb the stairs to the main entrance on a day the East German leadership was due to visit. Two burly security officials blocked their way without a word. The two soldiers turned to each other, shrugged, and walked away. The Soviets had a similar mission in West Germany. They also had the right to mount a 24-hour honour guard at the Soviet War Memorial in West Berlin, and Spandau Prison in West Berlin, used to house Nazi war criminals, where the only prisoner for 21 years was Rudolf Hess.

Hess was Hitler's deputy until 1941, when he flew solo to Scotland on a doomed mission to negotiate peace with Britain. He was arrested and taken prisoner, and eventually convicted of crimes against peace at the post-war Nuremberg trials. He was still serving his sentence when he committed suicide in the prison in 1987, aged 93, after which the jail was demolished to prevent it becoming a shrine to neo-Nazis. Previous pleas by the western allies to release Hess on compassionate grounds were rejected by the Soviets, who wanted to maintain their regular foothold in West Berlin when they provided the prison's military guard for three months every year.

Tiptoeing Through the Cold War

The office-flat in East Berlin was in a part of the city that still bore the scars of the ferocious fighting in 1945 as Soviet troops captured the city from die-hard Nazi forces. East Berlin's restoration programme started late, giving priority to the cultural landmarks in the centre – the State Opera, the Comic Opera, the university, the cathedral, and the world-famous museums. The one major building not restored was Berlin Castle, the main residence of Prussian kings and German emperors, badly damaged by Allied bombs during the war. The communist government saw the castle as a symbol of Prussian militarism and pulled it down in the early 1950s. After German reunification in 1990 the castle was eventually rebuilt according to its original design.

Checking in at the office, I introduced myself to the office manager/secretary/translator Erdmute Behrendt, a bubbly East Berliner who had served half a dozen Reuters reporters since the office was opened in 1959, including Freddie Forsyth, who became a best-selling author after his first novel The Day of the Jackal swept the world, and Anthony Grey, who spent 27 months solitary confinement in Beijing as Reuters correspondent accused of spying. In reality Grey, who also went on to write several fiction and non-fiction books, was held in retaliation for the jailing of eight pro-Beijing journalists in Hong Kong by the British authorities.

The opening of the East Berlin bureau was not particularly welcomed by the West German authorities, who saw it as some sort of recognition of East Germany. The decision to open may have been partly influenced by a pile of tens of million German marks that the domestic news agency ADN, which Reuters had helped set up after the war, had been paying for use of our services ever since. The money was sitting in an East German bank account, but it was in East marks, which were non-convertible, and could not be taken out of the country. It could however be used to fund the new bureau. I was reliably told of one, probably the only attempt by Reuters to get some of the money out, by buying an Old Master painting in East Germany. Someone was sent in, the authorities

23

saw him coming, looked on as he bought a painting supposedly by Lucas Kranach, the 15th century German master, complete with an export licence, for a large sum of East marks. Returning eagerly to London our man went straight to Sotheby's auction house, which declared it "a rather poor fake".

Erdmute was hired after she responded to an English-language ad in the communist-controlled press. The East German authorities were stunned by this "irregular" move as they already had someone lined up for us. When they queried "is this how you recruit for important jobs in Britain?", the disarming reply was "yes, that's exactly how it's done". She was bright, hard-working and loyal, and a few years later, when Reuters decided to open a German-language service, showed an untapped talent for writing colourful life-style features. Although it was assumed by all of us that she was regularly quizzed by the state security service, the notorious Stasi, there was no evidence over the 40-odd years she worked for Reuters that she divulged any information that could have seriously compromised the correspondents or local contacts.

The Stasi was regarded by many as one of the most effective espionage and security services in history. Founded in 1950, it kept watch on its own people through a network of thousands of citizen informers, arresting an estimated 250,000 people over its 50-year existence. A foreign section operated an active spy network abroad, particularly in West Germany, where it successfully infiltrated political and business circles. One of the most successful spies was Günter Guillaume, a top aide to Chancellor Willy Brandt, who was forced to resign in 1974 when he was unmasked. One popular infiltration method was to send in good-looking young men who would link up with some of the hundreds of young women working as secretaries for the various ministries in Bonn. In East Berlin we always assumed that our office was continuously bugged, a suspicion that was confirmed a couple of days after the Wall came down in 1989 when a mysterious door at the end of the main corridor in the office suddenly opened and a pair of Stasi operatives emerged to sheepishly apologise for listening in to our lives. After German reunification the Stasi files were opened to anyone who wanted to see them. Many ordinary citizens who took up the invitation were shocked to see some of their personal details included, and who had provided them.

Though many citizens lived in fear of the Stasi, they were also the butt of plenty of jokes, usually pointing to their stupidity. "Why do Stasi officers always go around in groups of three? One who can read, one who can write, and the other to keep an eye on the two intellectuals." Another favourite was: "Why do Stasi officers make good taxi drivers? Because they know your name and where you live." Anyone caught telling such jokes could face imprisonment in the early years of the state, though the situation became more relaxed.

Back in the office, I took possession of the office car, a Wartburg, with a three-cylinder, two-stroke engine, the up-market end of the domestic car market. The only other choice was the no-frills Trabant, with a 600 c.c. two-stroke engine and a plastic body for cheapness and easy repairs. Nicknamed "a spark-plug with a roof", the "Saxon Porsche" and "running cardboard", it was declared International Car of the Year in 1989 for carrying tens of thousands of East Germans to the West as communism collapsed.

# 5. LIFE IN THE GDR

In the office a work routine was introduced that always began with Neues Deutschland (New Germany), the official organ of the ruling Socialist Unity party, a tough read most days but required in case important political or economic decisions were announced or implied. While my German was reasonably solid, Erdmute would help out with some of the more arcane expressions, using her prized Socialist Dictionary. One day early on she came up with a translation that I found odd, and I asked to see the dictionary. Opening it at random, my eye fell on an entry for an inoffensive German word that should have translated as "bad lad", or similar. The dictionary version was "cock-sucking son-of-a-bitch". I gently carried the dictionary across the room and dumped it in the waste bin.

Other sources of information were severely limited. There were no Western embassies, pre-recognition, and with no normal direct phone connection to West Berlin, no immediate contact with the British, American and French Military Missions who followed events in East Germany. Some of the East European diplomats were helpful, particularly the Czechs, until the entire embassy staff were recalled to Prague. The Czech information officer used to come to our flat, insist that I play loud music on my gramophone, and pass on some useful details from foreign ministry briefings. It was only later that I learned that any sound engineer worth his salt could shut out the music. The best background for discreet conversations was a noisy cocktail party, I learned. Local journalists were occasionally helpful, and some of the East Bloc media were useful, particularly the Russians, who despite their protestations of socialist brotherhood, were for the most part deeply suspicious of the East Germans.

I did have regular access to diplomats in West Berlin during visits through the Wall to help out the bureau there which was manned by

Annette von Broecker, an attractive young blonde who later became Reuters' editor in Bonn. The main stories at the time were weekly demonstrations by members of the student-led APO (extra-parliamentary opposition), disillusioned with the state of West German politics, almost invariably ending in violence. Because of West Berlin's special status males did not have to do military service, a situation that attracted thousands of young men to the city. At each visit through Checkpoint Charlie I had a full page of my passport stamped. After I had run through two passports in less than a year, the authorities allowed me to have an insert, and eventually a document giving me preference over the dozens of tourists usually queuing to cross.

West Berlin, in contrast to the East, was a consumer's paradise, kept as a showcase of capitalism through regular injections of money. A huge department store known as KaDeWe, "Shop of the West", was the second largest in Europe after Harrods in London. Apart from a wide choice of local and foreign restaurants there was the French Officers' Club restaurant overlooking one of West Berlin's lakes, to which I was not entitled, but I bluffed my way to its excellent subsidised cuisine by pretending to be a British army officer.

Occasionally I attended meetings of the West Berlin Foreign Press Club, of which I was also a member, and at one of these had an interesting insight into Soviet power structures. It was a farewell party for the West Berlin correspondent of the Tass news agency, one of dozens accredited to the city, at the Soviet military mission. After several hours, as the vodka and conversation flowed, the head of mission, a diplomat, entered the room, announced the end of the party and thanked us for attending. He was completely ignored by the Tass correspondents, who continued pouring drinks as he walked out red-faced, realising he was out-ranked.

In the east one source I was keen to meet was a colourful member of the city's expatriate community, John Peet, a former Reuters West Berlin bureau chief who defected in 1950 to East Berlin, from where he dictated the news of his own flight to his stunned deputy back in the bureau. In an international press conference in East Berlin Peet, who came from an English Quaker family and had served in the International Brigade fighting for the Republicans during the Spanish Civil War, announced that he "could no longer serve the Anglo-American war-mongers". He was particularly concerned about the prospect of a West German army being created with Allied encouragement. His press conference was carried in full by Reuters.

Reuters management discouraged any contact with Peet, who published a weekly newsletter in English called German Democratic Report about events in the country which was sent to foreign embassies and media. Although it provided little headline news, and much of it was devoted to unmasking former Nazis in West Germany, it also included useful details about daily life in East Germany.

I became good friends with Peet, a true intellectual and a skilled journalist, and often turned to him for his encyclopaedic knowledge of Germany and the international communist movement. He was not a communist, rather an anti-fascist, and although we avoided discussing his views about the current East German system I had the strong impression he was quite disillusioned by the developments since its foundation. He never used me to carry information the authorities wanted published.

Another useful source with whom the bureau kept in regular contact was Wolfgang Vogel, an East German lawyer who, operating quietly under the radar, negotiated the exchange of political prisoners and the transfer of dissidents and failed escapees to West Germany. His most notable case was the 1962 swap of U.S. pilot Gary Powers, whose spy plane was shot down over Russia two years previously, and an American PHD student Frederic Pryor who had been seized on a visit to East Berlin. They were exchanged for a Soviet spy known as Rudolf Abel, a KGB colonel. Over three decades Vogel also negotiated the transfer to the West of over 30,000 political prisoners and 200,000 ordinary citizens, mainly relatives of escapees or defectors, paid for by the Bonn government. The lucrative business made him a wealthy man, and he drove a Swedish Volvo sports coupé, reputedly the only Western-made car in East Berlin. Vogel was always happy to talk to us, but there were no major swaps during my time – although I did spend a night in the Wartburg on Glienicke Bridge linking West Berlin to Potsdam, the usual handover point, amid rumours of an impending exchange. One of my successors in the East Berlin bureau had better luck in 1986 when, fresh from our Moscow bureau, he recognised Soviet dissident Anatoly Shcharansky as he was being exchanged on the bridge and was first with the news.

For interesting conversation, provided it did not involve politics, another expatriate in the city was Alan Winnington, a life-time communist who covered the Korean War and the Chinese civil war from the communist side, and who knew revolutionary leader Mao Tse Tung personally. He was stripped of his British citizenship after being accused of interrogating British troops fighting in the Korean war. An Australian journalist I met in Saigon in 1975 recalled meeting him when he appeared with the northern delegation at truce talks at the joint Korean border. To celebrate his birthday, a group of Western journalists presented him with an elaborate cake shaped like a penis with the words "Happy Birthday Alan, you big prick!" His views were hard-line communist, and his unwavering support for the invasion of Czechoslovakia put him at odds with other members of the small expatriate community in the city.

I did manage to get one high-ranking East German government contact, through the generosity and shared solidarity of a visiting Swiss journalist. He had been invited to the country and was impressed with the red-carpet treatment he was being given in the hope he would help influence his neutral homeland to recognise East Germany. Dropping into our bureau he described how his minder had cut through red tape in getting him direct access to top officials, gave me his number and suggested I identify myself as a friend. The contact was Hermann von Berg, a top aide of East German Prime Minister Willi Stoph who was involved in secret contacts with West German officials. He provided me with some of my best information about the inner workings of the party.

In the late 1980s he fell foul of the authorities after sending critical articles to the west, and eventually left the country -- with the help of Wolfgang Vogel.

In between the news stories I adjusted to life in the east, though I was aware I was spoiled by having access to West Berlin at any time. With East Germany having the highest standard of living in the East Bloc, people generally had enough to eat, though there were periodic shortages of staples such as butter, meat and coffee. There were quite serious food shortages in 1970 after two bad harvests and a severe winter that reduced coal supplies. For all consumer goods there was little choice, as in any centrally planned command economy where party officials rather than consumers decide what is on offer. There were a few "Intershops" selling Western luxury goods, but for hard currency only. East Germans, like their East Bloc neighbours, were paid in currency that could not be officially converted into U.S. dollars or West German marks, though it was possible on the black market for punitive rates, and could not be taken out of the country. The hard-currency shops, which were also available in some other East Bloc countries, were clearly used by the authorities to soak up hard currency received by ordinary people from friends and relatives in the West. Access to those in East Berlin was open to all, but there were reports that visitors to them could be pulled aside for questioning on how they came to the funds.

The lack of "proper" money for East Europeans was amusingly illustrated during the West Berlin Jazz Festival I attended where one of the star attractions was a group of leading players from all over the East Bloc calling themselves "The Non-Convertible All-Stars".

Service in shops and restaurants was patchy, with staff often chatting about their social lives and responding when challenged with "Can't you see we're holding a staff meeting." The first fully private restaurant opened a year after my arrival. Queues for shops were commonplace, you joined automatically assuming there must be something worth buying. Prices were controlled, and most things were affordable, if they were available. Very drinkable Hungarian and Bulgarian wine was available for east marks, and at the Havana Shop you could get Cuban rum and cigars. There was a six-year waiting list for a Wartburg, despite its high cost of 18,500 marks (around £5,000).

There was a guaranteed job for everyone, described by cynics as "we pretend to work and they pretend to pay us". There was similar resignation over the state of consumer supplies, voiced in the many black jokes doing the rounds. An example: "What would happen if the desert became communist? Nothing for a while, then there would be a sand shortage." Then there were the jokes about the socialist system. "What are the four deadly enemies of socialism? Spring, summer, autumn and winter."

Women's fashions were dictated by one man, 52-year-old Heinz Bormann, known in the West as "The Red Dior". Criticised by younger designers for churning out conservative fashion for the masses, he sold widely throughout East Europe and also West Germany, for much-needed hard currency, one of the very few East German products to find a ready market there. His main problem was the restricted choice of materials.

"In the West designers create a collection and then go out looking for material. Here it is exactly the opposite," he told me in his office in Magdeburg.

While there was officially no censorship of films or books, an extensive filtering process was used, starting with self-censorship, to block unacceptable material. There was a small group of dissidents, committed Marxists who directed their criticism against the East German authorities. They included playwright Heiner Mueller, whose works were popular in the west, folk-singer Wolf Biermann, who was eventually exiled while visiting West Germany, and author Stefan Heym, German-born who became an American citizen and returned to East Germany after World War Two after serving in the U.S. army. I used to visit Heym quite regularly, and one of these trips was noted by the Stasi. In a transcript of their report I received from our Bonn bureau many years later they noted in minute detail my telephone conversation with the author organising the visit, and my arrival at his house in an outer suburb of East Berlin, but then went on: "Nothing was known of the contents of their conversation." This suggested to me that the Stasi were not always as organised as people feared.

State television injected a strong dose of communist propaganda, particularly a regular spot called "The Black Channel", timed to go out just before or after popular programmes, which aimed to ridicule Western broadcasts. However most people preferred to watch western TV, which could reach all parts of the country apart from a small valley in the south-east of the country dubbed "the valley of the clueless". The most popular radio station in Berlin was Radio In The American Sector (RIAS), set up in West Berlin by the United States after the war. It provided a vital information service during the 1948 airlift to reassure West Berliners and was later used to beam across the Wall news about West Germany and some from the East ignored by its media, along with the latest popular music. There were also the BBC German-language service and the US-sponsored Radio Free Europe. For entertainment, the state-run DEFA company made films, mainly light comedies, in the same studios used by the Nazis to churn out propaganda.

Occasionally foreign films, particularly Soviet ones, would be shown. In one case, word went out on the grapevine that an interesting Soviet film would be shown for one night only at one suburban Berlin cinema. I joined a packed audience of mainly young people to watch a charming story about a travelling theatre group performing Shakespeare's plays to Russian villagers. The story itself was uncontroversial, the interest came when the interior of a villager's house revealed walls and ceilings covered with naïve murals of ordinary people and animals in glorious bold colours. There was a gasp from the audience, growing up against a background of strict Socialist Realism which condemned art for art's sake. An example of East German cultural restrictions at the time being tougher even than Soviet ones.

Among the most popular home-grown films were a series of Westerns in which the Red Indians regularly outwitted the U.S. cavalry. The films, based on a book by an East German female history professor who lived for years among the Dakota Indians, starred a Yugoslav actor playing the main character White Wolf. After three films he ended up dying in a hail of bullets to illustrate, he explained to me in an interview, that while the Indians fought bravely, they lost in the end.

East German interest in the Wild West may have had its roots in a bizarre museum located in a town near Dresden dating back to pre-communist times containing possibly the most extensive collection of Native American culture in Europe. The museum opened in 1928 was dedicated to Karl May, a highly inventive German author who won fame and fortune writing books about American Indians without ever visiting the country.

The remarkable accuracy of the books, including occasional passages of authentic native dialogue, were the result of May devouring a mass of scholarly works on Native American culture while serving a seven-year sentence for petty theft. East Germany, while supporting the museum as a means of depicting the Indians' struggle, banned all May's books on the grounds that they glorified imperialist ideals. One of his central figures, a blond blue-eyed immigrant German frontiersman called "Old Shatterhand" was considered by many to embody the Aryan "master-race" ideal later developed to its extreme by Hitler.

In Berlin the Comic Opera offered mainly operettas, musicals and ballet, while the State Opera struggled to compete with West Berlin's German Opera for the big stars. One of the most popular attractions was the Berliner Ensemble theatre set up by Marxist playwright Berthold Brecht, who wrote The Threepenny Opera among others, and his wife Helene Weigel.

I had a number of East German friends, as opposed to official contacts, mainly involved in non-political activities such as acting, publishing, photography and art. I was always aware of being monitored, at least some of the time, and always advised friends and acquaintances that contact with me could get them into trouble. As far as I was aware however none of those people suffered at the hands of the security authorities.

With a lack of real news about actual events in the country, and the ever-present threat of the Stasi and its informers, it was difficult to establish how many of the population genuinely believed in the communist system, or, particularly in the case of senior managers, officials and journalists, were guided by opportunism.

Occasionally I did a "vox pops", talking to ordinary people in the street, when they were on their own and could talk freely, to try to find out what they really felt about their country and specific issues. Unlike in neighbouring Czechoslovakia, where a recent genuinely popular movement to liberalise the whole communist system led from the top of the party had been crushed in 1968, the only rebellion in East Germany was a workers' revolt in 1953 fuelled mainly by the government's decision to increase productivity levels.

A common response to my questions was resignation, and a lack of enthusiasm for communism as a system, but quite often accompanied by a certain pride in the achievement of the country in rebuilding its economy literally from scratch after its new rulers had to send its entire manufacturing base, including railway tracks, to the Soviet Union as reparations. Some also noted the frequent reports in the East German press that West Germany still had former prominent Nazis in leading positions. There was also pride in the spectacular successes of the country in sport, of which more later.

East Germans could visit other East European countries apart from Yugoslavia, which broke from the international communist system in 1948 and became a founding member of the non-aligned movement. With its more de-centralised and less repressive form of government, it was regarded by East Berlin as the West. The most popular destinations were Hungary, with its camping sites around Lake Balaton, the largest lake in central Europe, and Bulgaria, with its Black Sea coastline. Hungary would eventually provide the springboard for the mass escape of East Germans, and the collapse of communism in Europe.

The Black Sea coast was a mixed pleasure for visitors from the East Bloc. An East German friend of mine was boiling with rage on returning from a Bulgarian resort after discovering that the main hotels and restaurants and even some of the beaches were restricted to those with hard currency, for western tourists and eastern ones with connections. The Bulgarian government had invested heavily in building upmarket resorts along its coast, dubbed the "Red Riviera", to bring in westerners and much-needed hard currency.

There was skiing in East Germany, though relatively low level with slopes rising to 1,200 metres. For those seeking more reliable snow there were the Tatra mountains in Poland and Czechoslovakia, with runs coming down from over 2,000 metres.

East Berlin itself was surrounded by a vast network of lakes and forests, similar to but more extensive than those in the west of the city, that provided plenty of opportunities for relaxation. I spent an afternoon cruising in a Dragon yacht owned by a friend of a friend, a classic boat built in the 1920s by one of pre-war Germany's leading boatyards. As we drifted past lakeside villas with neatly-trimmed lawns, some with Wartburg speedboats moored at the end, it was difficult to associate the scene with the communist East. I recalled a recent trip in a tourist ship around the lakes organised for the press corps by the foreign ministry, and watching the faces of the Russian journalists as the surveyed the scene in silence.

One of the top activities in the country was sport, both in active participation by ordinary people and support for elite athletes who were posting extraordinary successes in international events. In the Olympic games in Mexico City in 1968, East Germany, competing for the first time as a separate nation, finished fourth in the medals table, behind the U.S., Soviet Union and Japan. In the 1972 Games in Munich it came third, four years later in Montreal it came second behind the Soviet Union, ahead of the USA. It was sweeping the medals table at international swimming, athletics and rowing events. Some of the records set by its athletes and swimmers stood for years. The women's 400 metres record of 47.60 set by Marita Koch in 1985 still looks almost unassailable. Other countries looking for an answer noted that a large chunk of the nation's GDP was going into sport, partly to bring the country some of the international recognition it craved but was denied through diplomacy, but also to divert public attention from the underperforming economy. A system of elite schools was created specialising in individual sports, the pupils hand-picked at an early age by national coaches according to their physical attributes and potential. Other East Bloc countries were also sponsoring their athletes, making a mockery of the Olympics system and its millionaire president Avery Brundage, who fought against any hint of professionalism in the West but ignored full-time state sponsorship in the East. An East German acquaintance of mine told how a leading national athlete was on the payroll of his company, would arrive every day, clock in, and go off to train.

East German sports officials also made good use of its access to all areas of West German life through espionage. In the 1972 Olympics in Munich, wild-water slalom canoeing was introduced for the first time. As the host, West Germany should have had a clear advantage by being able to build and train on the Olympic course. However the East German national coach slipped into Munich pretending to be an official of the International Canoe Federation, came back with plans for the course, and an exact replica was built in Zwickau, East Germany. The result: East Germany won all four gold medals, three silvers and one bronze, compared to a silver and bronze to the West Germans.

After the collapse of the communist system in 1989 the world learned what many people had long suspected, that East Germany had been running an intensive doping system for years. It was centred on the National Sports University in Leipzig, and particularly its secretive Institute of Sports Medicine. When a Soviet sports delegation visited the university I asked a friendly Russian journalist who had accompanied them what they had seen. "We saw a lot of things – but not everything," he replied grimly. Hundreds of East German competitors who received huge doses of anabolic steroids suffered serious side effects, including infertility, unwanted hair growth, breast cancer and heart problems. Shot-putter Heidi Krieger took so many drugs she decided to have a sex change and became Andreas.

The first big political story broke early in 1969 after West Germany announced it was holding presidential elections in West Berlin, despite its special status which kept it outside mainstream West German politics, and East Germany banned western parliamentarians from crossing to the city. The Soviet Union also protested against the decision, noting that members of the neo-Nazi National Democratic Party would be in the city, raising fears of a major new bid to isolate the city. In the end the elections went ahead, an indication to Western diplomats that the East German leadership had been overruled by Moscow, which was engaged in negotiations with the West.

Not long after that two East Germans hijacked a Polish airliner to the French sector of West Berlin, armed with guns that later turned out to be incapable of firing, and were sentenced to two years jail. They were lucky, a year later the French government passed a law stipulating five years to life imprisonment for hijacking.

A much sadder story came a year later when a young married couple tried to hijack an East German airliner to the west from Schönefeld airport but were foiled by the crew after a stewardess persuaded them they did not have enough fuel to get to West Germany but would land in West Berlin. When the couple saw they were landing back in Schönefeld they shot themselves with pistols they were carrying. I reported some of the story after driving to the airport, which was outside Berlin city limits, and talking to staff, but the news of the suicide emerged later. The story illustrated one of many problems faced by East Germans. The couple had just married but were unable to get an apartment, allocated by the state like everything else, in an area where both could work.

One of our stories was the renaming of a street in East Berlin after wartime Soviet spy Richard Sorge, regarded by many as one of the most successful agents in history, attended by some famous names in the shadowy world of espionage. Working as the Tokyo correspondent of a leading German paper Sorge, who had German and Russian parents, was believed to have transmitted a mass of valuable information to Russia. These were thought to have included advance information on Hitler's invasion of Russia and Japan's decision not to attack Russia in 1941. Sorge was arrested in Tokyo and executed in 1943. The radio operator for his network, Max Christiansen-Clausen and his Finnish-born wife Anna, the group's courier, attended the renaming ceremony. Also present was Rudolf Abel, of spy-swap fame.

As the communications problems between the two Berlin bureaux became more acute, we decided to apply for a special telephone link between them. Waiting for a favourable opportunity, one came up when Neues Deutschland carried a long exposé of a West German middle-level politician because of his links with the past. It was not a big story, but I ran it fully, and was delighted to see us get a front-page mention in the paper the next day. Striking while the iron was hot, we called the authorities, and were promised a new line. A few days later it appeared, with a crank handle to alert the other office. The historic event was captured by a photo of me on the phone and Erdmute hovering over my shoulder that was sent to London and appeared in the Reuters house magazine. On a trip back to London shortly afterwards I noticed an undercurrent of mirth as I walked across the newsroom, and soon discovered why. The photo had been torn out and attached to a clip where notes were posted under the headline "this month's caption competition". I was told the competition had run to three pages, and the acknowledged winner was: "Darling, something big has come up but I think we can handle it together." I never told Erdmute, who would have been mortified.

Towards the end of the year I had one of my most unexpected stories, and my first real scoop. On the day of East Germany's 20th anniversary celebrations on October 7 I was walking to the city's central Alexanderplatz square to watch the main ceremony, with music and searchlights. Turned away by officials because I lacked the right ticket, I was walking back when I was almost bowled over by a running crowd of hundreds of young people being chased by baton-wielding police. Joining in on the trot I asked what was going on, to be told there had been a rumour the Rolling Stones would sing from the top of the huge Axel Springer building, erected two years previously in a deliberate act by West Germany's largest publishing house right next to the Wall. The rumour was the result of a throwaway remark by a RIAS disc jockey, but East German police were also aware of it, and moved in with truncheons, beating heads and making several arrests. The Stones' music was banned in East Germany but could be heard on Western radio and bought on the Black Market for big money.

Not for the last time in my career the scoop appeared in a number of papers as eye-witness reports by their own correspondent. Most of them were based in Bonn. Some papers carried a report from my AFP colleague quoting the government spokesman as denying that the clash ever happened.

Aware that my report was probably the only mention of the country's anniversary celebrations to appear in the Western press, I slunk into a reception that evening for foreign journalists covering the event expecting a cool reception but was assured by the foreign ministry spokesman that my posting was secure.

Early in 1970 I headed for Dresden in Saxony to mark the 25th anniversary of one of the most controversial Allied actions of World War Two, the fire-bombing of a city known as "Pearl of the Elbe" for its 17th and 18th century city centre, which was completely destroyed. Some 25,000 people were killed in the British-American attack, many of them refugees fleeing from the approaching Soviet army. The raid, between

February 13 and 15, was part of Britain's policy of area bombing of German cities rather than precision targeting, implemented by the head of Bomber Command Sir Arthur "Bomber" Harris. The policy was controversial, with many commanders arguing its effectiveness was limited and did not justify the huge civilian casualties and damage it caused. Many critics have argued that the strategic importance of Dresden was limited, while its cultural treasures were known world-wide. Even Britain's wartime leader Winston Churchill had some later reservations about the action. When I asked diplomats in Britain's military mission in Berlin for a comment before I left for Dresden, there was an embarrassed silence. The mayor of Dresden, in an interview, said he believed Churchill was worried by the Soviet advance across Europe, recognising it posed a future threat, and was trying to slow it down by creating confusion. Others believe the attack was in response to a 1940 Nazi raid on the English city of Coventry that destroyed its medieval centre and cathedral. There were later claims the Coventry raid was in retaliation for one by British forces on Munich six days previously.

In Dresden itself the baroque heart had been largely replaced by undistinguished 1950s buildings. One of the two best-known landmarks, the Zwinger art gallery, was severely damaged in the raid, and had reopened only in 1963. The Frauenkirche, with one of the largest domes in Europe, was just an enormous pile of rubble, following a decision by the East German government to leave it as a war memorial. It stayed that way until 1994, after reunification, when it was decided to return it painstakingly to its original state.

# 6. THE TWO GERMANIES START TALKS

Meanwhile the political scene had changed in Bonn with the election of the first Social Democratic government since the war headed by Willy Brandt, who broke with the previous government's combative stance towards East Germany in favour of more normal relations. It was part of his party's "Ostpolitik", a drive to improve relations with the countries of East Europe ravaged by the Nazis. In his inaugural speech to parliament he called for improvements in the humanitarian situation in East Germany and suggested relations between them should be settled by a treaty. But he ruled out international recognition of the GDR, arguing they were both parts of one nation. Early in 1970 premier Willi Stoph sent a letter to Brandt inviting him for talks on their future relations which would depend on official recognition of his country under international law, and preliminary negotiations were soon under way.

A few weeks after the anniversary, in one of the biggest stories in Europe since the war, East and West German government leaders met directly for the first time, in the East German city of Erfurt, to discuss ways of improving relations. The West Germans had wanted the meeting to be in East Berlin, allowing Brandt to return to the West via West Berlin, thus reinforcing the city's ties to the home country. This was opposed by the East Germans and the Russians, who argued that West Berlin had a special status. Almost certainly another reason was they feared the popularity of Brandt, a charismatic speaker who was well known in both parts of the city and the rest of East Germany as a former West Berlin mayor. His anti-Nazi credentials were flawless, having spent the war fighting with the resistance in occupied Norway, returning to Germany in Norwegian military uniform. He refused to reclaim his German nationality until 1947.

The East Germans' fears were justified as 2,000 people arrived at Erfurt station to greet Brandt's arrival. They called "Willy, Willy", as the party crossed the square to their hotel, changing to "Willy Brandt", to differentiate him from his host. As crowds called for him to come to the window, he made a brief appearance, and according to some reports responded with a wave. I could only see his window from the side, but he appeared to be trying to silence the chants, recognising that the reception he was getting was a serious embarrassment to his hosts.

In the talks Brandt suggested international recognition could come eventually after a long process of negotiations and proposed that the two states should join the United Nations. Stoph reiterated his demand for full official recognition under international law. The talks, as expected, made no real progress but the two sides agreed to meet again in Kassel, a city in West Germany roughly midway between Berlin and Bonn, in May.

After the Erfurt meeting the international press covering it were invited to an evening reception in nearby Weimar, an architectural and cultural gem with connections to writers Goethe and Schiller, musicians like Liszt and architect Walter Gropius, who founded the Bauhaus movement there. The reception was held in the city's most famous hotel The Elephant, built in 1696. A connection that was unlikely to have played a part in its selection was that it was Hitler's favourite hotel on his many visits to the city.

During the reception Alan Winnington approached me and said there was someone who wanted to meet me, and introduced a beaming Chinese journalist called Li from the national news agency Xinhua. I recoiled, unsure how to deal with representatives of a country currently holding one of my predecessors captive. Li dismissed the actions by Red Guards who stormed Anthony Grey's house in Beijing in 1967, smashed up the interior, killed his cat and left its body on his bed, as "just students". He then invited me to dinner at the Chinese embassy in East Berlin in two days' time. I returned to Berlin the next day, after breakfast at the hotel which saw the appearance of one of the rarest objects in East Germany, bananas, at least for the early risers. Offered clearly to demonstrate that everything was available, they had disappeared by the time most visitors were up. I was reminded of a popular joke doing the rounds in East Berlin.

How can you use a banana as a compass? Put it on top of the Wall – the bitten end always points east.

I almost forgot about the dinner with the Chinese, thanks to a heavy previous night and a thick head. I arrived in time to the embassy located in a suburb with a strong Soviet military presence. This was ironic at a time when relations between the two countries were at a low ebb over doctrinal differences and rivalry. As soon as I entered the embassy building, I realised that something was not quite normal. As we headed for the dining room, three immaculately dressed waiters stood stiffly. I recognised one as the culture and information secretary, a senior official on the staff. Anticipating that I had been invited to a banquet with many guests, I was stunned to discover I was the only one, and there was only one host. Over the delicious multi-course banquet Li and I chatted generally and amicably, avoiding Tony Grey's incarceration, and I left well-fed but bemused. The next day I sent a message to managers in London explaining exactly what had happened. I learned later that my report caused a huge stir, and after a few phone calls, the word came back that Grey was about to be released, and two senior editorial staff were sent off incognito on a mission to bring him home.

The story had an interesting follow-up for me when a couple of years later Grey returned to Berlin to make a BBC programme about his experience. I drove over to pick him up at our West Berlin office. As we headed back towards Checkpoint Charlie I glanced at him beside me in the front seat and saw he was sweating profusely and his hands were gripping the arm-rest. As he got out of the car, one of the least friendly of a not overly friendly group of border guards suddenly stopped and said in German: "Mr Grey, haven't seen you in a long time," and Grey relaxed immediately. Whether they really remembered him from over four years previously, or, more likely, had been listening in on our new office-to-office phone as we organised the pick-up, the answer probably lay somewhere in the STASI files.

Colin McIntyre

While Reuter bureaux in both parts of Germany prepared for the follow-up summit in Kassel, the 25th anniversary of the end of World War Two in Europe fell on May 8, 1970 and was marked in starkly contrasting ways in the two rival countries. In the West the day was associated with defeat and many people preferred to draw a veil over it. In East Germany, whose citizens had been told by their government since the state's formation they were the good Germans, it was hailed as a glorious day of liberation from the Nazi regime by the victorious Red Army. I attended a ceremony at the building where the unconditional surrender was signed by representatives of the Third Reich and the Soviet army, the officers' mess of the former spy training school of the German armed forces in Karlshorst, now a museum. An elderly Russian woman who had been present at the actual event described how arrogant Field Marshall Wilhelm Keitel had been as he signed for the Germans. The Allies insisted it be signed by the German military to avoid a repeat of the "stab-in-the-back" legend of World War One when the surrender was signed only by the government, leading some of the military to claim it had no responsibility for it.

In later years West Germany also started seeing May 8 as a day of liberation rather than defeat, and recently pressure has grown to declare it a national holiday, though there was opposition from the far right AFD party. At present the only national holiday connected to German history is October 3, marking reunification in 1990.

Two weeks later the follow-up meeting between Brandt and Stoph took place in Kassel, a city dating back to 900 A.D. which suffered severe bomb damage in World War Two on account of its tank factories. On the first visit to West Germany by an East German premier since the two countries were founded, Stoph arrived by train. The centre of the city was closed to traffic as a lone motorcycle courier in black leather sped between the two delegations with the latest proposals as both sides clearly lacked trust in the security of local phone and telex communications.

44

In an interview with the West German news agency DPA Brandt said the way would be open for negotiations on relations between both sides, with proposals covering trade, transport, cultural exchange and cross-border movement. This was in response to Stoph's demand for an international legal treaty and a full exchange of ambassadors, illustrating the wide gulf between the two positions. The meeting made virtually no progress and the two sides agreed it was time for a break.

Six months later Brandt addressed the other key part of his Ostpolitik when he travelled to Warsaw to sign a treaty recognising post-war borders that ceded nearly a quarter of Germany's pre-war territory to Poland, with an enclave that had been East Prussia further to the east going to the Soviet Union. A small minority of the 12 million Germans who fled or were expelled were still holding regular meetings in a forest stadium in West Berlin, some of which I attended, calling for the restoration of the territories. Haranguing the mainly elderly crowds, the speakers referred to East Germany as Middle Germany.

During Brandt's visit to Warsaw, on a visit to the monument to the 1943 Warsaw Ghetto uprising in which some 13,000 Jews died, Brandt unexpectedly dropped to his knees in a gesture that resonated around the world. One commentator wrote: "There are people who can say more with their back than others with a thousand words."

As the East-West German talks resumed, though only at expert level, parallel four-power talks were under way on a treaty to reinforce the position of West Berlin aimed at ending once and for all Soviet and East German blockades of the city. The West made it clear that a settlement of the Berlin problem was crucial to a détente process sought by Moscow to confirm Europe's post-war borders giving it control of the East Bloc. Moscow's interest in pursuing détente was behind the removal a few months earlier of  long-serving Ulbricht, who took a hard line on West Berlin and with relations with the West in general, and his replacement by Erich Honecker. According to East German sources Ulbricht felt his country was unprepared for détente because of its ailing economy and was still worried by the enthusiastic reception Brandt had received in Erfurt. Honecker was seen as closer to Moscow, a relationship dramatically highlighted by a classic photo of him greeting Soviet leader Leonid Brezhnev with a lingering kiss full on the mouth. The photo went around the world as a symbol of East Germany's subservience to Moscow.

The Berlin talks were held by the US, British and French ambassadors to Bonn and the Soviet ambassador to East Berlin, mainly in West Berlin, and lasted over a year. After each session the ambassadors were grilled by the foreign and domestic press, and invariably the Western trio had nothing to say. The Soviet ambassador Pyotr Abrasimov, a war hero and vastly experienced diplomat from Belarus, clearly took pity on us and always came up with a little piece of home-spun wisdom. "The further you go into the forest, the more wood you have to cut," was one. "You can't have a rose without thorns," was another. Each of these was seized on eagerly by the press, and gave us a lead paragraph, though we realised they added little substance to the story. However we were so grateful to Abrasimov that after the signing ceremony the West Berlin international press corps, of which I was also a member, presented him with a book of German aphorisms, and he accepted with good grace.

During one of these reporting trips to West Berlin, while the Queen's younger sister Princess Margaret was visiting as Commander-in-Chief of the British regiment currently garrisoned in the city, I discovered the soft spot of the hardened border guards at Checkpoint Charlie – royalty. Having covered the briefing after a regular four-power meeting I had to rush back to East Berlin to don a black tie for a reception for the royal visitor at West Berlin's Charlottenburg Palace. As I passed back through the checkpoint I handed my passport to the guard and asked if they could speed it up as I was due to meet Princess Margaret. All hell broke loose as he seized my passport, raced across the room, opened the door and threw it in, shouting: "Quick, quick, he's meeting Princess Margaret." There was a brief scuffle inside and the sound of a date stamp being pounded several times at speed, and 10 seconds later the door burst open and my passport was thrown back to me as I stood open-mouthed. My passage through Charlie normally took at least 10 minutes.

The Berlin agreement was finally signed at the end of September 1971. As well as defining West Berlin's road, rail and telecommunications links with the west, it also allowed West Berliners to cross to the east for the first time since the Wall. The agreement gave fresh impetus to negotiations between the two Germanies, and preliminary talks on a Basic Treaty setting out future relations began.

At this stage I was joined by a second Reuter correspondent, a friend from one of my visits to Vienna when he was posted there, as Reuters had just opened a German-language service and wanted more from the east. Derek Parr had swum for Oxford and could barely believe some of the performances of East German swimmers not yet in their teens. He went on to become European and world masters champion and a record holder in his age group, right up to the over-75s, in the 200 metres butterfly, one of the toughest races in the sport.

While the two of us kept an eye on the German-German talks and all the other news, one major story broke in the autumn of 1972 as we were half-way out of the door at the end of the day. Alerted by the pinging of the telex, indicating an urgent ADN story, we rushed back to read that a passenger jet of the state airline Interflug taking East German tourists to Bulgaria's Black Sea coast had crashed near Berlin. There were reported to be no survivors among the 156 passengers and crew. As we were the only western journalists officially accredited to East Germany, and therefore able to travel outside East Berlin, Derek headed off while I phoned around. The plane, a Russian-built Ilyushin IL-62, came down near a town called Königs Wusterhausen just outside Berlin which was covered by the Berlin phone directory. I began calling random numbers asking if anyone had seen or heard anything and was eventually directed towards a street close to the crash where residents told of hearing an explosion and seeing a plane on fire passing overhead. It emerged later that the crash, the worst in German aviation history, was caused by a fire in the rear cargo bay from a leak in a hot-air tube. As we had the only eye-witness report of the crash scene Derek recorded a piece in German for West Berlin TV and radio on his return. An interesting angle on the crash was provided by our colleague from Polish TV, who when he called Warsaw to alert them to the story was asked: "Got any more good news for us?" For many in the region, World War Two was clearly still painfully fresh.

As 1972 drew to a close the two German negotiating teams announced they had reached agreement on a Basic Treaty, and it was signed on December 21 in East Berlin. At a press conference East Germany's chief negotiator Michael Kohl was bombarded by the national and international media. As the questions became more and more detailed a lone British voice came from the back, from the BBC's veteran Bonn correspondent Bob Elphick. "Does this mean the Wall will come down?" We locally-based press who had been following every step of the negotiations in minute detail and knew the Wall was never on the agenda rolled our eyes in astonishment over such a naïve question as it met with a resounding "no". But Bob was right, it was the question everyone would be asking, and it inevitably appeared at the top of all our reports. It was an early lesson for any journalist, avoiding getting too close to the story, and an example I regularly cited decades later when I was training journalists across the world for the Reuters Foundation.

The treaty paved the way for diplomatic relations to be opened with East Germany, and Western countries arrived soon to set up embassies in East Berlin. The two German states meanwhile established permanent missions, de facto embassies, but formal diplomatic relations were not established and were overtaken by German reunification in 1990.

Shortly after Christmas I was called back to London to work on the World Desk, bought a house and set up home with my girlfriend Sigi from Berlin, who had her own dramatic back story. Born in East Prussia, Germany's easternmost province now part of Russia, she fled the oncoming Soviet army with her mother and three brothers. An attempt to cross an ice-covered stretch of the Baltic to get to ships taking them further west was abandoned as many families disappeared through the ice, and they turned back and finally got one of the last ships out of the capital Königsberg taking them to Danzig, a German enclave partly surrounded by Poland. Along with thousands of other refugees from the east they were booked on a former cruise liner Wilhelm Gustloff to take them to the rest of Germany. They missed the departure of the Gustloff, which was sunk by a Soviet submarine shortly after leaving harbour and went down with 9,400 people, the largest loss of life in a single ship sinking in history.

History came back to haunt Sigi in 2002 when we visited Königsberg, now renamed Kaliningrad, to try to retrace her family home in the country outside the capital. In a city park I took a picture of a bronze plaque which seemed to suggest a marine incident, and discovered it commemorated the captain of the submarine that sank the Gustloff. Asking around, we discovered that the plaque was only erected after a statue to Bomber Harris was unveiled outside St Clement Danes church in London in 1992. One of Bomber Command's most destructive raids was against Königsberg in 1944, wiping out most of the historic centre of the city.

In London, after finding an 1850s terraced cottage in north London with no heating, proper kitchen or bathroom and putting ourselves in debt for 20 years to buy it, we set about trying to make it habitable. It was not just a question of décor, there were structural problems involving plastering. Just when we were getting on top of the work the Conservative government was forced to introduce a three-day working week to conserve electricity as coalminers went on strike. One result was a serious shortage of plaster, which affected our whole street as several other people were working to restore these old properties. News of a new delivery of plaster to a builders' merchant several miles away went along the street and amid the sound of revving car engines we managed to race off and get a few bags before they disappeared.

The other major shortage caused by the three-day week was toilet-paper. For several weeks pubs and restaurants chained their rolls to the wall.

We were putting the last lick of paint on the walls 18 months later, and had got married, when the call came to travel again. This time to Jakarta, the capital of Indonesia, and to be thrown into another Cold War as communism took hold in regional neighbours Vietnam, Cambodia and Laos.

*Map of Europe*

*A young man holds a Czech flag next to a burning Soviet tank. CIA, Wiki Commons*

*Berlin map. Author Gzen 92, Creative Commons Attribution*

*East German soldiers block Brandenburg Gate as Wall goes up (13 August, 1961).*
*Heinz-Peter Junge, Creative Commons Attribution.*

*Berlin Wall, Thierry Noir, 1968, GNU Free Documentation License*

*A 1986 model Trabant*

*Dresden's historic centre after the Allied bombing. Cassowary Colorization, Creative Commons Attribution*

*East Berlin office celebrates the installation of the phone line to West Berlin*

*Karl May Museum Photographer Paulae, Creative Commons Attribution*

# 7. COLD WAR IN A HOT CLIMATE

The Cold War in Asia was a part of the global freeze as the superpowers the USA and the Soviet Union, and increasingly China, battled for influence over Southeast Asian countries seeking independence from colonial rule, particularly from the French in Indochina, after Japanese occupation ended in 1945.

My experience with that region was to come, but first I had to familiarise myself with Indonesia, a vast country of 17,000 islands, hundreds of distinct ethnic and linguistic groups and 250 million people, the world's largest Moslem population. I had little time to read up on the country, or learn the language, as I replaced a correspondent who quit suddenly to return to Australia. I did have some familiarity with the language having spent part of my childhood in Singapore, speaking some Malay, the basis of Indonesia's national language. I also spent a few weeks in Jakarta during one school holiday when my father was in the Australian embassy there.

Indonesia gained its independence from 400 years of Dutch rule in 1945 after a four-year armed struggle. The Dutch were attracted to the area because some of the outlying islands in the huge archipelago produced exotic spices that were highly prized in Europe as medicines and to mask the taste of badly preserved food. A tiny island producing nutmeg, which was thought to cure bubonic plague behind the Black Death of the Middle Ages, was traded by Britain to the Dutch in exchange for Manhattan Island, then known as New Amsterdam, now New York.

Indonesia's recent history was turbulent. After a failed coup by a left-wing military group in 1965 blamed on the powerful PKI communist party, which was backed by China, army commander General Suharto instigated a violent anti-communist purge in which between 500,000 and a million people died. Suharto took over from Sukarno, who led the country to independence from the Dutch, and headed a military regime for the next 31 years.

On the way to Jakarta we stopped off in Singapore, Reuters' reporting centre for Asia, to get a briefing. I was told by Sydney Schanberg of the New York Times, who had an office in our building, how lucky I was to be going to "the real Asia". Our paths would cross a few months later when he came out of Cambodia after its takeover by the hard-line communist Khmer Rouge.

We settled into our new home, a single-storey house in a quiet street in a suburb outside the city centre. We had a cook, a cleaning lady, a nanny (superfluous), a night-watchman and a driver, a normal contingent in Indonesia where foreigners were expected to provide as much local employment as possible. Apart from the driver, none of them spoke English and it was left to Sigi to make herself understood. The cook had been taught by previous correspondents to provide Western dishes, and he was reluctant to produce the Indonesian cuisine we loved as it invariably involved chopping lots of individual spices and ingredients.

The house was located next to someone who kept geese, which presented a problem when I was trying to send radio reports from a makeshift sound studio made up of sofa cushions. We were providing these broadcasts under a short-lived contract Reuters had with a U.S. company to provide rolling voice reports from around the world. Like most houses in Jakarta it was also within range of a mosque, with the usual call to morning payers just before sunrise and others at midday and early evening. The house, while modest, was upmarket by Jakarta standards. It was bounded by properties where families paid more for their drinking water than nearby generals watering their immaculately groomed lawns.

There was an early problem when the phone line went down. Visiting the local switching centre I discovered that connections were in short supply, and our line had been handed out to a general who had just moved into the area. After my protests it was restored, but over the next few months I had to stop off regularly on my way to work to be reconnected. I only needed to show my face at the door for an official to race into a back room to switch us back on.

A few days after our arrival in Jakarta in October 1974 our luggage arrived, and I decided to get a taste of Indonesia's notorious corruption, rated among the world's worst. Declining the offer of an agent to take the luggage through the customs process, I decided to do it myself, to the dismay of the officials. Each process required a different stamp from a different official, some of whom demanded payment. Others were probably too embarrassed to ask. I counted 27 stamps.

I was also introduced to the marginal economy in which many people operate. As I was being driven through Jakarta by a local journalist I noticed a lorry in front in which two men were constantly shovelling sand, in the middle of the tropical day. Puzzled by this, it was explained that the driver was paid by bulk rather than weight, so after paying two men to fluff up the sand during the trip he could still made a profit.

My first major task was learning to live with Indonesia's communications with the outside world, or lack of it. With no telephone or permanent telex connections with Singapore, our reports were sent in two daily 30-minute radio telex casts at noon and five p.m. They were often wiped out due to sunspot activity and had to be repeated. This procedure was already an advance on the one used by my predecessor. His reports were tapped out in morse code.

I faced a major communications problem months later while covering the Indonesian Golf Open, part of the Asian tour attracting golfers from all over the world. I had been using the local PTT to file my stories to Jakarta, but when I tried to send the result on the final day was told the office had shut at 5 p.m. After making a fuss a uniformed motorcyclist arrived at my hotel, I was ordered onto the pillion seat and driven at high speed to the local military headquarters where I was allowed to use their system.

# 8. TIMOR

Before we had time to make contact with the various ministries and the diplomatic community, I was on the move again, an unexpected trip to a little part of Portugal. In April 1974 a group of young army officers had succeeded in overthrowing the right-wing Estado Novo dictatorship that had ruled Portugal and large parts of Africa since 1933. The largely bloodless coup was known as the Carnation Revolution after citizens put the flowers in the muzzles of the guns. With the country returned to democracy the new rulers quickly began the process of pulling out of their African Colonies. These were Angola, Mozambique, Cape Verde, and São Tomé and Princip. And then there was East Timor, a pinprick of a country at the farthest end of the island chain making up most of Indonesia. Located 16,000 kilometres from Lisbon and just 500 kms from Australia, with a population of 600,000, 90 per cent of them illiterate, it was an almost forgotten colonial anachronism propped up by regular aid from the homeland. Full-bodied Portuguese red wine flowed freely, drunk chilled, and a telephone call to Lisbon cost the same as one to the other end of the island.

When Portugal's Minister for Overseas Territories announced that he was heading for Timor, I needed to get there in a hurry. One choice was a flight to the western end of Timor island, which was Indonesian, and a Portuguese airline light plane to East Timor's capital Dili, but it would not get me there in time. The alternative was one of the world's least-publicised scheduled airlines called Zamrud, operated by a former American CIA pilot from Bali, south of Java, flying to Dili once a week in a 32-year-old DC-3 airliner. Jack Rife, from Turkey Creek, Kentucky, kept one plane flying every day with spare parts from other veterans bought in a job lot from a small American airline. After I was weighed along with my luggage, we had an easy flight in clear skies. In the wet season, without weather checks or radio controls to guide them, "we just fly blind for most of the way, then come down under the clouds and start looking for the islands," Rife said.

Arriving at Dili's airport, a grass strip, we were met with a large proportion of the town's 30,000 inhabitants, as the plane's arrival was always a major event. I was quickly introduced to leaders of the three main political parties that had come into being following the revolution, representing the three clear alternatives for the country's future. The Timorese Democratic Union (UDT), for staying with Portugal until it could become independent. Fretilin, formed by young left-wingers, for full immediate independence. And the Timorese Popular Democratic Association (APODETI), for joining with Indonesia, the giant to the north, which appeared to have little popular support. Officials of all three parties came from the educated elite of Dili, many were related by marriage, and several had studied in Lisbon.

There appeared to be strong backing for continued links with Lisbon, at least in some parts of the country. In the rolling hills above the town, after a bone-crunching ride in a four-wheel-drive, I met up with a young American anthropologist living with the local tribespeople. She explained how allegiance to Lisbon was rooted in folk legends, the Portuguese were revered as saviours who arrived to restore order after centuries of fighting on the island and the Portuguese flag was venerated in tribal ceremonies, one of which I watched.

In Dili the Portuguese minister, addressing a colourful gathering of bare-chested mountain warriors and Dili's multi-ethnic citizens, appeared to rule out full independence, saying Timor was too weak to stand alone. Other countries in the region, particularly Indonesia and Australia, were known to regard the prospect of a left-wing but economically dependent country emerging in a relatively stable region with concern. On integration with Indonesia, the minister said it seemed illogical to exchange one controlling power for another.

I filed my story by telegram to our Lisbon bureau – there was no connection with Indonesia or Australia– at commonwealth rates, i.e. for virtually nothing. It arrived in Lisbon where a puzzled local staffer who had never received traffic from Timor brought it to our correspondent, who whisked it to London. A veteran news editor wrote that it was the first time in his memory he had handled a story from Timor. I learned on my return to Jakarta that the article was circulating as an official document at the United Nations while it was discussing the Timor situation. I recognised this was based less on the quality of my reporting than the fact I was the first outside journalist to visit for some time.

Flying back to Jakarta I missed the Zamrud flight to Bali, opting instead for a TAP Portuguese airlines flight in a 10-passenger Norman Islander light plane to Koepang, on the Indonesian side of Timor Island. The pilot was a young Australian with whom I had been sharing many drinks together with a few foreign tourists the previous evening. As I waited nervously at the air strip the crowd parted and our pilot, wearing dark glasses, advanced slowly, announced "I don't feel so good" and ordered me to sit in the co-pilot's seat. We had a trouble-free flight across the mountainous island.

Back in Jakarta, an odd little story dropped in on us when the Indonesian air force discovered a former Japanese soldier hiding out on the remote Indonesian island of Morotai. He was flown to Jakarta after giving himself up 29 years and three months after his government surrendered in 1945. Teruo Nakamura was the last of dozens of Japanese "holdouts" who either doubted the veracity of the surrender report, rejected demobilisation on ideological grounds or were simply not aware the war had ended because communications had been cut by the allies.

# 9. VIETNAM, LAOS, CAMBODIA

Soon after my return to base I got new marching orders, this time to Vietnam, where the 20-year-old war between Chinese- and Soviet-backed forces in the north and US-backed forces in the south was limping on, to join a small team of reporters. It was one of three civil wars going on in the region, the others being in Laos and Cambodia which also involved North Vietnamese intervention. The conflicts were known as the Second Indochina War, following an earlier one bringing an end to French colonial rule in the region.

In Saigon, American troops had left two years earlier, but there were plenty of restaurants and bars to cater to the journalists and NGOs, the only foreigners left after non-essential personnel had made their exit. The daily U.S. military briefings, known locally as the "Five o'clock Follies," were still going on, although they became briefer by the day as designated military zones disappeared off the map, swallowed by the advancing North Vietnamese/Viet Cong forces. Trips to the front for journalists were becoming scarcer. The absence of the huge U.S. military back-up system made them increasingly risky as the hard-pressed South Vietnamese military struggled to reassure the West that they were in control.

After I arrived, the local army PR worked hard to persuade a group of foreign journalists to do a day trip to a strategic South Vietnamese army base. Some of the less experienced journalists went, and they returned three days later, shell-shocked, after the base came under heavy bombardment. In Saigon itself, a 6 p.m. to 6 a.m. curfew meant that journalists and others were confined to barracks, although the Caravelle and Continental hotels where most were staying were comfortable enough. For a carton of cigarettes or a couple of dollars, you could hire your own military escort to take you back to your hotel.

The Reuters operation in Saigon — later renamed Ho Chi Minh City — was still reeling from the death of the two correspondents in the 1968 Tet offensive. As the security situation worsened, there was a reluctance to get out into the field. Still, it was eventually decided to send me north in a light plane shared with the New York Times to Danang, a major U.S. air force base threatened by communist forces. On arrival I hitched a ride on the back of a local motorcyclist headed north. From the booming of artillery and the stream of people streaming to the city, it was clear the communists were close. Back at Danang airport, we were told our plane had been commandeered by the U.S. military to fly a wounded American pilot to hospital. We were ushered onto a C47, a cargo version of the DC-3 built in the 1930s that was supposed to take a maximum of 34 passengers and were joined by a few more.

A New York Times journalist aboard, something of an aviation buff, had a front-page story the next day announcing a new world record for the plane of 94 people on board. That record was broken a few weeks later when 98 orphans were flown out of the town of Du Lat in a similar plane. A day later, a Boeing 727 belonging to World Airways, brought in by its swashbuckling owner Ed Daly, flew into Danang just as communist forces entered the city to pick up passengers. The plane with a normal capacity of 120 left with over 300 after South Vietnamese soldiers fought to get on board.

An American journalist on board, Paul Vogle of UPI, filed a memorable story:

*DA NANG, March 29 (UPI) – Only the fastest, the strongest and the meanest of a huge mob got a ride on the last plane from Da Nang Saturday. People died trying to get aboard and others died when they fell thousands of feet into the sea because even desperation could no longer keep those fingers welded to the undercarriage.*

The fall of Danang sent journalists scurrying for news from the city, now under communist control. Our ever-resourceful translator came up with the goods a couple of days later from a Vietnamese Red Cross worker who had fled the city by boat a week after its capture and who recounted life in the city under the new communist rulers, with cinemas already showing patriotic films with titles like "The Revered Flag", "The Woollen Vest" and "Battlefield in Quang Duc". He said North Vietnamese currency was being used alongside the South Vietnamese piastre, and already commanded a black-market rate three times higher than normal as people hedged against a future currency change. As for the mood of the people, he said: "Of course they are worried about economic hardship, a changed life-style and political restrictions. At the moment however they are just glad to be out of the war."

It is hard to believe today when we consider the extreme risks that journalists run covering current conflicts, but in Vietnam there were no restrictions on journalists' movements. "Embedding" reporters with troops had not even been thought up by the authorities. In the early years of the Vietnam War, journalists wore battle fatigues with "PRESS" stamped across their chests following the practice used during World War Two and Korea covered by the Geneva Conventions on the conduct of wars. That all ended when the U.S. forces pulled out in 1973.

When London Daily Mail editor Sir David English arrived in Saigon in the dying days of the war on an "Operation Babylift" to ship out Vietnamese orphans sponsored by the paper, he stepped out of the plane in immaculately tailored fatigues with "bao chi" (press) across his chest, to the bemusement of waiting journalists who had long since moved to shorts, sandals and tee-shirts.

In the next big war — the first Iraq War — the United States military banned journalists completely, recalling that it was graphic press coverage of the Vietnam conflict that helped turn the American public against it. That decision to ban journalists backfired when freelance correspondents doing their own thing, often at great personal risk, uncovered stories that contradicted official reports. In subsequent wars, the generals turned to embedding as a way of allowing in journalists but keeping them under control.

During my five-week stint there was an attempt by a lone South Vietnamese pilot to bomb the presidential palace, which produced a classic attempt by a New Zealand journalist to find a local angle.

*"A lone South Vietnamese airman flew over the New Zealand Embassy in Saigon today on his way to bombing the presidential palace."*

As the plane screeched overhead, a group of Western reporters walking in the city hurled themselves to the ground, mistaking it for incoming artillery. Some Vietnamese men stood around laughing at them, until the bombs exploded next to the nearby palace and the locals threw themselves down.

I booked a flight to write a feature story and ended up reporting a major humanitarian and aviation disaster. I had heard the authorities were flying hundreds of refugees streaming from the advancing communist forces to a remote offshore island and decided to have a look. Arriving at the airport, I was immediately directed to a cargo plane being loaded with sacks of rice. After sizing me up the co-pilot ejected one sack, and I boarded, standing up. The American pilot turned to greet me before take-off, and I could not fail to notice he had only one eye. I was assured by the rest of the crew that he was well up to it, and he proved it by landing the heavily laden plane on a grass strip covered by metal fencing.

On our return, I noticed heavy smoke rising from close to the airport and learned that a U.S. military C-5 cargo plane carrying hundreds of war orphans as part of "Operation Babylift" had crashed shortly after take-off, killing 78 children and around 150 adults, while there were 170 survivors. It was the first flight in the operation ordered by U.S. President Gerald Ford to evacuate 4,000 thousand orphans, most of them fathered by American soldiers.

After I had been in Saigon for five weeks, Reuters decided to rotate me out for a week's R & R in Singapore in preparation for what everyone expected would be the final push, and I left on a plane filled with other reporters on a similar mission. As it happened, the push came earlier than expected as South Vietnamese forces in the Central Highlands collapsed during that week, along with any major resistance.

As we flew over the Mekong Delta south of Saigon, which by this stage was firmly in Viet Cong control, the pilot had just announced our altitude when a man in the next seat handed me, without an introduction or comment, a sheet of paper detailing the weapons known to be available to the insurgents, particularly surface-to-air capability. Noting that several of them brought our plane well into their range, I handed it back, without comment.

Six days later the big evacuation came. Between April 29 and 30, 1975, some 6,000 people were evacuated by the U.S. military and more than 130,000 escaped by boat, South Vietnamese army helicopters and fixed-wing aircraft. Reuters staff ended up on a U.S. aircraft carrier patrolling off the coast. By then, it was too late for me to return, and my flight back in was cancelled. Reuters sent in a French reporter to be "rolled over" by the communists, and he joined several other foreign reporters who decided to stay. They were able to function in a restricted manner for a couple of weeks before they were ordered out as the new rulers clamped down, setting up "re-education" camps for South Vietnamese government officials and soldiers.

With Vietnam under new management international media attention turned to the other conflicts in the region. Cambodia had just fallen to the hard-line communist Khmer Rouge, so that left Laos. From Jakarta I few to Singapore and on to the Laotian capital Vientiane with a veteran Reuter correspondent, the only passengers on the Royal Air Lao airliner. Driving through the sleepy city of just 187,000 inhabitants, there was a large presence of Buddhist monks in their orange robes and a sprinkling of Western hippies attracted by cannabis openly sold at the city's outdoor food market. My first thought after looking around, it was an ideal place to quit smoking, a habit that had rocketed to 60 a day in Saigon. After checking into the Lane Xang hotel overlooking the Mekong River, I unpacked the carton of 200 Marlborough cigarettes I had bought on the plane, opened the bedroom window and hurled them out, unopened, with a cathartic roar. I never smoked again.

As far as the war was concerned, it was effectively over. In what was known as the "secret war" royalist troops had been battling communist Pathet Lao troops, backed by North Vietnam, for 10 years. The royalists were supported by the Americans, covertly as the country was officially neutral, who recruited a 30,000-strong army of hill tribesmen and flew bombing raids against North Vietnam's Ho Chi Minh trail supply route to its fighters in the south, which ran through Laos.

Everything changed in 1973 when the two sides signed a ceasefire calling for joint rule and the removal of all foreign forces, and the Americans left. The truce lasted only two years. The North Vietnamese stayed and the Pathet Lao refused to disarm, and in May 1975 the two communist allies attacked royalist positions. With neighbouring South Vietnam and Cambodia having fallen to the communists, and with no more U.S. support, the royalists bowed to the inevitable and agreed to a peaceful takeover. There were joint police patrols in the cities, and across the country towns were taken over in carefully orchestrated events organised by students and left-wing groups following what officials called "uprisings by the people".

I flew to the town of Savannakhet, the country's second largest city, in a Royal Lao Air Force Hercules transport plane, to watch the whole population turn out to greet the arrival of Pathet Lao tanks, with soldiers leaning on their gun barrels in heroic poses. A group of residents stood behind a huge banner proclaiming "The Chinese community of Savannakhet welcomes the Pathet Lao."

I had another reason for visiting the city, to talk to a group of Americans working for USAID and their families who were under house arrest following anti-American demonstrations across the country. While there was no sign of any guards around the complex as I walked in, I was assured by the families that their confinement was real. A few weeks later the USAID operation in the city was shut down and they flew home. At the time the U.S. government provided half of the $32 million annual international fund which kept the impoverished country afloat.

Despite initial promises to uphold the freedoms people had enjoyed under the old system, the Pathet Lao gradually tightened its rule. The joint police patrols gave way to Pathet Lao alone. An order went out that night-clubs were to close. On the last night before the ban I joined foreigners and locals in one of Vientiane's most popular nightspots. As midnight sounded, the French DJ played a patriotic Laotian song, and there was quiet. After 15 minutes he declared "that should keep the Pathet Lao happy", and we danced on for several more hours. Two days later, the club was ordered to close "or else". In December the Pathet Lao took full control of the country, abolishing the monarchy, sending King Savang Vatthana into exile and declaring a Lao People's Democratic Republic. Soon afterwards it signed an agreement allowing Vietnam to station troops in its country and send in political and economic advisors.

Well before this however I had pulled out of Vientiane, after paying my hotel bill, which was a major operation in a country where the only denomination of the Laotian currency in circulation was a 100-kip note, worth around 20 English pence. The receptionist at the hotel desk asked me how long I had been staying, and on hearing three weeks, reached into a cupboard with a wide selection of paper bags and produced a very large one capable of carrying several days' worth of food shopping. I was then directed to the state bank around the corner where after paying dollars several bundles of kip were packed into my bag, whereupon I returned to the hotel, handed them over and left for Jakarta.

Soon afterwards I was summoned to Bangkok, our central bureau for covering Indochina, and sent to the Cambodian border to meet a group of foreigners caught up in the Cambodian capital Phnom Penh when it fell to the Khmer Rouge in April, who were being shipped out. I was joined by Sigi, as we were on holiday in Malaysia when I got the call.

When the Khmer Rouge arrived some 800 foreigners, mainly French nationals, and 600 Cambodians sought refuge in the French embassy in the capital. They included a small group of foreign journalists, including Sydney Schanberg, who decided to ignore an order to evacuate the city. A British journalist Jon Swain was in Bangkok but on hearing that foreigners were gathered in the embassy and appeared to be safe, persuaded a Thai pilot to fly him into Phnom Penh the following morning, and joined the group. It included American photographer Al Rockoff, known for taking risks, who had been badly wounded in a shrapnel attack and had technically "died" while being treated in a Swedish Red Cross hospital. He was fond of responding to warnings he risked death with "won't be the first time".

The Khmer Rouge had a fearsome reputation, particularly among journalists. Made up mainly of young uneducated men, they were raised on an extreme form of communism inspired by Mao Zedong's cultural revolution. During the Cambodian war 37 foreign and Cambodian journalists were killed, the majority executed without trace.

After two weeks in the embassy half of the group were ordered into open trucks and driven to the Thai border, where I was waiting to receive them. They arrived after a gruelling four-day journey but announced that we could not report anything about their trip or their time in the embassy as it could endanger the lives of the rest of the group still to come. In an emotional address to the waiting journalists Schanberg threatened to personally pursue any of us breaking the information embargo. I talked to a few of the group, particularly a Scottish Red Cross doctor who had kept a diary of his time in the embassy and their journey across the country, and he agreed to talk to me once the embargo was lifted.

Returning to Bangkok, the bureau continued to cover developments in the area. A few days later reports emerged that a French official who had been in the embassy was quoted in a newspaper describing some aspects of life there. I got a call from the Red Cross doctor saying that as the embargo appeared to have been broken, he would speak to me. Meeting in his Bangkok hotel he described in meticulous detail life at the embassy and the grim situation in the country outside of the Khmer

Rouge takeover. After discussions with Reuters and other news organisations we decided not to use the story yet but sent a long report for London to prepare.

A few days later word came that the second convoy was heading out and I drove to the border with Sigi in a hotel taxi. As soon as we saw the dust of the approaching trucks I sent her back to the telegraph office to occupy the single phone line while I stayed to meet the second group. I arrived at the telegraph office to a scene of total chaos. Sigi had been chatting to our Bangkok bureau chief John Rogers when a young AFP journalist who had been in the embassy burst through the door, saw the line was occupied and launched himself over Sigi's head to pull out all the plugs. This enraged a New York Times journalist whom I had promised to let file a few lines – Reuters had an arrangement with some U.S. papers – and a fight broke out. The head of the office, a tall Thai speaking good English, ordered everyone out of the room, declaring he would select the reporters at random. Reuters came up first, but we had already sent word to London to release the story. It was an extraordinary tale but gave only a slight indication of the horrors to come over the next four years of genocide.

The report told of ghost cities and towns emptied of people as the new communist rulers ordered everyone to work in the fields. "The houses were all empty, the capital was empty," said one Frenchman. Hospital patients, including thousands of bed-ridden war victims, were pushed, wheeled and carried out of the city at gunpoint. Earlier the inhabitants had stood beside the road waving to the incoming troops as loudspeakers declared: "The war is over, do not resist." A French photographer in the embassy commented: "Little did they know it had only just begun."

Other towns they drove through were almost deserted, with half-eaten meals in some of the houses, indicating a hasty departure. A radio announcement had ordered town-dwellers to take food for two days, any possessions they wanted, to leave their doors open and head for work in the rice-fields. The doctor said that more than 90 per cent of the paddy fields seen on the journey had not yet been planted even though the monsoon season was approaching, raising the prospect of severe food shortages down the line. And this was in a country where over 25% of the population had been displaced and 20% of property destroyed by war.

In the embassy itself the Khmer Rouge ordered Cambodians, Vietnamese and Chinese nationals to leave the embassy, apart from a few women married to Frenchmen. Three marriages were performed in the embassy, one for a French journalist marrying his girlfriend, the others of convenience to allow the women to remain. Those expelled included members of the Cambodian royal family and a few government ministers. Later information revealed that some senior government ministers managed to escape the country, but others, including Prime Minister Long Boret, were captured and executed, along with former government soldiers. Schanberg and Swain were taken away by a group of young Khmer Rouge soldiers and were about to be shot but were saved by the persistent intervention of Schanberg's translator Dith Pran. I knew Swain from Saigon and he told me later in Bangkok that he had given up hope but Pran's beseeching eventually wore down the soldiers.

In the embassy the remaining group of over 800 from 21 different nationalities, sleeping in cars, the garden and the cinema, suffered shortages of food, water and sanitary facilities, by drinking water from air conditioners and occasionally skinning and eating a cat. After five days the Khmer Rouge handed out beer, cigarettes, whisky, rice, and muddy water from the Mekong River. Once they dumped half a dozen live pigs, which were slaughtered by a French doctor turned butcher.

Over the next few years the full extent of Khmer Rouge leader Pol Pot's experiment in communism became clear as he sought to create a socialist agrarian republic free from outside influences. Targeted were all professionals, intellectuals and ethnic minorities such as Vietnamese, Chinese, Thais, and anyone connected with a foreign government.

Wearing glasses and having soft hands was often enough to deserve the death sentence.

During Pol Pot's rule an estimated 1.5 to 2 million people died, the great majority of them executed and buried in mass graves, the remainder through hunger and disease. Some 20,000 mass grave sites were eventually discovered, the "killing fields" coined by Pran that became the title of a film largely about him. A large proportion of the dead were killed by scythes, clubs and sharpened bamboo sticks, to save ammunition.

The Khmer Rouge maintained their brutal rule until 1979 when newly unified Vietnam invaded and installed a rival communist government. The Khmer Rouge retreated to the jungles of Cambodia and waged guerrilla war against the new government for 10 years. The monarchy was restored to Cambodia in 1993 and the Khmer Rouge had largely dissolved by the mid-1990s. Pol Pot died in 1998, but two former leaders were sentenced to life imprisonment by a United Nations-backed court in 2014 for crimes against humanity.

# 10. TIMOR REVISITED

Back in 1975, it was time to return to Indonesia, where our first task was to find a new house as the owner of ours wanted to reoccupy it. We eventually found a delightful little house with a small enclosed garden set above street level – but only after Reuters had to fork out three years' rent in advance, the usual practice in Jakarta that had made a lot of people, particularly the military, very rich in a short time.

The situation in East Timor was developing rapidly. Early in 1975 the two pro-independence parties had joined in a loose coalition which lasted until August, when policy differences came to the surface. Civil war broke out after the UDT staged a coup which sparked a three-week civil war that left Fretilin in control for three months after the Portuguese military garrison backed them.

In September and October Indonesian special forces began operating secretly across the border from West Timor against Fretilin troops. With Zamrud no longer operating to Timor I tried to fly in on a Portuguese flight from Koepang along with an Australian freelance journalist based in Jakarta. As we tried to persuade the Portuguese pilot to take us, the governor of the region, an admiral, arrived in full military uniform and threatened to shoot down the plane if we tried to take it. The pilot turned us down, with regrets.

On October 16 our local Jakarta staffer Soeharyono was tipped off that five Australian TV journalists had been killed while covering the Indonesian incursion into East Timor, and we broke the story of what became known as the Balibo 5. The journalists were based in the provincial town of Balibo, and, believing they would have protection as Australians and journalists, had painted a large national flag on the side of their building.

The official Indonesian version was that they were killed in crossfire during fighting. The bodies were burned beyond recognition. The remains of the five were sent by the Indonesians to the Australian embassy in Jakarta and examined by a doctor who declared they were "probably" human bones. The remains, which fitted easily into a cigar box, were buried in a windswept cemetery in Jakarta in the presence of Australian diplomats and the small foreign press corps.

In a sombre mood after the ceremony we retired to a local chicken restaurant. As we ate in grim silence we watched as Tony Joyce, a correspondent for the Australian Broadcasting Corporation, was piling chicken bones on the side of his plate. Pointing to them, he remarked "that's the entire Melbourne branch of the AJA" (Australian Journalists' Association), injecting a much-needed burst of black humour. He was to die himself four years later in Zambia after being shot in the head at point blank range by an unknown assailant while sitting in a police car.

The killing of the Balibo 5 sparked huge popular protests in Australia, but its government kept relatively silent, and did not officially challenge the Indonesian version of events, indicating that they shared Jakarta's concern over the prospect of a left-wing state in the region and wanted to keep on good terms with their nearest neighbour.

In December the Indonesians staged a full-scale invasion of East Timor, taking over Dili and the second town of Baucau in a lightning operation in which hundreds of civilians were killed. Australian freelance Jill Jolliffe who was reporting for Reuters at that time managed to flee the city in the nick of time with the International Red Cross. Not so lucky was another Australian freelance Roger East, who had flown in weeks earlier to try to find out about the Balibo killings. He was lined up and shot along with a group of around 50 civilians, including women and children, and their bodies were dumped in the sea.

The invasion began a bloody 25-year occupation of the territory in which an estimated 100,000 to 180,000 people were killed or starved to death. It ended in 1999, after the 30-year-old military regime in Jakarta was overthrown, when a referendum was organised by the UN and the overwhelming majority voted for independence. After the result pro-

Indonesian militias went on the rampage, terrorising civilians and destroying homes and factories in what amounted to a scorched earth policy. I went back to Timor 25 years after my first visit for the Reuters Foundation training journalists in the territory, many of whom wrote and fought under Indonesian occupation, living in the mountains, and noted sadly that Indonesia had provided more infrastructure in a quarter century than the Portuguese in 500 years, then trashed much of it in a fit of pique.

With Timor gone quiet, the main story for the next few months was the rise and fall of Indonesia's giant state oil monopoly Pertamina. In early 1975 the company could do no wrong, controlling Asia's largest private airline, a shipping line with its own tanker fleet, and vast rice and cattle estates. It produced its own annual budget figures, and the finance minister never knew until the last minute how much he was getting in revenue. It all came apart when a small US bank called in a relatively small loan and revealed that the company was over $3 billion in debt.

In late autumn 1976, after I had got a call to return to London as a sub-editor on the World Desk, I was hosting a farewell lunch for press colleagues in our favourite Chinese restaurant when the ABC's local staffer rushed in to announce there had been a coup d'état. Leaving our groaning banquet untouched we stumbled out expecting to see tanks in the streets. All was quiet as we returned to our offices to discover what was going on. It was, in the end, a very Indonesian coup, based largely on Javanese mysticism and superstition. It turned out that an obscure former official in the agricultural department called Sawito Kartiwibowo had published a number of documents, backed by a couple of former senior politicians, one of which accused Suharto of allowing his family and friends to enrich themselves and of betraying the trust of the people. Sawito, who had apparently convinced himself he would become president after receiving a flash of light while meditating, was arrested.

The affair was dismissed by Suharto's security chief Ali Murtopo as a storm in a teacup, but the president was worried enough to issue an unprecedented statement denying he and his family were enriching themselves at the nation's expense. While Suharto himself was not thought to be personally avaricious, his family were notorious for taking their cut, particularly his wife Tien, known as "Mrs Tien Percent" for the amount she was believed to have sliced off every major business transaction.

# 11. RETURN TO THE "COLD" COLD WAR

After two years on the World Desk I was back in Vienna, this time in a permanent posting joining three other journalists, including a trainee, and with a roving brief allowing me for the first time regular visits to all the East Bloc countries.

I drove from London in a battered Volkswagen Beetle with Sigi and a five-month old daughter on the back seat and a pram strapped to the roof. After two days in the Intercontinental Hotel we moved into our predecessor's flat in a leafy district of Vienna. In what proved a godsend for the family it was just around the corner from the Türkenschanz Park, with a large playground, marking the spot where Ottoman Turks dug their trenches during their unsuccessful two-month siege of Vienna in 1683. The closeness the besiegers came was underlined by my daily bike ride to the office in central Vienna, which took just 15 minutes.

While the main focus of the bureau was East Europe, Vienna was also the headquarters of three United Nations organisations – The UN Development Organisation (UNIDO), the Office on Drugs and Crime (UNODC), and the International Atomic Energy Agency (IAEA), which checks on countries' peaceful nuclear programmes to ensure they are not being diverted to make weapons. The city was also the headquarters of the Organisation of Petroleum Exporting Countries (OPEC), the scene of frantic activity by financial reporters when major meetings were called to discuss issues affecting the global oil price. This was an organisation that proclaimed an oil embargo in 1974 in retaliation for U.S. support for Israel in the 1967 Middle East War that drove up the world oil price by 300%.

I had some experience of the tension surrounding these meetings, going back to an oil ministers' meeting in Bali, and when OPEC called a conference of oil ministers I was roped in to try to interview them as they emerged from the talks. Standing alone in a square outside the Hofburg Palace where the conference was held I confronted Saudi Oil Minister

Ahmed Zaki Yamani, an influential figure within OPEC, as he slipped out of the meeting early. Dodging my question on whether the group would raise prices with a non-committal answer, he drove away. I strolled back to the Reuters booth in the conference press centre, waited until our oil correspondent arrived shortly afterwards, and told him what had happened. "Have you sent it out as an urgent", he shrieked, to which I replied that Yamani had not said anything of substance. I was then given a very quick lesson in the realities of the rarefied and high-octane world of oil reporting. The fact that such an influential figure had left the conference early would have been taken by thousands of nervous financial traders across the world as an indication of how it was going, and they would have acted according to their experience and instincts.

Vienna was also a popular venue for major international conferences, partly due to the efforts of the country's long-serving chancellor Bruno Kreisky. He decided the best defence strategy for his small landlocked country, sharing borders with eight others divided between East and West, was to turn it into an essential meeting point where both rival groups could discuss outstanding issues. He cited Britain's wartime leader Winston Churchill as declaring "meeting jaw to jaw is better than war". One result of this policy was that my first major story on arriving in Vienna was to cover a summit between US President Jimmy Carter and Soviet leader Leonid Brezhnev on 18 June 1979. It ended with the signing of the first agreement between the superpowers to limit long-range missile launchers to 2,400 on each side.

Kreisky, a social democrat who ruled the country from 1970 to 1983, also brought his country into the volatile world of Middle East politics by supporting Palestinian demands for proper representation and seeking an end to terrorism in the region. The Austrian leader, a non-practising Jew, invited Yasser Arafat, head of the Palestinian Liberation Organisation (PLO) set up to win independence from Israel through armed struggle, to Vienna in 1979 and granted full diplomatic status to the PLO office in the capital. Israel, which regarded the PLO as a terrorist organisation, reacted with outrage. Kreisky's decision came back to haunt the country two years later when guerrillas from the rival militant Fatah faction that split from the PLO attacked Vienna's main synagogue, killing two people and wounding 18.

Meanwhile we covered seven countries including Austria. It was a busy bureau, even at a time when, to the outside world, not a lot seemed to be happening in East Europe. The bureaus with full-time correspondents mainly filed their reports directly to London but were frequently called on by Vienna to contribute to stories reflecting regional developments or reactions to major news stories. Opportunities to travel to the less well-reported countries were limited but were seized on as an opportunity to contact Western diplomats and the odd dissident.

Some trips in the early days were to cover sports events, particularly football, at a time when Reuters was still committed to providing major news of British clubs travelling abroad to British regional newspapers.

# 12. CZECHOSLOVAKIA

I got to Prague for the first time in July 1969, driving from East Berlin and filling in for a month before the first anniversary of the invasion while our hard-pressed correspondent took a few weeks leave. The heady days of the Prague spring and the intense emotions of the invasion had given way to a widespread feeling of resignation. Dubček, who had been allowed to stay on as Communist Party leader, had been forced out in April and given a job in the forestry commission. He was made the scapegoat of a sudden outpouring of national pride and anti-Soviet feeling which burst from the World Ice Hockey Championships held in Sweden in March and April.

The Soviet Union had entered the tournament as hot favourites having won the previous six championships and three out of four Olympics. But for Czechoslovakia, where ice hockey is the national sport, this was clearly about much more than sport as it beat the reigning champions in both matches, becoming the first hockey team to overcome the Soviet Union twice in the same tournament, while losing to the Swedish hosts. It was the first time in international ice hockey that body checking was allowed in all sections of the ice, and the Czechs took full advantage of the new rules as they turned their bodies into human missiles in one of the most violent matches ever recorded.

When news of the second 4-3 victory was relayed to Czechoslovakia thousands of citizens took to the streets in celebrations that in some cases, particularly in Prague, turned to anti-Soviet protests with signs saying "there were no tanks so they lost", and "Czechoslovakia 4, occupation forces 3". During the disturbances the Prague office of the Soviet state airline Aeroflot was ransacked, and while there was widespread speculation this was the work of the state security police StB it provided the evidence the occupiers needed to claim the leadership had lost control.

Anti-Soviet feeling was ingrained in the country since the invasion. A Western journalist who had worked in Moscow and spoke good Russian, but was desperate to learn Czech, had complained to a Czech friend in English about the lack of toothpaste. Remarking that there was no shortage, she asked him to speak his order in Czech, responding: "Oh no, that sounds way too Russian." In another case we were drinking at his local bar, where he was well known, and he ordered a second round of drinks in Czech. After being ignored several times by the waiter, he said to me "over to you". I asked for two beers in German and got the immediate response "straight away, sir", and they arrived promptly.

Dubček was replaced by Gustáv Husák, a Slovak who had been an early ally of the reformers but changed course to head a group of party conservatives calling for a reversal of the Prague Spring. In the first steps in a process of "normalisation" that grew gradually more authoritarian over the next two decades, he re-introduced censorship and overturned moves to liberalise the economy, allow political opposition groups and more free speech, and reduce the activities of the secret police. Early victims of the new laws were writers, artists and filmmakers who had thrived during the reforms, including internationally known playwright Vaclav Havel, whose works were now banned.

With legal outlets for ordinary people's anger and frustration closed down, they turned to humour, for which the country was famed, much of it directed at the Soviet Union, state security officials and the stuttering economy, particularly the lack of choice in food and other consumer goods. In one joke doing the rounds a fairy godmother offers a man three wishes, to which he replies for all three "the Chinese army to invade Czechoslovakia, and then return home". The puzzled fairy grants the three wishes but asks for the reason behind them. "They will have to cross the Soviet Union six times", was his response. Jokes about police were popular across the East Bloc, but particularly in Czechoslovakia where the StB was starting to crack down on any signs of dissent. Someone walks into a Prague bar announcing "I've just heard a great police joke", at which point a man rises from the back warning that he is a policeman. "In that case I'll tell it very slowly and repeat it if necessary." An old woman asks a butcher for a variety of prime cuts, from sirloin steak to calves liver, which had not been seen for years as they were destined for high party officials or export to the West for hard currency. As she leaves one butcher remarks "What a silly old woman", while the other says "But what a memory".

Two years later I was back in Prague, this time as full-time Reuters correspondent for Czechoslovakia, a posting that lasted a year before I was called back to Berlin for the final stages of the German-German talks. The political situation had hardened, with an active dissident movement disseminating news, views and banned literary works through "samizdat" clandestine publications, under the radar of the StB. Many political figures, writers and journalists associated with the reform movement were eking out a living cleaning windows, stoking boilers in apartment buildings and other menial jobs. The economy had not improved, and relations with the Roman-Catholic church, among the most troubled in the East Bloc since the 1950s, appeared to have worsened.

We regularly received the samizdat reports, which often included news of the latest arrests and jailing of dissidents, from a former Moscow correspondent for Czechoslovak TV reduced to stoking a boiler in a large block of apartments after being sacked. His visits followed a similar pattern: a knock on the door, we would open it and point him towards a typewriter, without a word being exchanged, as we assumed our office was bugged. He would tap away on a report and when finished would rise, bow to the rest of us in the office, and leave. We would race to the typewriter and usually find a story worth sending out to the wider world.

These reports would inevitably be followed by an increase in interest from the StB, but their agents were relatively easy to spot when they followed us as they insisted on doing their shadowing in foreign cars rather than Czech made Škodas. The preferred vehicle was a white Citroen, which made spotting them even easier.

Colin McIntyre

I was able to thank our samizdat provider Luboš Dobrovský nearly 20 years later when he was appointed Defence Minister in President Havel's government. The irony was not lost on either of us when I was ushered in to see him and we spent the first few minutes laughing uncontrollably.

Despite the attentions of the security services I was able to meet local people, and became friends with a group of students at Charles University and a few others. They were aware there was some risk in associating with me but dismissed it. One of the students, Michael Žantovský, would play a major part in national events and Reuters' coverage of them two decades later.

My assistant/translator was Johnny Krčmař, whose background reflected the political changes in his country over the past couple of decades. The son of a Czech diplomat and Italian mother, he was barred from a university education because of his bourgeois background. Speaking accent-free English after schooling at private Dulwich College in London, he was working in a steel factory until his language skills brought him to a job with CTK. Thrown out of the agency after writing the report of Soviet troops entering the agency's newsroom, he was picked up by Reuters.

He made it clear from early on that he was expected to report to the StB on my actions. One day during a lull in activities he asked me if I had anything to report that he could pass on to "the boys". Wracking my brains, I recalled visiting the American Embassy recently for a social drink on Friday with the US marines guarding it. The next day he arrived at work to declare "they loved the marines".

My first task was to find someone to teach me Czech, outside office hours, and after the word went out we were visited by Jan Šling, whose father Otto was one of the 11 leading Communist Party officials convicted of nationalism in a Stalinist show trial in 1952 and executed. Jan's mother was English, so lessons went smoothly for a couple of weeks until he disappeared, sent to jail for speaking out about the situation in foreign broadcasts, particularly the BBC and Radio Free Europe. Recalling the

84

troubles my colleagues had experienced during my last trip to Prague, I decided to stick to English and German, which, although it brought back memories of the brutal six-year occupation of the country by the Nazis for many older people, proved to be a useful neutral lingua franca.

My next task was to get a license plate for my car, a battered Renault 4, and was surprised to see that the ever-vigilant security authorities made what I considered a small blunder. Foreigners were given colourful number plates that could be spotted at a distance, red lettering on a bright yellow background, with numbers allocated to their embassy. As there was no Australian embassy in Prague, the authorities decided to issue me with plates for the International Organisation of Journalists (IOJ), a communist front grouping set up by the Soviet Union and based in Prague. The result of displaying these plates meant that I was often waved through regular checks by the security police as a friendly figure.

A major news challenge came with the parliamentary elections of 1971. Like all East Bloc elections they were largely meaningless as candidates were dominated by the Communist Party and there was no genuine opposition. The only way for voters to register their opposition to the party programme was to spoil their ballot, a brave move that involved crossing the polling station to a single curtained booth in full view of officials. But as they were the first elections since a constitutional reform in October 1968 created a Czechoslovak federal Republic from individual Czech and Slovak states, and the first since the Warsaw Pact invasion, the authorities were clearly taking them seriously. This presented a problem for journalists trying to accurately report the situation. After trying to assess the mood of the public by talking to people, and unsurprisingly discovering widespread apathy, I agonised for hours while writing a preview of the polls and sent a carefully worded piece to London. It came back with few changes, but with the apathy angle moved to the opening paragraph. I sensed trouble, and immediately took a copy of my outgoing report and waited for a phone call, which came a few hours later from the foreign ministry press department requesting my presence immediately. I received an official warning, and an apology from London.

On election day I sent an early report and waited for Johnny to join him at the voting process. As an indication of how seriously the authorities were taking the poll his home was visited three times by the authorities warning his mother he would get into trouble by failing to vote. With 10 minutes to go before polls closed we raced to his local polling station, he marched straight to the booth, put a line through the ballot paper and left.

Not surprisingly all 350 seats in the bicameral parliament were won by candidates of the National Front made up of the Communists and a mixture of small parties. The reported victory margin was 99.45 per cent.

Czechoslovakia was known for producing and consuming some of the best beers in the world. At the time I was there the country ranked second in the world behind Belgium for annual per-capita consumption, at 29 gallons. Excluding mainly wine-drinking Slovakia from the equation, the Czech lands of Bohemia and Moravia headed the world. The best-known brews were Pilsner, from the town of Plzen close to Prague, and Budvar, from České Budějovice in south Bohemia. While Pilsner went on to lend its name to a certain type of beer produced all over the world, Budvar, also known as Budweiser after the town's German name, became involved in a long-running trademark battle with the giant U.S. brewery Anheuser-Busch over the use of the name.

After spending some time in Prague trying out the two brews, along with a few others, I was invited for an official tour of the Pilsner brewery, founded in 1842 and in continuous production ever since, despite damage by British bombs during World War Two. The only time production was paused was during the country's first free elections in 1990 after the fall of communism, when the authorities ordered all beer production and bars to close to avoid any alcohol-fuelled incidents.

In the Middle Ages, when hereditary brewing rights were enjoyed by individual houses, Pilsen town councillors would make regular spot checks to test quality. This involved a sample being poured on a bench and when dry was sat on by local worthies in leather trousers. If they stuck it was a good brew. If the bench came up with them as they stood, it was an outstanding one.

After a tour of the brewery and sampling the brew, strongly encouraged by my hosts, I had lunch and left for Prague six hours later after touring the city, hoping my alcohol level would have disappeared by then. Czechoslovakia had a nil level for car drivers. I was picked out by a policeman at the edge of town, narrowly failed a breath test, and was taken to a local clinic where the doctor was clearly on my side, suggesting "have you been eating apples". I had to leave the car and return to Prague by train with Johnny, who had also failed the test. A few days later we were visited by a policeman who took away my license for six months.

One of the more unusual stories we handled involved a young Czech woman who had fled to Sweden with her husband following the Warsaw Pact invasion, leaving their daughter behind with her grandmother. The woman flew back in a light plane piloted by Swedes in a bid to bring out the girl, was arrested after their car was stopped for speeding and put on trial in Brno, the capital of Moravia. We drove down to attend the trial but as we waited to enter the courtroom it was filled by secretaries and other staff summoned from all over the building, and we were told there was no room inside. The woman, who was pregnant with her second child, was found guilty and put under house arrest but after three years and pressure from the Swedish press and government allowed to re-join her husband with their daughter.

The daughter Paulina Porizkova, six at the time of the trial, went on to become one of the world's top models, an actress and writer.

In the summer of 1971 Czechoslovaks, or the vast majority of them, were stunned to learn that Emil Zátopek, possibly the greatest distance runner of all time and a vocal supporter of the Prague Spring reform movement, had recanted his opposition to the Communist Party. Zátopek, a national hero after winning the 5,000 metres, 10,000 metres and marathon at the 1952 Olympic Games and setting 18 world records during his long career, had been expelled from the party and stripped of his army rank of colonel after the 1968 Warsaw Pact invasion. He worked in several jobs including dustman, where he was often recognised by passers-by who emptied his bins for him.

In an interview with the party daily Rude Pravo he said: "I would consider it to be a shame to be an enemy of the Communist system."

"I was like one of those wild people who really poured oil onto the flames, which could have turned into a fire able to endanger the Communist world," he was quoted as saying. He was invited back into the party and allowed to travel.

Zátopek, whose ragged running style was once described as "wrestling with an octopus on a conveyor belt", lost much popular support for his decision, though many recalled his competitive spirit and generosity. He handed one of his Helsinki Olympic medals to Australian distance runner Ron Clarke who broke a string of world records but never won a championship medal. When Zátopek died in 2000 a private ceremony at Prague's National Theatre was attended by the Czech Prime Minister, a decision that caused something of an uproar in the country.

Just before Christmas, I got a call from a policeman speaking perfect English suggesting we meet at a local café. After an hour of polite conversation which included what I felt was a heavily veiled inquiry into whether I was prepared to help them, he reached in his pocket, handed back my passport with "Happy Christmas" and left.

In January 1972 a report came through CTK late at night that a Yugoslav Airlines (JAT) DC-9 with 28 people on board had crashed in Czechoslovakia after a mid-air explosion. A friend who was visiting called a hospital in a town near the crash site and learned that, miraculously, one of the stewardesses had survived. The next day we set off for the site, managed to get through a police road block in the back of a local workman's van and discovered that the plane, flying from Stockholm to Belgrade via Copenhagen, had broken up into three sections. We learned that the stewardess, Vesna Vulović, had been found in the wreckage by a local villager who had been a medic during World War Two and kept her alive until she reached hospital, where she remained in a coma for 27 days.

The Belgrade authorities immediately blamed Croatian ultra-nationalists who had carried out several attacks on Yugoslav civilian and military targets over the years. This appeared to be confirmed when on the day of the crash a bomb exploded on a train travelling between Vienna and the Croatian capital Zagreb, injuring six people. The following day a man describing himself as a Croatian nationalist rang a Swedish newspaper and claimed responsibility for the airliner bombing. A German newspaper report claiming the airliner had been brought down by Czech fighters mistaking it for a military plane was eventually dismissed.

Vesna Vulović, who was left with a limp, went back to work with JAT as ground staff. She became something of a celebrity in her own country, particularly after she was cited by the Guinness Book of Records as setting a new world record height for surviving a fall without a parachute, 10,160 metres (33,330 feet), receiving the award from Paul McCartney of the Beatles. She was fired from JAT in 1990 after taking part in protests against Yugoslav leader Slobodan Milošević, a Serb nationalist who eventually broke up the country.

A few months later I was back in Berlin. I returned to Czechoslovakia in 1979 as Prague correspondent but based in Vienna, while covering other East Bloc countries. Reuters had downgraded the bureau to local correspondent level due to the difficulties of operating under Husák's increasingly harsh regime.

The situation in the country had worsened on all fronts. An economy in free-fall, relations with the Catholic Church at crisis point and the StB cracking down hard on dissent. This followed the emergence of a loose civil movement that broke new ground by challenging the government to keep to international pledges on human rights and individual freedoms which it had signed up to. The Charter 77 group may have had limited support in the country, particularly outside Prague, but it gained increasing exposure abroad as its clandestine reports reaching Western newspapers and radio stations continued to embarrass the government.

Although the signatories of the manifesto were careful to emphasize they were not an organised political party, which would have made them illegal, the government condemned the group as anti-state and anti-socialist and subjected signatories to several forms of harassment including jail. Their treatment led to the formation of a second group The Committee for the Defence of the Unjustly Persecuted (VONS), and in October 1979 six of its members including Havel were jailed for up to five years.

In 1981 around 40 people were detained in a major roundup following the arrest and expulsion of two French lawyers accused of smuggling in émigré material and money for dissidents, and some were later jailed. The crackdown was seen as indicating the government's anxiety over recent events in neighbouring Poland, with the establishment of East Bloc's first free trade union.

My student friends from 1971 had faded into the background, and I was reluctant to try to contact them.

On the economic side the lack of consumer goods that people actually wanted had led to a sort of barter system in which anyone able to offer a service, such as a doctor, plumber or electrician, was likely to jump the queues for food and other services. The system existed alongside straightforward corruption with bribes for everything from trying to gain a university place to buying land for a country cottage and obtaining scarce goods in shops.

The government even acknowledged that corruption was a problem. An army-run magazine came out with the startling revelation that a West German businessman caught trying to smuggle cameras and watches into the country said he needed them to bribe foreign trade officials. The squeeze on consumer goods was compounded by a poor grain harvest and the Soviet Union's decision to cut its oil deliveries which made up 90 per cent of Czechoslovakia's needs by 10 per cent.

The parlous state of the economy prompted the Communist Party Central Committee to recommend in mid-1982 that more people be allowed to work as independent artisans as their main job. Up till then only pensioners, housewives and invalids could be licenced as full-time private dressmakers, shoemakers and carpenters, and only on a limited basis. Since the communist takeover in 1948, when farms were collectivised and businesses nationalised in a frenzy of ideological purity, private industry had not gone much beyond tiny garden plots growing fruit and vegetables. Even orthodox East Germany had allowed some private businesses and restaurants, and Hungary enjoyed a thriving private sector helping make it run East Europe's most successful economy.

Details of the new recommendations were vague and initial interest quickly gave way to scepticism. As one Western diplomat remarked: "There seems to be less in the proposals than meets the eye."

Meanwhile the communist authorities were continuing their crackdown against the Catholic Church, both the officially recognised body and a "secret church" which appeared to be still thriving despite being driven underground by three decades of tough anti-religion policies. Church sources reported that priests were being stopped in their cars by police and failing breathalyser tests after sipping communion wine. Vatican Radio reported that some priests who had been exempted from military service were being called up. The moves appeared to be a concerted drive to restrict the numbers and activities of Catholic priests.

The secret church was reported to be strongest in Slovakia, which has a predominantly Catholic population, but was spread throughout the country. Vaclav Maly, a spokesman for Charter 77, said that at least 30 priests were celebrating mass privately, and there were also reports of secret convents where women shared the same apartment, living like nuns, but dressing normally.

Despite repeated attempts the authorities were unable to silence one outlet for protest in Prague, the so-called "democracy wall". Erected originally as a memorial to former Beatles star John Lennon shortly after his shooting in New York in December 1980, the wall turned into a protest for democracy and free speech in graffiti that was painted over as soon as it appeared but re-written just as quickly. The cat-and-mouse game seemed likely to continue as posters appeared in the surrounding area in central Prague, which contained several foreign embassies.

# 13. ROMANIA

My first visit to Romania was in July 1970, while I was posted to East Berlin, when Soviet Prime Minister Alexei Kosygin visited Bucharest to admonish Romanian communist leader Nicolae Ceausescu for failing to join other Warsaw Pact states in the invasion of Czechoslovakia two years earlier. Ceausescu had taken over the leadership of the Party in 1965, added the role of head of state in 1967, and immediately began setting the country on a relatively independent course in foreign policy while easing censorship of the press and the arts at home. In condemning the invasion of Czechoslovakia he rejected Moscow's self-proclaimed role as the sole arbiter of world communism, and joined Western organisations such as the General Agreement on Trade and Tariffs (GATT) and the International Monetary Fund (IMF). On the economic front, the country was a significant oil producer benefitting from soaring world prices.

Ceausescu's stance soon brought the country to the attention of the West, particularly the United States, and in 1969 it became the first communist country to be visited by a U.S. president with the arrival of Richard Nixon.

All of this made Bucharest a pleasant contrast to my current East Berlin experience. The cafés were full, many of them outdoors, and ordinary people were happy to talk to foreigners. Food seemed plentiful in the shops, and the streets of a city which between the two World Wars was described as "Paris of the East" due to its elegant architecture and sophistication of its elite were throbbing with activity.

After a perfunctory greeting of the Soviet premier at the airport by Ceausescu, with none of the embraces and bear hugs reserved for trusted allies, the two men sat down to discuss a new friendship treaty. After a long wait that went well into the night with my AP colleague we managed to get a copy of the communiqué, in Romanian, at around midnight after taking a taxi to the office of the national news agency Agerpres. With no translators available at that hour we were forced to ask the bouncer in the night club in the basement of our hotel, with no more than basic English, to help us out. Working through the night we had something available in the early hours, only to find that our Moscow bureaux had come up with a rounded version based on a full Russian text.

The text of the agreement was fairly bland, committing the two countries to cooperation on a number of levels. However it omitted any reference to the Brezhnev Doctrine, which had been included in a similar friendship agreement with Czechoslovakia signed a few months earlier. The omission was widely seen as Moscow's reluctant acceptance of Romania's go-it-alone policies, comforted by the knowledge that despite Ceausescu's limited reforms, the Communist Party was still firmly in control of the country. For Moscow, there were possible advantages in being able to show the West that the Communist bloc was not monolithic but prepared to tolerate the odd maverick.

Nearly 10 years passed before I visited Romania again from Vienna, and the country bore no relation to the one I experienced, albeit briefly, in 1970. Ceausescu, now 61, was running one of the most oppressive regimes in the East Bloc, with full control over the media, a state security service that monitored and terrorised the people and a cult of personality surrounding himself and his wife Elena. The economy was in tatters and saddled with huge hard currency debts due to mismanagement.

The transformation came after the Ceausescus visited China, North Korea and North Vietnam in 1971 and returned fired by Chinese leader Mao Zedong's cultural revolution which aimed at purging the remnants of capitalist and traditional elements in society and North Korean leader Kim Il-Sung's policy of "Juche", achieving true socialism through building national self-reliance. On his return home Ceausescu issued a series of edicts known as the "July Theses" setting out his plans for an ultra-nationalist revolution led by the Communist Party.

It was against this background that the Romanian Communist Party held its 12th congress in 1979 which re-elected Ceausescu to a fourth five-year term, called for continued emphasis on heavy industry over increasing the supply of consumer goods and reaffirmed the country's independent line on foreign policy.

The congress passed a resolution calling Ceausescu among other things "most beloved son of the people, a brilliant leader and remarkable revolutionary, a highly prestigious and authoritative personality of present-day political life". It was typical of the cult of personality created around him and his wife, who had enjoyed a meteoric rise through the party ranks to become the undisputed number two in the country.

When Ceausescu appointed himself President of the Republic in 1974 he had himself presented with a bejewelled sceptre clearly influenced by European royalty, a gesture that was greeted by Spanish artist Salvador Dali in a telegram saying "I deeply appreciate your historic decision to establish the presidential sceptre". The national press, either missing or choosing to ignore the obvious satire, put it on the front page.

An exhibition in the national history museum in Bucharest devoted two whole floors to presents Ceausescu received from the nation on his 60th birthday the previous year. They included large tapestries of him from different parts of the country, some showing him carrying the sceptre, many bearing the title "omagia" (homage). One exhibit was a record-player, a gift from the Securitate secret police, with a note "made in our workshops".

The Securitate was one of the largest secret police forces in the East Bloc, compared to the population, making its presence felt through informers. At the time there was reckoned to be one agent or informer for every 43 of Romania's 22 million population, which made it virtually impossible for a network of dissidents to survive. According to Western diplomats the Securitate's influence was enhanced by spreading rumours through the population. One was a supposed new clause in the penal code making it obligatory for any citizen having contact with a foreigner, whether by accident or design, to immediately contact the police. I had several experiences trying to talk to local people who shied away, clearly reluctant to have anything to do with the security forces. I questioned the authorities about the new clause, whose number was well known in the population, and was shown the latest copy of the code - which made no mention of it.

After two days of the party congress the small group of foreign journalists attending it decided to skip the third day, traditionally a quiet one at such pre-programmed meetings, and took off to retrace the history of the 15th - century warrior-prince Vlad Dracul whose cruelty inspired the vampire legend. Encouraged by a spate of Dracula films and books appearing in the West, the Romanian tourist authorities were seeking to cash in by organising tours to Bran Castle, in the province of Transylvania, thought to have been Dracul's home.

The BBC correspondents and myself decided to check with the tourist authorities before we went, and an embarrassed official admitted that Dracul, known as "The Impaler" for putting his enemies on wooden stakes as a deterrent to others, had never lived at Bran Castle.

"We know we are sitting on a potential gold mine," the official said, "but we cannot allow a flood of superstition to be transferred onto the shoulders of an important figure of our history." Dracul was credited with halting the advance of the Ottoman Empire in this part of Europe and of being ahead of his time in working to centralise the state.

The official said Irish novelist Bram Stoker, who wrote Dracula in 1897 without ever visiting Romania, took a name and added his own imagination and 19th-century Irish superstition.

Visitors to the castle were clearly unaware of the castle's disputed past, and the visitors' book was full of entries like "To Dracula, with love", and "At last I have visited Dracula's lair, and enjoyed it". Not so happy was the little German girl who wrote: "I came to see Dracula, but he wasn't at home."

Returning to Bucharest in the late afternoon we learned there had been an extraordinary incident at the congress when an 84-year-old veteran Communist official attacked Ceausescu verbally, accusing him of putting personal interests before those of the country and ignoring real problems. The president retorted by indirectly accusing Constantin Pirvulescu, a founding member of the Romanian Communist Party, of being a Soviet agent, and party officials briefed correspondents that he was senile.

While playing down the incident officials were clearly alarmed by it, and I was followed everywhere the following day by a Securitate operative, clearly recognisable by his ill-fitting clothes and habit of spinning around or bending to tie his shoelaces every time I looked back.

Western diplomats pondered whether the incident, which was not reported in the strictly controlled Romanian press, was an isolated outburst by an angry old man or the tip of an iceberg of discontent. While there were few obvious signs of resentment in a population under constant surveillance, Western embassies reported an increase in applications from Romanians to emigrate, hoping that by the act of applying they would be regarded as troublemakers and eventually allowed to leave.

With consumers already forced to buy imported low-grade meat while top-quality produce was exported to the Middle East for hard currency, the future looked anything but rosy.

The regime was still recovering from the shock of a strike by thousands of coalminers in Transylvania's Jiu Valley two years previously, the first big challenge by ordinary workers to the party's authority. Some 35,000 of 90,000 miners downed tools in protest against an extension of their working hours, low pay, an end to disability allowances and bad conditions. The miners refused to deal with anyone but Ceausescu, who eventually arrived and tried to settle the crowd with a rambling five-hour speech interrupted by booing, but finally gave in to several key demands. The concessions were quickly withdrawn and a major crackdown on the strike organisers saw hundreds jailed or sent to other areas and Securitate agents drafted in as miners to inform on others.

Colin McIntyre

On a reporting trip to Romania several months after the Party congress, the situation in the country had visibly worsened. As the government sought to repay nearly $6 billion debt to Western commercial banks, it was forced to step up exports of agricultural products to the West and Middle East for hard currency. Much of the debt was money borrowed to finance an ambitious programme of building refineries to handle its own and other oil arranged when world crude prices were sky-high. When prices slumped Romania was left with more capacity than it could use.

Rationing of bread, cooking oil and sugar was introduced, for the first time since World War Two. As the government's years of neglecting agriculture in favour of heavy industry was highlighted by a poor grain harvest, long queues formed for milk, eggs, and meat, mainly of poor quality. A joke doing the rounds was that pig's trotters had been renamed "patriots", as the only meat not going abroad. In the following years heating and electricity were also added to the rationing list, and in 1985 regional radio stations were closed and television was cut to one channel broadcasting just two hours a day.

Ignoring growing popular discontent over the shortages, Ceausescu went ahead with a grandiose plan drawn up in the late 1970s to transform Bucharest and other cities into showcases of communist rule influenced by his trips to China and North Korea. In the face of opposition from planners in 1983 he destroyed nearly 400 hectares (4 square kilometres) representing some 20 per cent of Bucharest's old city centre to make way for the Palace of the People, one of the world's largest buildings covering 385,000 square metres, and a huge boulevard leading to it flanked by apartment blocks with impressive frontages but little behind. Among buildings destroyed were 27 orthodox churches, eight of which were relocated, six synagogues, three protestant churches, an Art Deco theatre and two museums.

# 14. ALBANIA

Like just about every foreign correspondent, I had long considered Albania the Holy Grail of reporting destinations. In self-imposed isolation after breaking with former allies and mentors Yugoslavia, the Soviet Union and China, in that order, the world's first officially atheist state did not welcome visitors from anywhere, particularly journalists. No Reuter journalist had managed to visit for 16 years. Part of the Ottoman Empire since the 15th century, Albania achieved independence in 1912 following the Balkan Wars, and was ruled by a former tribal leader who became prime minister in 1922 aged 27, president a few years later and King Zog the 1st in 1928. When the country was invaded by Mussolini's Italy in 1939 the royal family went into exile, and a year later the Nazis took over.

In 1944 communist leader Enver Hoxha, a committed Stalinist, took control of the country of just 2.7 million people, the poorest in Europe, and introduced a system he trumpeted as the only pure form of communism in existence. The system, which remained virtually unchanged for the next 45 years, banned private cars, religion, beards and long hair for men. Hoxha set up a secret police force, the Sigurimi, which was reported to have 30,000 officers and ran forced labour camps across the country for suspected dissidents. It was thought that one in three Albanian citizens had either spent time in a camp or had been questioned by the Sigurimi.

In the early 1950s right-wing guerrillas including emigres backed by the U.S. and British secret services landed in Albania in a bid to topple the regime but were betrayed by British double agent Kim Philby and all were killed or captured. Philby, who was eventually unmasked and fled to Moscow in 1963, insisted in a later interview on East German TV that his action had prevented a major confrontation in Europe by dissuading the West from undertaking similar operations in other East Bloc countries.

Meanwhile Hoxha, who was educated in France but had not left Albania since 1961, cut all links with former friends and neighbours. First with Yugoslavia, a close ally during World War Two but an enemy when it broke away from the Stalinist Soviet Union in 1948. Ties with Moscow were cut soon after Nikita Khrushchev denounced the late dictator in 1956. And finally with China for continuing to deal with the "revisionist" Soviet Union. This left the impoverished country completely self-reliant economically.

My first experience of Hoxha was wading through an 800-page political diary published in 1979 shortly after my arrival in Vienna in three languages and writing a report on it. He revealed that the country's 17-year link with China, which had formally ended the previous year, was anything but a love affair. After coming down on Beijing's side in the Sino-Soviet split during the 1960s the Albanian leader made clear that his new ally treated his country little better than the old one.

As the diary told it, Hoxha was from the start suspicious about Chinese policy "which has always been characterised by vacillations and opportunism," and despite his warning to Beijing "revisionism in China grew steadfastly stronger day by day." He also accused Chairman Mao of creating a personality cult around him almost like a religion, adding: "Are we dealing with Marxists or with religious fanatics?"

Extolling Stalin as "a great man, a great revolutionary" whose mistakes, "if they exist, are minor ones", he recalled that the Soviet leader, blamed in the West for millions of deaths from executions, Gulag labour camps and famine, "took the greatest care of me...even over the hat I should wear to avoid getting a cold, and going so far as ...to show me where the toilets were if I needed them".

My eagerness to visit the country was whetted by the experience of British journalist James Cameron, who recalled in a memoir finding a small item in a West German newspaper in 1963 advertising an eight-day visit to Albania. Filled with excitement over a possible scoop he arrived at Munich airport to discover to his horror that all the 17-strong group waiting to take up the offer were journalists. Their Albanian hosts, quickly realising these were no ordinary tourists, kept them on a very short leash during their time in the country, and nearly sent Cameron home early after he cabled a brief story to his paper calling the country "isolated".

Worse was to happen to the last Reuter journalist to visit Albania at around the same time as Cameron. Eager to get his experience into print he filed a story on his first day in the capital Tirana describing the centre of the city as resembling a medieval Turkish village. That evening there was a knock on the door of his hotel room and he was advised he was booked on a plane to fly him home early the next day. Another early Reuter visitor found his hosts were only interested in finding out the radio frequency we were using to transmit stories to some countries. He discovered later that the national news agency ATA had been illegally tapping into Reuters World Service, but the company had changed the frequency.

With the economy in serious trouble following the break with Beijing, there were signs that Albania was starting to look elsewhere for trade partners. One day the Vienna office was contacted by the Albanian embassy's press attaché Mr Bejo, a young man speaking good German who expressed interest in what we were doing. We continued to cultivate him, waiting for the moment to suggest a trip to Albania. That moment eventually arrived when Austria was drawn to play Albania in a World Cup soccer match in Tirana. After lengthy negotiations, it was agreed that I could fly into Tirana the day before the match, book into a hotel, attend the match the following afternoon and fly back to Vienna in the same plane as the national team. I was under strict instructions from Mr Bejo – you can look around, but you can't talk to anyone.

After flying to Belgrade I joined a Hungarian flight to Tirana, one of only four a week to the Albanian capital. The fortress mentality of the reclusive country became apparent immediately as the plane had to make a big curve and come in from the Adriatic Sea since foreign flights were banned from overflying Albanian territory. However as an indication that the country was starting to open up to the outside world, passengers included Hungarian chemical experts, Czechoslovak businessmen and a Yugoslav working for a West German company buying Albanian crude oil.

Leaving Tirana's tiny one-story airport in a rickety van my attention was drawn immediately to the sight of concrete bunkers, shaped like pillboxes, littered across the country, many newly built. Over 170,000 of them were erected as part of the country's "people's war" defensive strategy based on the partisan model used successfully during Albanian resistance to the Nazis led by Hoxha. One could not fail to notice that they were positioned to face an invasion from any quarter, as Albania had no allies, just enemies.

We passed fields where no trace of mechanisation could be seen, with men ploughing behind oxen as brigades of women attacked the earth with spade and hoe.

Tirana revealed itself as an attractive city of well-tended parks and tree-lined streets that were spotlessly clean. The city's architecture could be divided into four main groups – the narrow streets and compact buildings harking back to Turkish rule, the faded elegance of the inter-war period under King Zog, the formal Brutalist showpieces of Mussolini's rule and undistinguished post-war apartment blocks. In the giant main square named after national hero Skanderbeg, a 15th-century warrior who resisted Ottoman expansion, a lone policeman directed virtually non-existent traffic with agitated whistling and vigorous arm movements. Facing the square was a mosque carrying a sign declaring it to be a cultural monument. The gates were bolted shut, according to a local official because of renovation work on the murals inside. When Albania abolished religion in 1967 an estimated 70% of the population were Muslim, 20% Orthodox Christian and 10% Roman Catholic.

After checking into the Hotel Dajti in the city centre, with dusk falling, I persuaded the elderly lady at reception to let me look at a list of embassies – there were only 10 -- and a map of the city. Noting the addresses of the Italian and French missions, I headed off on the dimly lit streets intent on breaking my promise to Mr Bejo. At the Italian embassy, a building like all the others in the street, the ambassador was away, but his nervous young assistant told me that many Albanians, including the young, could speak Italian and could pick up Italian TV stations.

At the French embassy, I knocked at the door and it was opened immediately by a tall, distinguished looking man of middle age who hauled me eagerly inside, produced a bottle of Johnny Walker Black Label whiskey and we chatted for several hours. I had the feeling that my charming host, who was fluent in English, was happy to pass up his regular bridge game with the Greek, Italian and Turkish envoys. I speculated as to what may have sent such an apparently highly qualified diplomat to what must have been seen as the ultimate backwater. I decided it probably involved some senior French official's wife, mistress or secretary.

Among other things we discussed the question of who might succeed the 72- year-old Hoxha, in power for 36 years. My host said Hoxha was expected to be replaced by prime minister Mehmet Shehu, 67, his right-hand man for three decades, with his position boosted by the appointment of his brother-in-law as defence minister and a nephew as interior minister. Diplomats did not expect any major changes in policy. As for trying to find out what ordinary Albanians felt, particularly the young, there was little opportunity in such a secretive society.

There had been reports in the mid-1970s of unrest among the country's youth, with a growing desire for more Western music and fashions and the chance to travel abroad. The immediate consequence of this was that the few Albanian students abroad were called home immediately. The programme had only recently been revived and there were now some 100 Albanians studying abroad.

The next morning I visited an exhibition entitled "Albania Today" which was clearly aimed at showing both foreigners and ordinary Albanians that the country could go it alone economically without foreign credits, concessions or aid. The exhibition showed Albania could produce the whole range of essential goods, everything from ploughs to pins, needles and buttons. It also showed a few manufactured goods such as drills and X-ray equipment of basic quality, but these were unlikely to find ready markets in Western or Eastern Europe.

Albania's ban on accepting foreign credits or allowing foreign concessions and joint ventures was not the result of some passing whim. The policy was enshrined in the country's 1976 constitution drawn up personally by Hoxha, ensuring that his policies would be continued after his death.

"You can't run a household on borrowed flour," one Albanian official was quoted as saying. "It's just colonialism under another name."

There appeared to be enough basic food in the shops, a local Skanderbeg brandy was quite drinkable, and the country was proud of their wines containing no chemicals. This gave the wines an attractive natural taste, but without additives to stabilize the process left them open to going off quickly. I witnessed a dinner for a party of officials where the waiter lined up a row of bottles, opening them one by one and sniffing each one, setting several aside for later use in cooking.

In its search for ways of boosting the economy Albania was reported by diplomats to be looking to the West, not for aid, but for compensation. Albania was reported to be demanding some $2 billion in war reparations from West Germany for damage during the Nazi occupation, and around $40 million worth of Albanian gold which fell into British hands during World War Two. Britain refused to return it until Tirana paid compensation for the sinking of two British warships by mines in the Corfu Channel in 1946.

After attending the football match in the national stadium, won by Austria 1-0, I flew back to Vienna with the team and filed my stories.

Several days passed without a word from Mr Bejo, and I began to wonder whether something I had written had upset them. This was confirmed a few days later when I was walking through central Vienna and met him coming the other way. He immediately crossed the road to the other side. After several calls to the embassy went unanswered I arranged a meeting at which he complained furiously about my mention of Prime Minister's son-in-law becoming defence minister, which he denied, and saw as an accusation of nepotism in the leadership.

Eventually normal relations were restored, and we heard nothing unusual from Albania until almost exactly a year later when Prime Minister Shehu was reported by the Albanian news agency ATA to have committed suicide "in a moment of nervous distress".

Speculation of a rift between the two leaders over policy was underlined when there was no declaration of national mourning, and only a terse obituary in the party daily Zeri I Popullit. Albanian diplomats in Vienna said there was no national mourning because suicide was considered a disgraceful act "directed against the party".

Confirmation of a major rift came in 1982 when Hoxha accused Shehu in a book of spying successively for the United States, Soviet Union and Yugoslavia. A few years later the party daily revealed for the first time that Shehu had been "liquidated" for espionage.

In the same year there was a curious report of another abortive landing on Albania's coast by armed emigrés, 30 years after the previous such attempt. The government announced that heavily armed "runaway criminals" equipped with radio transmitters and foreign and Albanian currency had landed, were discovered the following morning and were "totally liquidated" by soldiers, security forces and local residents.

A day after the announcement the exiled claimant to the Albanian throne Prince Leka was quoted as saying in Paris that commandos from a royalist National Liberation Army had staged the landing. Leka, 43, told a French newspaper he had been against the operation because it seemed suicidal.

# 15. BULGARIA

Bulgaria had been de facto ruled since 1956 by Todor Zhivkov, who followed the Soviet line faithfully and cracked down on dissent through his feared CSS secret police. The country gained international notoriety in 1978 when dissident writer Georgi Markov, who had defected to London 10 years previously, was assassinated in broad daylight in the city with a poisoned umbrella.

The major story from Bulgaria in the mid-1980s, when I had moved to Ireland, was the regime's forced assimilation of the country's 800,000-strong Turkish minority, a hangover from the Ottoman Empire that ruled the country for 500 years. In 1984, Sofia ordered that all of them must adopt Christian names and renounce their Muslim religion and customs. Even Turkish names on gravestones were ordered changed. One man complained that he had been forced to change his grandfather's name, "which was absurd as he had died 16 years before I was born". There were protests, but they were quickly snuffed out as the authorities deployed tanks and water-cannon and issued arms to ethnic Bulgarians in the area.

The government official justification was that the minority were originally Bulgarians who had been forcibly "Turkified" under Ottoman rule, and claimed they were changing their names voluntarily. There was a widespread view that Zhivkov was worried the higher birth-rate among the minority threatened to destabilise the country.

I visited Bulgaria infrequently, as there was little hard news coming out of the country. Despite its hard-line image, I found the mood among ordinary people quite relaxed, particularly compared to that in Romania across the border. Most of my visits to the country were confined to covering football matches involving British clubs, or the English national side on one occasion. There was an unwritten system under which the Reuters correspondent in the region would contact the manager of the home side for team news and quotes, which would then be passed on to the travelling British press in exchange for similar information about the visitors. The journalists would then spend hours and large sums of money phoning their match previews back to the UK through the hotel's system, struggling to spell out Slavic names over a bad line which was cut when, almost inevitably, they tried to get a Georgi Markov angle into their report.

One interesting story from Bulgaria involved an interview with Zhivkov's daughter Lyudmila, an enigmatic 38-year-old who had enjoyed a meteoric rise through the party and was responsible for education, culture and science. This had led to widespread speculation that she was being prepared to take over from her father in what would have been the first dynastic succession in the East Bloc.

When I interviewed her in the presidential palace along with a local translator, a charming diplomat's son who spoke fluent English and German called Tony, she shrugged off the suggestion, saying: "The question is of no concern to me, only to journalists. Only time will provide the answer."

Lyudmila certainly had plenty of influence in the country. We were originally told our interview would be held the following day, so we headed off by car to visit a town over 100 kilometres away, Gabrovo, billed as the humour capital of Bulgaria, after setting up an interview with town officials by phone. Passing through a remote village a policeman leaped into the road, flagged us down and told us Lyudmila wanted to see us in an hour. We asked him how he knew we would be in that village, and he replied: "Police in every village between Sofia and Gabrovo were told to look out for you." With a wide grin Tony said "I've always wanted to do this", put the warning lights on, pressed the horn and we rushed back, making it just in time.

During the interview Lyudmila showed her practical side by recalling how she had opened the country to outside culture, including much more from the West, and re-vamped the education system to emphasize work-related training. She was also keen to talk about her pursuit of an abstract ideal she called "new socialist man" which appeared to combine oriental mysticism, European philosophy and Marxist doctrine that even some of her admirers found puzzling.

"Nature has created all possibilities for man to corresponded with his environment, the problem is ensuring that man develops in an all-round manner," she said as Tony struggled to make sense of it.

When we completed our broken journey the next day Gabrovo, a bleak industrial town, turned out to be a disappointment. The site of an annual humour festival, whatever passed for jokes were based mainly on the meanness of the inhabitants. The symbol of the town was a cat with no tail, due to the inhabitants shutting their doors too quickly in winter to save energy. The standard Gabrovo joke was of two men attending a show, and when someone comes around asking for contributions one of the men faints and the other carries him out.

# 16. POLAND

On July 8, 1980, the State Aviation Works in Swidnik, a small town on the outskirts of the major industrial centre of Lublin in eastern Poland, went on strike over higher meat prices. The action came after Prime Minister Edward Gierek's government, facing a major economic crisis after borrowing heavily in the West in a bid to modernise the economy, raised prices of basic consumer goods while slowing wage growth. According to the strikers, it all began after one worker noticed that the price of a pork chop dinner in the factory canteen had soared by 80% overnight. The strikes soon spread to other factories in the Lublin area, and by the middle of July an estimated 80,000 workers from over 170 factories in the Lublin area were on strike. Railway workers in the city were reported to have welded a locomotive to the track. Their demands were limited to bread-and-butter issues -- the price of food, salaries and working hours. The government sent a delegation to the strike area, most of the demands were met, and by the end of July the strikes were over.

But on August 14, another strike broke out among shipyard workers in the Baltic port of Gdansk, an action that would have far-reaching consequences for the country, the government and the Communist system as a whole. The initial reason for the strike was the sacking of a popular crane operator and union activist, Anna Walentynowicz. But in contrast to their colleagues in Lublin, the Gdansk strikers were also demanding far-reaching political reforms, including the right to form independent unions with freely nominated and elected leaders, and the abolition of censorship. These posed a direct challenge to a system where the unions had almost no power, rubber-stamping decrees coming from the party. Communist ideology dictates that in a system in which the worker is supposed to own the means of production, going on strike is striking against himself. The shipyard workers were in effect calling for the formation of a pluralistic society in which the unions would become an established source of power outside party control.

The strikes across the country were not organised by one central body, but the strikers did get help from dissident intellectuals who had looked on in horror as a short-lived workers' strike in 1976, over food prices, was brutally put down by the government. The shipyard workers were led by an electrician, Lech Walesa, who had lost his job after the 1976 strike.

In Gdansk the situation developed like wildfire. Four days after the initial strike shipyard workers in the port of Czczecin went on strike, setting off a wave of stoppages that shut down activity along the coast, and in the coal mines of Silesia that fuelled industry and domestic heating, and brought the economy to a standstill.

As the embattled government offered to talk to the strikers, I was ordered to fly to Warsaw, and then to Gdansk, while our correspondent manned the office in Warsaw.

I arrived in the port city, along with dozens of other journalists from all over the world, to be greeted by the news that the city authorities had ordered a total ban on the sale of alcohol while talks with the government were taking place. With tension high over dwindling food stocks in the shops and fears of Soviet intervention, the move, though hardly popular, was accepted as one way of heading off popular outbursts. Recalling the alcohol ban to an Irish journalist years later, he said he had always wondered why the events in Poland were so well covered by the press.

The next day a delegation from the government led by deputy Premier Mieczyslaw Jagielski arrived for a first round of talks with the strikers during which he conceded that the authorities might be willing to permit strikes when all other avenues of redress had become closed. This concession, unheard of in the rest of Eastern Europe, was the strikers' second major breakthrough. The first was to force the government to the negotiating table in Gdansk, and not Warsaw.

Appearing to stand firm on the strikers' demands, which now included the reinstatement of Walentynowicz and the erection of a monument to the dozens killed during a major workers' strike in Poznan, western Poland, in 1956, Walesa told journalists: "We are demanding, not pleading."

After a second round of talks, broadcast by loudspeakers across the shipyard, the two sides came up with the Gdansk Agreement signed on August 31. It accepted most of the strikers' demands headed by the right to set up an independent trade union, the first in the Soviet Bloc, which soon developed into Solidarity, a social movement that eventually swept the country. The agreement also provided for the right to strike, limits on censorship, salary increases, the broadcasting of Sunday Catholic mass on state radio and TV, and the freeing of political prisoners.

"We have not got everything we wanted," Walesa said after signing the document with a large pen decorated with an effigy of the Pope.

"But we have got what was possible in the current situation, and we will get the rest later," he added before declaring the shipyard strike over and joining Jagielski in singing the national anthem.

Celebrations of the successful end of the talks were muted after the authorities decided not to lift the alcohol ban. However in at least one Gdansk restaurant diners were offered tea, in china pots and cups, which turned out to be wine, if requested.

Before flying back to Warsaw the next morning I dropped by the union's new office, proudly announcing the first independent trade union in the Soviet Bloc, to watch Walesa open it, eventually, after coming without the key and sending for another one.

On arrival in Warsaw I was sent straight down to Silesia, where striking coalminers had helped bring the economy to its knees and were having their own negotiations with the government. Poland was a major producer of high-quality coal for both domestic use and exports. Hailing one of the hotel's limousines, I headed south for the 350-kilometre journey to Jastrzębie-Zdrój, the centre of the strikes. Arriving a few hours later, we headed for the main mine where the talks were going on. Climbing a hill leading to the mine we came up against a police checkpoint, and I was seized by panic as I realised that my Polish visa, which was valid for only a few days, had run out. In East Bloc countries this was regarded as a serious misdemeanour usually resulting in expulsion from the country or worse. A young policeman got into the car and we drove to the local police station where he asked me to wait as he went inside. After a quarter of an hour he returned, opened the door and handed me my passport, saying in perfect English with a smile "That's fine, everything is in order". At that point I realised that the movement that became Solidarity had already spread its influence into all aspects of Polish life.

As dusk fell I joined the crowd of miners outside the main building to listen to the negotiations, which were broadcast by loudspeakers. As they went on through the night I listened to them, translated for me by waiting miners into English or German, until the moment shortly before dawn when agreement was reached and the strike was called off, a major development for both Reuters general news and financial services. After filing a report to our correspondent in his home in Warsaw I headed back to the capital, and after a few days back to Vienna.

I returned to Warsaw three months later to spell our correspondent Brian Mooney, taking a holiday after working virtually 24/7 to cope with the fast-developing situation. The Polish authorities only allowed international news organisations one foreign reporter at a time to operate in the country, meaning that I flew in on the plane taking him out, throwing me the keys to the office and the car as we passed each other at the airport.

My working conditions had improved dramatically with the introduction of new technology into the Warsaw office, a simple computerised keyboard linked to the system allowing us to tap out and correct stories, store them on a drum for later use, and send them to London with the press of a button. Up till then we had to write our stories on a typewriter, punch them onto tape on a telex and feed that through. The local staff would sometimes do the punching but with my experience of Vienna and other East Bloc bureaus I could type a lot faster when speed was essential.

The new technology was introduced in London a few months later, after the power of the Fleet Street print unions who had resisted it had been broken – Warsaw was used to try it out – which resulted in dozens of staff facing redundancy. Reuters offered aptitude tests and retraining for all sectors affected, including messengers. As a result several tape-punchers, many of whom had shown sharp intelligence in picking up mistakes and sometimes poor grammar in stories handed to them, found jobs elsewhere in the company. At least one became a regional manager, while one of the messengers, the bottom of the pecking order, found his way to becoming a foreign correspondent.

The situation in Poland had changed dramatically as what began as an independent trade union exploded into Solidarity, a national movement with a membership of 10 million, the bulk of the country's work force. It now had branches in all the regions, moving into offices provided by the state and taking over membership of the old discredited official unions, most of which had disbanded.

"There was a gap to be filled, and since the party was not able to fill it, Solidarity jumped in," one Polish official said.

The union was selling Solidarnosc (Solidarity) lapel buttons, calendars, posters and tee-shirts. Recently a ship was named after the movement.

But with large sections of the country on strike the food situation was dire, shelves were empty in the shops, and in April ration cards were introduced for meat. For those who could afford to go out to eat, the first call to a restaurant was "Do you have any food?"

At the local branch office in Warsaw, housed in a crumbling building entered through a courtyard, a largely volunteer staff struggled to cope with increasingly complex problems and a flow of people threatening to engulf them. A delegation from the Geneva-based International Metal-Workers Federation (IMF) said after a visit to Solidarity that the new organisation faced problems because people turned to it to settle complaints that would not be considered part of trade union work in the West.

However the union still had plenty of routine business. Shortly after my arrival millions of workers stayed at home in protest at the government's decision to offer Polish workers only alternative Saturdays free, in apparent contravention of the Gdansk agreement promising a 5-day working week. And farmers in south-east Poland went on strike to protest harassment of union activists and demand the registration of a private farmers' union called Rural Solidarity, as well as punishment of communist officials involved in putting down the 1976 food price riots.

In a bid to prevent union activists across the country from coordinating their actions the authorities had cut phone lines to the major industrial sites. But they forgot about telex machines, installed in most major factories as well as the Reuters bureau, enabling them and us to communicate by teleprinter.

Unlike other East Bloc countries, where land was owned by the state and agriculture collectivised, nearly 80 per cent of Polish farms were privately owned. Attempts to collectivise the land in the 1950s following the Stalinist model were soon abandoned, partly due to opposition from the powerful Catholic Church. While many farmers worked uneconomically small plots and were starved of equipment and fertilizer by the state, they still managed to outperform state farms.

While pushing reforms into new territory, Solidarity's organisers had been careful not to challenge the leading role of the Communist Party in the country's life, and the party itself appeared to be following a Moscow-approved course. However things changed in March, 1981, when a meeting of the party's central committee saw a revolt of the rank-and-file against the old guard. This was followed a month later by an unprecedented conference of grass-roots members in Torun, Poland, which called for further liberalisation, greater press freedom and far-reaching democratic reforms within the party.

The political developments in Poland prompted the Soviet news agency Tass to accuse the Polish party of "revisionist elements", one of the most serious charges in the Kremlin book, and similar to those levelled against Czechoslovak leaders before the 1968 invasion.

Gierek, whose government had allowed the creation of Solidarity, had already been replaced as party chief by Stanislaw Kania, under pressure from hard-liners in Moscow who feared Poland was preparing to leave the communist trading bloc Comecon. The prime minister portfolio was handed soon afterwards to General Wojciech Jaruzelski, who had fought with Soviet forces in the battle to capture Berlin. In October he took over from Kania as party leader and his first act was to form a Military Council of National Salvation.

On December 13, Jaruzelski went on television to announce the introduction of martial law across the country. Demonstrations broke out across the country as army, citizens' militia and ZOMO special units took to the streets armed with water cannon, tear gas and clubs. Thousands of demonstrators were arrested and dozens killed. In a coal mine in Katowice nine pro-Solidary miners were killed by ZOMO forces. Speculation over whether Jaruzelski ordered martial law to prevent a Warsaw Pact invasion similar to 1968 in Czechoslovakia continued for years.

Martial law was lifted in 1983, but many political prisoners were not released until a general amnesty in 1986. While the crackdown spelled the end of Poland's unique reforms, Solidarity's challenge to the authority of the Communist Party, though short-lived, set an example that other countries in the region were soon to follow as the pillars of communist rule began crumbling.

I received word of my next move, to Ireland, an abrupt change of subject-matter as I left the Cold War behind – but not for long, as it turned out. What little I knew about the island of Ireland was that it was divided between an Irish Republic in the south where daily life was dominated by the Catholic Church and a British-ruled part in the north where a Protestant majority was fighting a seemingly never-ending war against minority Catholics seeking reunification.

However what appeared to be entrenched positions in both parts of the Ireland which seemed unlikely to produce much in the way of news stories began to change shortly after my arrival as a new Irish government decided to take on the Catholic Church over its ban on abortion, divorce and contraception, while in the north there were moves by Britain to bring the Dublin government into the search for a peaceful solution for the territory.

# 17. IRELAND

Learning that I was heading for Ireland my initial response was unenthusiastic. I had visited the divided island briefly once, knew little about it, and had no family connection with it, as far as I knew. All that changed within a few weeks. Firstly, Sigi informed me, out of the blue, that she had always wanted to visit Ireland. She based this on reading "An Irish Diary" by German novelist and Nobel laureate Heinrich Böll, who visited the country in the 1950s, one of the poorest in Europe at the time, and eventually bought a cottage on a remote island off the coast. The book, which was translated into English and 16 other languages, was a huge success, particularly in Germany where it had shaped the perception of Ireland for decades. Describing a country he saw as quite different from the rest of Europe, coming out of World War Two, he was particularly struck by its attitude to poverty. In his opening paragraph he wrote: "Here Europe's social order took on different forms: poverty wasn't just 'no disgrace', it was neither an honour nor a disgrace."

A few weeks later my father, who was in semi-retirement and had begun for the first time to look at our family's background, broke the news that the McIntyre ancestor who went to Australia in the 19th century came from Ireland, not Scotland as we had always assumed. So now I was not going to a new country, I was going back to my roots.

Arriving in London for a briefing, my role was not simply taking over a bureau, but creating one from scratch. Because of the strong position of British newspapers in the Republic of Ireland, with most British dailies producing Irish editions, Dublin had hitherto been covered by the British national news agency The Press Association.

While this arrangement had served Reuters well over the years, the reporting tended for obvious reasons to concentrate on issues of interest to Britain. With Ireland joining the European Union in 1973 there was growing interest for Irish news from its European partners. There was particular interest for less Anglocentric news from troubled British-ruled Northern Ireland, the only continuing conflict among the bloc's members.

I was sent to Dublin on a pre-assignment trip at the end of 1982 to cover the general election, always a good opportunity for journalists to examine rival parties' dirty washing. The elections saw the Fianna Fail government headed by Charles Haughey ousted by a Fine Gael administration led by Garret Fitzgerald.

The elections provided an opportunity to try out new technology gradually being introduced into reporting and editing as the Fleet Street unions were losing their hold over the printing process. I was among the first London-based Reuters reporters to use a device called a Teleram Portabubble, the size of a large typewriter with a built-in basic computer, small screen and a cradle for transmitting copy by telephone. Bulky and heavy, requiring users to carry up to 30 metres of cable to plug into an available socket, it nevertheless changed the lives of travelling reporters. Instead of banging out a story on a portable typewriter and phoning it through or punching it out again on a teleprinter, reporters could tap out a story, editing as they went along, and send it in seconds down a phone line to London, where it could be processed immediately. The machine could also store old stories and background details in its memory. Hailed as a breakthrough in communications technology, the company that produced it went bust three years later as other firms moved in with smaller, lighter, cheaper and faster devices powered by batteries, particularly the Tandy.

We even learned eventually how to transmit our reports from a Tandy through a public phone on the street, an operation that entailed unscrewing the microphone and attaching wires with crocodile clips. This worked well until I discovered that in some countries this procedure was classed as espionage with heavy penalties. One also ran the risk of angry would-be callers banging on the windows of the phone box, and in one case desperate fellow-journalists tried to drag me out by force.

Back in London, I packed up the family's goods and we headed for Dublin, with our daughter now four and a two-year-old son. We had already found a place to live after Reuters wisely allowed us to spend a few days in Dublin to find a property as we were the first foreign staff to be seeking accommodation. It was ideally located near St Andrews College, a non-denominational school offering an alternative to the Catholic system established across the country. It also had a kindergarten over the back fence where our daughter was enrolled, which proved invaluable when Sigi and I decided to have our first evening out without the children, watching a play at Dublin's famous Abbey Theatre. Calling home at the interval to check there was no answer, and in a panic I called the head of the kindergarten who said "hold the line" before racing around the block, knocking at our door, finding the baby-sitter playing happily with our children, and returning breathlessly to report.

Shortly after our arrival the company organised a major reception in the city's top hotel to announce our arrival in Ireland. It was a lively event that went on well into the night. One guest was taken to hospital, which was widely seen as the sign of a good party. However I also learned that a potential scandal was brewing, and that I should plan an early start the next morning.

I arrived very early with a sore head on my first real day at work at the Reuters office, a small operation of technical and sales staff looking after customers of the company's financial services.

I was confronted with one of the biggest political scandals in the country's history. The biggest in fact since what was known as the Arms Crisis of 1970 in which Haughey, then finance minister, and other senior Fianna Fail figures were alleged to have helped smuggle arms to the Irish Republican Army (IRA), fighting to end British rule in Northern Ireland.

The new story broke as the incoming justice minister announced that the previous government had authorised telephone taps on three leading Dublin journalists. The taps, normally used only to investigate serious crime or threats to national security, were introduced after consulting the nation's police chief following growing suspicions within Fianna Fail that senior figures were leaking information about party infighting. The scandal led to a major reshuffle within Fianna Fail and came back to haunt Haughey nine years later when it contributed to his resignation as prime minister.

I had a brush with the murky world of Irish politics a few days later at a gathering of journalists in a pub near the parliament. Confronted by an attractive woman "of a certain age" who had noted my reported arrival in the country she asked me how Haughey was regarded in Britain. I was searching for the right diplomatic words when I was elbowed sharply in the ribs by an Irish journalist I knew from shared drinking sessions in London, Paddy Clancy, who whispered "Terry Keane". She was Haughey's mistress for 27 years, wrote a gossip column in a leading daily newspaper, and my non-committal reply to her query may have saved me serious embarrassment.

While the country was digesting the wire-tap story, another one broke from an unexpected quarter. On February 8 a news flash announced that Shergar had been kidnapped at gunpoint by a balaclava-clad gang. It meant nothing to me until I learned that the victim was one of the most successful racehorses of all time, winning seven of his last races including a 10-lengh victory in the English Derby, the biggest winning margin in history. The horse, owned by the Aga Khan, had then been put out to stud on a farm he owned in Country Kildare, not far from Dublin. At up to £80,000 for each cover, Shergar was not just famous, but also very valuable.

While it was a huge story globally, for Reuters financial reporting desk there was a more important task for me, Ireland's annual budget. So while my journalist colleagues in Dublin were joined by dozens from abroad in following up the Shergar story, I spent the day in parliament handed the budget speech page by page by a treasury official, to avoid any leaks, and sending the key points to London as urgent news on my Portabubble. The appearance of this machine was greeted with hilarity by colleagues in the parliament's press centre who sent their stories in the traditional way by phone. Despite their insistence that they would never need such technology, within a couple of years they were all using Tandys.

The next day I was able to join the hunt for Shergar, which took days, then weeks, as the kidnappers demanded a £2 million ransom which was refused by its new owners, a syndicate of 34 which required proof the horse was still alive and was anxious not to set a precedent. There were rumours it had been abducted by mercurial Libyan leader Muammar Gaddafi, who had been accused of providing explosives to the IRA and had allegedly been spotted riding him across the desert. As the investigation trail went cold the police chief running the investigation began deploying an unconventional range of detention techniques, including clairvoyants, psychics and diviners.

Neither the kidnappers nor the body were ever found. Years later a former IRA member claimed the organisation was behind the action, designed to raise money for arms, but the horse had injured itself soon after the kidnapping and had to be put down. Another later version had an uninjured Shergar machine-gunned to death after the IRA realised the new owners would not pay up and the kidnapping had horrified Ireland's horse-loving public.

Before I had got my feet firmly under my desk an event came along that turned upside down all my pre-conceived ideas about Protestant-Catholic relations on the divided island. It was the 1983 Five-Nations rugby match between Ireland and France, and I was reporting it for the world. In the build-up to the match supporters flooded in from Northern Ireland and the pubs around Dublin's Lansdowne Road rugby stadium filled up, before and after the game, with Protestant Unionists drinking shoulder-to-shoulder with Southern Catholics, sometimes joining in singing Republican songs. For, as I quickly learned in my confusion, the Irish rugby team was and remains an all-Ireland affair, and it gets plenty of support, and some of its players, from the North.

While primarily played by the Protestant middle class in the 19th century, when Britain ruled the country, rugby continued to thrive after the country split in 1922 as the Catholic majority played Gaelic football and hurling, a fierce form of hockey. Gaelic football was taken to Australia by Irish immigrants, voluntary or not, to form the basis of Australian Rules football.

The rugby international began with the Irish national anthem Amhran na bhFiann (Soldier's Song), which talks of Irish independence, and Northern Unionist players were not expected to sing along. In the inaugural Rugby World Cup in 1987, in the face of Unionist objections to the national anthem, the Irish captain produced a tape of "The Rose of Tralee", a 19th century ballad about a girl called Mary, and it was played after no acceptable alternative could be found. For the 1995 World Cup the team sang a new politically neutral anthem "Ireland's Call" specially composed by Northern Irish pop musician Phil Coulter, and this is now sung alongside the official anthem at international matches.

*Vietnam evacuation*

*Human skulls bear testimony to mass killings by the Khmer Rouge in Cambodia (Adobe Stock).*

*War graves in Cambodia. (Adobe Stock)*

*Belfast peace wall (Adobe Stock)*

*Orange parade in Bangor, 2010. creative Commons Attribution*

*Belfast wall art. (Adobe Stock)*

# 18. GOING NORTH

After Shergar fever finally subsided I decided to make my first trip to Northern Ireland, wracked by sectarian violence as IRA guerrillas sought to unite the British-ruled province with the Irish Republic. With a 60 per cent Protestant majority favouring continued British rule and the bulk of the 40% Catholic minority hoping to join the Republic in the south, Northern Ireland was a tinderbox ready to catch fire at any time. Official British policy was that London had no strategic interest in the province and would relinquish it if the majority of its population decided on reunification with Ireland. The fervently pro-British Protestant majority were determined that would never happen.

In the border town of Dundalk an hour's drive from Dublin I entered a world dominated by smuggling. With prices of many goods considerably cheaper in the North, business was booming across the border in the town of Newry while shopkeepers in Dundalk complained the whole area south of the border was dying.

"The only thriving business around here is smuggling," one said.

Officially travellers from the South were allowed to bring back only a very limited amount of goods duty-free, but the overstretched Irish customs post on the main roads could do little more than operate spot checks. At the height of the troubles these posts were regularly blown up by IRA guerrillas. And there are 300 major and minor crossings along the 500-kilometre border.

Armed British troops were never far away and would occasionally break cover to stop and search a particular vehicle.

In Newry, one delighted shopkeeper said: "A few months back you could play football in these streets. On Thursdays and Saturdays the shops are so full with southerners that locals can hardly get in. We do our shopping on Fridays."

127

Heading to Belfast, I checked into the Europa Hotel, carrying the unwelcome title of the world's most-bombed hotel after 36 attacks during the troubles. I met up with Reuters part-time correspondent Jim Campbell, who worked for the Sunday World, a tabloid produced in Dublin but also sold in the North, the only popular paper with cross-community appeal. He accompanied me to the headquarters of Sinn Fein, the IRA's political wing, in the Falls Road in the Catholic section of Belfast. I was welcomed by its leader Gerry Adams, looking more like a college professor than the head of an organisation that represented one of the world's most effective guerrilla organisations. Adams was the party's leading strategist behind Sinn Fein's new policy of "the ballot and the bullet" combining the threat of armed force with political campaigning. Recognising that my reports would be picked up in the United States, source of much of the party's financial support, he offered full cooperation in my work. After dropping in regularly during my visits we were soon on first name terms, a slight embarrassment a few months later when Sinn Fein held its annual congress in Dublin and Adams, a controversial figure at the best of times, greeted me with "Hi, Colin" as he passed. On the Protestant side there were a number of paramilitary organisations pledged to combat the IRA, but most were outlawed and none would have declared themselves openly to a neutral journalist. I did call in on the spokesman for the Ulster Unionist Party, the main political organisation representing the Protestant majority.

In the centre of Belfast, life carried on as a new normal. But it was anything but. The entire inner-city shopping area was surrounded by a "ring of steel" metal fence closing the area to car traffic and allowing access to pedestrians only after a thorough body-search at the gates. The fence went up after "Bloody Friday" in 1972 when the IRA set off 26 explosions in the centre, killing 11 people and injuring 130.

British armoured cars roamed the streets around the centre, and heavily armed British soldiers patrolled, their presence welcomed by the Protestant majority but shunned by most Catholics. And across the city

Protestant and Catholic areas were separated by "peace walls", thrown up as temporary measures following violence between the two communities in 1969, but since extended and refined. One stretch of the wall was topped with a line of rotating metal spikes known locally as "German razor plating", recalling the Berlin wall. But in contrast to that wall, the Belfast version was built with the consent of many of the people affected by it.

The walls were not limited to Belfast, but also featured in other Northern Ireland towns with divided communities. If all the walls were placed end-to-end, they would have stretched to over 34 kilometres, with the longest single wall adding five kilometres by itself.

Despite the dividing walls, after 14 years of sectarian violence people were still dying in the streets of Belfast and elsewhere in the province, so regularly that most incidents received only a few lines in British newspapers. Someone coined the term "an acceptable level of violence". But by the end of 1983 over 2,300 people had died since "the Troubles" erupted in 1969. Of these 191 were policemen, 507 soldiers and 1,642 "civilians", including guerrillas fighting on each side of the sectarian and political divide, and politicians. Several leading politicians had narrow escapes, and those who were also members of the Parliament in London were provided with bodyguards as a matter of course.

The continuing violence had affected many as it had moved from the streets and country lanes into places once considered sanctuaries – bars, churches, hospitals and universities.

The violence by Republican guerrillas was directed mainly at British soldiers, members of the overwhelmingly Protestant police force, and other people considered to be working for the government, directly or indirectly. Protestant paramilitaries mainly targeted Catholic community politicians and leaders.

Ordinary citizens on both sides of the divide were not immune to violence as paramilitary groups often took on the role of "community police" to mete out punishment for repeated criminal and anti-social behaviour, often at the request of the community. Among these was "knee-capping", shooting the victim in the legs, which could lead to permanent disability, amputation and occasionally death. For some in the Catholic community guerrilla justice was preferred as police were regarded as a hostile force. And for both communities, instant justice for local troublemakers was often preferable to long drawn-out court cases. For many young criminals, a limp was often a better option than months or years in jail.

At the end of the day Jim suggested that I might like to meet some active IRA members, unofficially, and we headed for a taxi, one of a fleet of black London cabs that provided a regular secure service up and down the Falls Road and Protestant Shankill road for ordinary citizens. They ran like bus services, which were considered too vulnerable to attack, and cost about the same.

After a brief journey we stopped off at a pub full of drinkers and started talking to a group of men at the bar about current issues, none of them controversial. I told a few East European jokes, which went down like a lead balloon. After a friendly parting we returned to the city centre and I asked Jim when I would meet the IRA. "You just did", was the reply.

Back in Dublin my family, after almost three months of steady rain, demanded to fly to somewhere warm and sunny. Taking an early holiday I booked a flight and a hotel in Spain's southern Costa del Sol overlooking a beach, and we arrived at Dublin airport late on Friday evening to be told that while my the family with German passports could board, I could not as Australians needed visas. This came as a complete surprise as I had visited Spain as a student without any formalities. The next morning, a Saturday, I called the Australian Embassy and finally reached a diplomat who gave me a name and address of a Spanish colleague who might be able to help. Driving to a housing estate outside central Dublin I rang the door of the address and was told my man had moved to another estate some distance away. Asking around there I was about to give up when a woman walking with her child said that "Javier" lived next door to her.

Racing to the house he was just leaving when I screeched to a halt outside, gabbled my story, and he agreed to accompany me to his embassy and stamp a visa in my passport. After driving him back I went home to pack, took a taxi to the airport and managed to buy a ticket on the same flight my family had taken the previous evening. I turned up at the hotel in Fuengirola at midnight, much to the surprise of my family who had not expected to see me until Monday at the earliest.

Back in Dublin, the country was soon caught up in a campaign aimed at putting an existing legal ban on abortion into the constitution, and beyond the range of reformist courts. The campaign to insert an amendment into the constitution, which had become the most acrimonious in Irish history, was led by a small but determined conservative pro-life pressure group. Although there appeared to be little support for it, since most people felt a legal ban was good enough, the sponsors had taken advantage of political turmoil in recent months to get backing for the amendment from all political party leaders.

The campaign was a particular embarrassment for Prime Minister Fitzgerald, who on taking office had announced a "constitutional crusade" aimed at ridding the constitution of elements dictated by the powerful Catholic Church. Fitzgerald, whose father was a Southern Catholic and mother a Northern Ireland Protestant, believed these moves were necessary to encourage Northern Protestants to even consider joining the Republic. Foremost among these targets were Ireland's bans on abortion, contraception and divorce.

Fitzgerald was a former economics lecturer and journalist who once wrote for a number of British publications. A favourite story about him was getting a call from the London Financial Times several years ago asking for a story, to which he replied it would be a bit awkward as he was now foreign minister. Pressed by the paper, he agreed to knock out several hundred words. At a social pre-Christmas meeting with him a couple of years later with the Dublin foreign press he was asked about the story. When he began to equivocate we howled him down, and, recognising a good story that did nothing to tarnish his reputation, accepted it.

As anti-abortion campaigners took to the streets, some wearing tee-shirts proclaiming "Hang on in there baby, I am voting for you" under a picture of a foetus, feminists said it would do nothing to stop the average 30 Irish women a day travelling to Britain for abortions. In the end the amendment was passed by 67% to 33%.

It took 35 years for Ireland to overturn the abortion ban by a landslide, seen as a historic victory for women's rights. It also sealed the country's transformation from a bastion of religious conservatism to one of Europe's most tolerant democracies, the first country to legalise gay marriages by popular vote.

In 1983, the battles for divorce and contraception were still to come.

It was time to head back to Northern Ireland for the annual summer Marching Season, when members of the conservative Protestant Orange Order march, often through Catholic areas, and sectarian tensions are regularly inflamed. The order is closely linked to ruling Unionist political parties determined the province remains part of the United Kingdom. The main march on July 12, known as "the Glorious 12th", marked the victory of Protestant Dutch King William III over English King James II in the Battle of the Boyne in 1690. The other main parade was in Londonderry to commemorate the action of Protestant apprentice boys shutting the gates of the walled city in 1689 against James's Catholic army. The parade regularly led to trouble as Orangemen, and it was only men, insisted on marching through a city which had long had a majority Catholic population, which they call Derry.

The night before the 12th parade Protestant families built huge bonfires in the streets, which sometimes turned into sectarian demonstrations as Irish flags and other republican symbols were burned. Often drink was behind these demonstrations, despite pleas from the organisers that "it's about the battle, not the bottle".

The march, or "walk" as it was officially called, took place unchanged as it had for decades. The men, in suits and bowler hats clutching rolled umbrellas, shuffled by to the music of a pipe band which included young children. The time was beaten out by huge Lambegg drums, one of the loudest acoustic instruments in the world measuring up to a metre in diameter. The deafening sounds were seen by Catholics, probably correctly, as sending out a sectarian and triumphalist message as the parade passed through their areas.

Crossing the street while the parades were marching, known as breaking the line, was strongly disapproved of.

Heading back to the south, I decided to visit the town of Crossmaglen, dubbed the most dangerous in Europe, with a huge British army base surrounded by a population of Catholics and fervent Irish nationalists. A story I wrote after the visit began: "In this fortress army outpost, 200 British troops risk their lives to defend a flag no one recognises." The town lies close to the Irish border in south Armagh, a part of the province known as "bandit country" because of its strong Republican tendencies.

Knowing of the dangers of travelling in the area, in a car with a Dublin registration, I had sought and was given advice. This was to call a local publican and explain I would like to visit the town. Responding that I would be very welcome, he also asked when I planned to come, the exact time, and details of the car I was using.

Arriving at the town, one was struck by the sight of the Irish Republican flag flying at the entrance, and slogans on the walls hailing the IRA. The inhabitants read Irish papers, used Irish money in most of the shops and bars, listened to Irish radio and did most of their drinking across the border.

The only British Union Jack flag fluttered above the army barracks in the centre of town where the soldiers had to put up with constant hostility from the townspeople and occasional bomb and shooting attacks by Republican guerrillas. So unsafe were the country lanes that the soldiers, assigned for only four months at a time, were flown in and out by helicopter. Even the base's rubbish went out that way. In a three-year period during the 1970s 30 British soldiers were killed in and around Crossmaglen, most of them blown up by booby traps and bombs hidden in ditches.

"I really can't understand why the soldiers are here," a local teacher said. "They don't perform any useful function except to provide targets for the IRA."

Looking for some lunch I spotted a sign for a Chinese restaurant, and intrigued as well as hungry, went into Chi Chuong Ly's establishment to eat his food and hear his story. Ly, renamed John Lee for the benefit of local people who flock to his restaurant, fled Vietnam in 1979 with members of his ethnic Chinese family and 300 others in a six-metre boat which was eventually picked up after a week at sea by a British freighter.

Asked why he had chosen to come to one area of violence and tension after fleeing another, the 26-year-old said: "The bombs don't worry me, I heard plenty in Vietnam."

As for the British soldiers patrolling the streets of Crossmaglen with faces blackened and automatic rifles at the ready, periodically stopping people for questioning, he replied: "I don't care about the soldiers, we had plenty of those in Vietnam. Soldiers' uniforms all look alike, only the police look different here."

Heading back across the border, I decided to make one more detour, this time to the site of the Battle of the Boyne which looms so large in Ireland's history, particularly in the North. My interest was aroused after hearing that a 290-hectare estate complete with stately home and contents, claiming to be the battle site, was up for sale.

This came as news to Irish-American millionaire James Delaney, a two-metre tall Texan who had bought a 12-hectare plot on the other side of the River Boyne after being assured it was the battle site, and planned to build a "reconciliation museum".

However it was the first estate, known as Oldbridge, that was eventually chosen by the Irish government to house a Battle of the Boyne visitor's centre after it was sold by 28-year-old Nicholas Coddington, whose ancestors fought in the battle.

Coddington was selling the property before emigrating to Canada, ending an unbroken line of ownership going back nine generations. He said their departure was not prompted by a terrifying experience earlier in the year when masked gunmen held him and his Canadian-born wife for 12 hours while stripping the 15-bedroom house of over £150,000 worth of silver and art.

"That hurried us along a bit, but we had already decided there was no way we could run the house and estate," he said. One of the estate's unique features was the right, granted under an 1842 act of parliament, to lay traps on the river that on a good day could bring in a dozen salmon.

While I was back in Dublin I heard the news that Jim Campbell had been shot at point-blank range after answering the door-bell and was in hospital in critical condition. I rushed to Belfast to find him able to talk in his bed despite receiving five bullets in the stomach. He had been rushed to the city's Mater hospital and was carried in just as a top surgical team was heading out after a major operation. One look was enough to persuade them to head back inside for an operation during which Campbell died, but was resuscitated, leaving one bullet lodged against his spine. One of the medical team pointed out the irony of the situation in that he would almost certainly have died anywhere else in the UK, but Belfast hospitals were at the cutting edge of dealing with gun-shot wounds on an almost daily basis.

He was almost certainly attacked by members of a hard-line section of the Protestant paramilitary group the Ulster Volunteer Force (UVF) after he had accused its leader of killing Catholics with apparent impunity, suggesting possible collusion with British security forces, and of financing his operations by drug trafficking. It was a local story for his newspaper and had not been used by Reuters. Police admitted any side could have

135

been involved in attacking Jim as his columns addressed extremists on both sides of the sectarian divide.

He was the first journalist deliberately targeted by paramilitaries during The Troubles. The first journalist killed by them was another Sunday World reporter Martin O'Hagan, a former IRA man, in 2001.

Jim was back on his feet a few months later and I made full use of his recent experience when showing Belfast to our then editor, a financial news specialist with little background in general news and none in hostile environments. With Jim as guide, we toured some of the main trouble-spots along the Falls and Shankill roads, driving into some notorious complexes before leaving hastily when shown we were not welcome. They included the Divis Flats on the Falls Road, a major IRA stronghold while the army occupied the top two floors of a 20-story tower in the estate. At the height of the troubles the troops could only get in and out by helicopter.

With my encouragement Jim would occasionally let out a little groan, complaining that the bullet had moved again. I allowed myself a little smile as the editor paled and sweated.

We also took in some of the murals shouting from the walls of the Falls and Shankill roads, mainly depicting paramilitaries on both sides killed in the sectarian fighting. The best-known of these was dedicated to Bobby Sands, an IRA prisoner who led a 66-day hunger strike in 1981 in which he and nine others starved themselves to death in a bid to force the British government to restore special political status to Republican inmates. The hunger strike followed a "dirty protest" in which the inmates smeared excrement on the walls of their cells.

Sands' funeral was attended by 100,000 people, and his death was widely seen as giving impetus to the Republican cause and boosting the influence of Sinn Fein as a political party.

Ironically a tour of Belfast's hotspots during The Troubles has in recent years become a major tourist attraction in this city of 400,000 inhabitants, with the black cab firms offering full tours of the sites, often with a guide with direct experience in the sectarian strife. The only other major tourist attraction in the city was the Titanic museum on the site of the former Harland and Wolff shipyard where the liner was built and launched in 1912. The ship, hailed as unsinkable, struck an iceberg on its maiden voyage and sank with the loss of over 1,500 passengers and crew.

On my way back south I made a detour to the village of Bushmills, in Northern Ireland's County Antrim, to check out the latest move in the long-running "whiskey war" between Ireland and Scotland. Bushmills, site of the world's oldest whiskey distillery founded in 1608, had just announced the launch of Ireland's first pure malt whiskey for over 50 years in a bid to capture a larger share of the market long dominated by Scotch. It was the second time the Irish were forced to play catch-up to their rivals. In the 19th and early 20th century pure malt Irish whiskey, with Bushmills and leading Dublin distillers Jameson and Powers, dominated the home and world markets due to its consistent flavour.

According to Bushmills managing director Billy McCourt its reversal of fortunes came with the development of a new, lighter type of whiskey made from grain, rather than malted barley. The new product, despite being developed by an Irishman, was rejected by Irish distillers but seized upon by their Scottish rivals sensing a new market for lighter blended whiskey more suitable for mixing. The new product found instant success, particularly in the United States, leaving the Irish producers struggling to catch up. They were left behind again when the Scots returned to the old methods by producing high quality pure malt whiskeys from a single distillery aged in oak casks for at least three years.

Crossing back into Ireland armed with new knowledge of whiskey production I decided to check out the unofficial, read illegal version that had been produced in Ireland for centuries. After some discreet inquiries among journalist colleagues I was directed to a pub in the Connemara district of County Galway and tasted my first "poteen" (pronounced pocheen), a colourless liquid that brought tears to my eyes. With the festive season approaching a strange, heady aroma hung over some of the more remote and rugged parts of Connemara as the illicit spirit was produced in dozens of home-made stills hidden outdoors. With the moonshine selling for less than half the price of a commercial whisky, there was plenty of demand, particularly around Christmas. Police make sporadic attempts to control production but could not cover all the rocky hills and remote islands in Connemara, where traditionally the best poteen was made.

Traditionalists in Connemara lamented what they saw as a general lowering of standards in the product over the years.

"When my family was doing it we took three weeks for each batch and used only the best barley," said one old man whose face bore witness to some fierce bouts with the bottle. "Now they use any old rubbish like potato peelings and make the stuff in two days."

Responding to a claim by a group of Connemara producers to have driven to Dublin and back, a distance of 480 kilometres, in a vehicle fuelled by poteen, one local commented: "Now why would anyone in his right mind waste 10 gallons for good poteen on a silly stunt like that."

Back in Dublin the big news in early 1984 was the impending visit of U.S. President Ronald Reagan on a sentimental journey to the tiny village where his ancestors lived until the potato famine drove them abroad. While most Irish people welcomed the visit to Ballyporeen, County Tipperary, a minority who criticised his nuclear, Middle East and South America policies saw it as a blatant pitch for the Catholic and Irish American vote in his re-election bid in November. Critics noted that Reagan appeared to have discovered his link with Ballyporeen only after his election in 1980, when it was drawn to his attention by a leading British genealogical organisation.

The visit, only the third by a U.S. President in office, passed off relatively smoothly despite 500 protesters at Shannon Airport on his arrival. Irish government officials were relieved he made no call for Irish reunification, strongly supported by Irish Americans, expressing instead the hope that "tolerance and reconciliation will one day unite Catholics

138

and Protestants in Northern Ireland". A further 4,000 protested outside parliament when he addressed both houses of parliament.

In Ballyporeen its 300 inhabitants were cashing in on the visit by selling souvenir tee-shirts and posters and even packets of Reagan homestead mud. Introducing the president to the assembled townspeople, the master of ceremonies noted that had Reagan's great-grandfather known that packets of the village soil would be selling for a pound he would never have left Ireland.

# 19. THE STATE TAKES ON THE CHURCH

In Dublin the main focus was on the next stage in the government's crusade against the power of the Catholic Church, this time over contraception. Under an existing 1979 law, described as "an Irish solution to an Irish problem", contraceptives could only be obtained for "bona fide family planning" with a doctor's prescription, and only at a pharmacy. Many pharmacies, particularly in country areas, refused to stock them on religious grounds. The new law would make contraceptives freely available to anyone over 18 without a prescription, available at pharmacies, doctor's surgeries and family planning clinics.

The Catholic Church, which recognised only the natural "rhythm" method for family planning and had already shown its muscle in the abortion referendum, was quick to throw down the gauntlet.

"The path to moral decline is a one-way street – once permissive legislation is passed it is almost impossible to undo it," thundered Archbishop Kevin McNamara of Dublin, a conservative newly appointed to Ireland's biggest diocese.

"The choice lies clearly between opting for education in self-control and encouraging self-indulgence in young people," he said.

On February 20, 1985, the new law was passed by 83 votes to 80. It was the first-ever defeat of the Catholic church in a head-to-head battle with the government on social legislation.

The government took on the Church a year later when it introduced a referendum to end a constitutional ban on divorce in Ireland, the only country in Europe apart from Malta where it was still illegal. Some 70,000 people were reported to be in broken marriages.

Deputy Prime Minister Dick Spring, announcing the referendum, said: "None of us like the breakdown of marriage but we know it's a reality and we have to deal with it."

A 24-year-old woman profiled in a Dublin newspaper before the referendum set out the bleak choice facing her, a life spent alone or in an illicit liaison with illegitimate children and all the social and legal complications that brings in an overwhelmingly Catholic country. She found it hard to accept having to pay the rest of her life for one wrong decision made when she was 17.

As expected the Catholic Church strongly opposed the move, proclaiming the sanctity of marriage, while opposition politicians highlighted possible financial problems for wives deserted by their husbands.

The vote was defeated overwhelmingly, 63.5% to 36.5%.

Not surprisingly the leaders of Northern Ireland 's Protestant majority were quick to condemn what they described as the "stranglehold" of the Catholic Church over Irish life.

"A state that is not prepared to respect the rights of its individuals is not to be trusted itself," said Nigel Hamilton, General Secretary of the Democratic Unionist Party.

It took another nine years for the country to vote to amend the constitution to allow divorce after couples had been separated for four out of the previous five years. As opponents of the new bill campaigned under slogans like "Hello divorce, goodbye Daddy", suggesting that men would desert their wives in droves, the Catholic Church came out strongly against the amendment but assured Catholics they could vote for it in good conscience and would not be committing a sin.

The amendment was passed by the narrowest of margins, 50.28% to 49.72%. Prime Minister John Bruton was widely credited with saving the day with a last-minute intervention addressed to Protestants at a vital juncture in Northern Ireland peace talks. Pointing out that the referendum was about equality for minorities he said it was important "we show the State respects the minorities in its own midst".

The first divorce in Ireland was granted in January 1997, to a dying man who urgently wanted to marry his partner.

The expected rush for divorces never happened, and Ireland remains at the bottom of the table in Europe. And this despite another easing of the divorce laws in 2019 when a whopping 82% of the country voted to further liberalise divorce laws by cutting the time couples had to be apart to qualify.

This decision, coming four years after the country led the world by voting by a 62% majority for gay marriages, showed clearly how far, and fast, the influence of the Catholic Church had waned.

I returned to Belfast in the summer of 1984 on hearing word that an official of the Irish Northern Aid Committee (Noraid) who had been barred from entering Northern Ireland planned to address a nationalist rally in the capital. Martin Galvin, a New York lawyer, was publicity director of the organisation accused by the British and Northern Ireland governments of providing funds for the IRA. The organisation claimed its sole purpose was to provide financial support for the families of jailed Irish republicans.

I joined the rally, to mark the anniversary of the introduction of a policy of internment without trial by the Northern Ireland government in 1971 in a desperate bid to stem rising violence in the country. The move was widely blamed for a rapid worsening of the situation, leading a year later to Bloody Sunday, when British troops opened fire on a civilian protest in Londonderry against internment, killing 14. A few months after that the Northern Ireland parliament was suspended, then abolished, leading to the province being ruled directly from London for the next 26 years.

The Belfast rally was going peacefully, despite a heavy police presence, until there was uproar at one end as Galvin appeared and began to address the crowd. The police charged in an unsuccessful attempt to arrest him, and during scuffles with protesters one was shot in the chest with a plastic bullet and died.

Sean Downes, 22, was the 15th person to be killed by rubber and plastic bullets, a 10-centimentre round intended to maim rather than kill, during Northern Ireland's troubles. His death led to a mainly silent protest march by thousands of people two days later.

# 20. NEW ANGLO-IRISH AGREEMENT IN TROUBLE

In 1985 all interest was focussed on a new Anglo-Irish agreement aimed at bringing Northern Ireland's warring communities together. The landmark agreement, signed in November by British Prime Minister Margaret Thatcher and Fitzgerald gave Dublin an unprecedented consultative role in how the province was run, particularly in matters affecting the Catholic nationalist minority, through an inter-governmental conference chaired by the Irish Foreign Minister and the United Kingdom's Northern Ireland Secretary. In exchange, the Republic shelved its aspirations to a united Ireland, for the time being, by formerly recognising the North had a right to stay British as long as most of its people wanted this.

Predictably the agreement was greeted with horror by Protestant leaders who saw it as a first step towards a united Ireland. They regarded it as even more radical than a 1974 initiative known as the Sunningdale agreement which set up an executive with power shared between the two communities backed by an Anglo-Irish council. That agreement collapsed after five months when Protestant workers backed by Unionist politicians and paramilitary organisations staged an all-out strike which paralysed the province.

This time Unionist leaders staged a rally at Belfast's City Hall attended by around 100,000 who heard the head of the hard-line Democratic Unionist Party Ian Paisley charge that terrorists were operating with impunity from the Irish Republic "and yet Mrs Thatcher tells us that the Republic must have some say in our province. We say never, never, never, never!" Paisley later compared Thatcher to "Jezebel who sought to destroy Israel in a day," while moderate Unionist leader James Molyneaux spoke of "the stench of hypocrisy, deceit and treachery". The agreement was also opposed by Sinn Fein, who saw it as confirming Northern Ireland's place in the United Kingdom.

Despite their strong opposition Unionist leaders appeared to have ruled out the strike option this time around, for several reasons. Firstly, unemployment in the province was nearly 23 per cent, compared with less than 10 per cent in 1974. As one Unionist politician put it: "You would be unwilling to ask someone who had a job to put it at risk." Secondly, the 1974 strike succeeded mainly because the British Army, called in five years earlier to quell intercommunal violence, was unable to operate the power stations. It was a skill the troops had since acquired.

Unionists did manage to hold a Day of Action which brought most of the province to a standstill, but it was mainly peaceful. A decision by the 12 Unionist MPs to boycott the London parliament made little difference in a chamber of 650. However there were several scenes of violence during the marching season, some of which I witnessed, involving Protestants clearly angered by the new agreement.

In the town of Portadown, a regular flashpoint as Orangemen insisted on marching to a Protestant church through a largely Catholic part of the town, I waited with two British journalists to witness the parade. Spotting the leader of the Orange Order in the town, with his splendid regalia in full view, we approached him for a comment. A big man, immaculately dressed in a suit, tie and bowler hat, he pointed to the top of the hill where a large group of marchers were gathered and said: "If you're not out of here in two minutes I'm going to call them down and tell them to give you a good kicking." I left Portadown that evening before my report, which used his words in full, was picked up by the local media.

Worse was to come a month later at the Apprentice Boys march in Londonderry/Derry. As I waited on the bridge crossing the river Foyle that separates the Protestant and Catholic parts of the city with two British journalists, I needed to return to my hotel not far away to check in with the London desk, this being before mobile phones. On my return there was no sign of my two colleagues. After checking with others I learned that the two were in hospital after being badly beaten by marchers who peeled off when they spotted them and laid into them. One of the two, from the PA, was a big man, a former junior swimming champion. At 1.71 metres, I would not have fancied my chances.

The agreement limped on for a few years but in the end failed to bring an immediate end to the political violence in Northern Ireland, nor did it reconcile the two communities through devolved power-sharing. However it did succeed in improving cooperation between the British and Irish governments, and paved the way to the Good Friday agreement 13 years later which brought in both the Unionists and Sinn Fein.

With my time in Ireland running out there were two more stories to cover, both peculiarly Irish involving alleged miracles.

Out of nowhere in rural County Mayo an international airport was emerging, despite criticism that it was in the wrong place, a "foggy, boggy hill", and would become a white elephant. Experts believed the airport would be the world's third smallest international airport, after Bujumbura and Ouagadougou in Africa. This did nothing to sway the determination of its creator, a canny local priest Monsignor James Horan, who had long dreamed of flying in tourists from abroad to his local church in the village of Knock, a major local pilgrimage site. In 1879 a village girl passing the church claimed to have seen figures of the Virgin Mary, Saint Joseph and Saint John the Evangelist against a wall, ran home to tell her parents, and a small crowd collected.

In 1981 Father Horan told a journalist from Irish radio: "We're building an airport, and I hope the Department of Trade doesn't hear about it, now don't tell them...We've no money, but we're hoping to get it next week."

True to his word, he managed to persuade then Prime Minister Haughey to come up with funds, playing on the relative lack of development of the west of Ireland compared to the east. When his Fianna Fail lost the elections the new government under Fitzgerald stopped the money, but Monsignor Horan sought funds in Ireland, the United States and Australia and raised enough to complete the control tower and passenger terminal. A thorn in the side of the government, he was a folk hero to many, and his story was turned into a musical "On a Wing and a Prayer".

When I visited Knock and met Monsignor Horan, the huge 2,530-metre airstrip, capable of carrying jumbo-jets, had been completed, and he was charging local youths to race their cars and motorcycles on it. With few buildings and no equipment, he was already looking forward to its first flight, using local farm tractors to tow the planes into position if necessary.

Monsignor Horan complained that since drastic cuts in regional rail services his area had the worst communications in the country.

"No company in England or Europe is going to invest in this region when it takes them two days to get here and two days to get back," he said. Dismissing the view that the airport must pay its way, he said: "An airport is like a road: it is a service."

The airport, renamed Ireland West Airport, opened officially in May 1986. Despite doubts about its viability, particularly due to its 200-metre elevation above sea level, it is now the fourth busiest in the country after Dublin, Cork and Shannon, and last year carried over 800,000 passengers. Sadly Monsignor Horan never lived to see it in full operation. He died on a flight to the major pilgrimage site in Lourdes, France, whose popularity he hoped to emulate through his airport.

The other claimed miracle emerged when reports appeared from all over the country of statues of the Virgin Mary moving. The first came from Ballinspittle, County Cork, when a man reported seeing a roadside statue of the Virgin Mary move spontaneously. Similar apparitions were reported from County Waterford, and from 30 other destinations around the country. Not all involved Mary, some involved other divine figures who appeared in stains on walls and other manifestations. While thousands of people gathered at some of the sites, including this correspondent, the Catholic Church refrained from comment, though one bishop dismissed the whole phenomenon as an illusion. Meanwhile a team of psychologists at Cork University explained the visions as optical illusions caused by staring at objects in twilight. The moving statues phenomenon soon faded, though a few cults persisted.

# 21. THE MOTHER OF PARLIAMENTS

Before the end of the year I got the call to move back to London, this time as UK Political Correspondent based in parliament. It would be a complete change of direction, from a generalist reporter covering everything that moved to a specialist working within a specific framework and rules. While most of my reporting covered British politics, I was briefly thrown back into the Cold War when Prime Minister Margaret Thatcher paid a historic visit to Moscow at the invitation of Mikhail Gorbachev, whose appointment as Soviet leader was to have wide-ranging implications for the future of communism in Eastern Europe.

I arrived to take up my new position in the autumn of 1986 as Thatcher appeared to be riding high after experiencing the worst two years of her seven-year rule, and gearing up to win an unprecedented third term in elections expected the following year. With unemployment falling and industry apparently picking up after a severe recession, she also faced opposition parties calling for an end to nuclear weapons, a stance that did not seem to be going down well with the public.

It was a remarkable turnaround in the government's fortunes after the ruling Conservatives lost heavily in local elections in May and had been trailing Labour in opinion polls. After returning to power in 1983 with a huge majority boosted by Britain's defeat of Argentina in the Falklands War, Thatcher lost popularity over a decision to ban union membership at Britain's spy centre, her bitter year-long battle with striking miners and her hard line on teachers' pay which led to 12 months of classroom disruption.

My first task was to move house, as our little Victorian terrace had only two bedrooms, and find schools for the children, always a major consideration for any family move. I had little time to look around as I was taking over from a colleague who had suddenly resigned to join the newly founded Independent newspaper. Unable to get our children into a school within easy walking distance we bought a house in Highgate further to the north and got them into the local primary.

My first task was to find my way around the Palace of Westminster, the official name of the Houses of Parliament, rebuilt in 1834 in the Gothic Revival style after the medieval Royal Palace was largely destroyed by fire. The fire was caused by burning wooden tally sticks, used as part of the accounting process by the government exchequer. Without a guide to help me, I struggled to navigate the building's 1,000 rooms, 100 staircases and nearly five kilometres of passageways, spread over four floors. Reuters shared a room with two other media organisations, close to the main press room where speeches and statements were delivered and parliamentary proceedings relayed on television screens.

In the debating chamber itself Reuters were allocated two of the best seats at the front of the press gallery, a hangover from the days of the Empire when much of the proceedings would have involved countries under British rule, hanging on every word from the homeland. Our seats were often empty as Reuters was now mainly interested in major stories of interest to the outside world. This was a cause of some irritation to British media organisations, some of which had teams of reporters following every word.

Reuters was also a member of the "lobby", a tight group of journalists allowed access to the members' lobby next to the chamber where MPs could congregate for discussions during or in between parliamentary sessions. In an arcane system dating back to the late 19th century, lobby journalists were briefed twice a day by the prime minister's spokesman, but unattributably. In the morning we were summoned to the PM's residence in 10 Downing Street, in the afternoon we clambered the stairs to a tiny room under the eaves, which I was told did not show up in any plan of the building, for our briefing.

The system had come under regular criticism that it encouraged secrecy, led to unprofessional conduct by forcing journalists to quote weak sources such as "friends" and "people familiar with", and created a cosy relationship between political journalists and the political establishment. Foreign journalists complained they were excluded. The spokesman we dealt with, Bernard Ingham, came under fire for regularly abusing lobby briefings by criticising individuals in Thatcher's cabinet, calling one a "semi-detached member". Over the years since several attempts have been made to reform the system, usually at a time when the government of the day felt it was getting a bad press.

One benefit of lobby membership was access to Annie's Bar, the only one of several bars on the premises where journalists and MPs could get together on equal terms. Another perk was access during the summer months to the outside restaurant and bar on the huge terrace overlooking the Thames.

A third benefit was the right to join the Prime Minister on trips abroad, and I took early advantage of it as Thatcher announced a visit to Oslo to meet Norwegian leader Gro Harlem Brundtland, Europe's only other female prime minister. The trip looked like an attempt to smooth over relations between two traditional allies and two strong women, following some thinly veiled criticism from Brundtland over Thatcher's policies, particularly on the environment. Britain was accused of poisoning Scandinavia with acid rain caused by the sulphurous smoke belching from British coal-fired power stations.

On the appointed day I took a taxi to London's Heathrow airport and reached a secluded section to board the PM's official plane, a Vickers VC-10 jet airliner flown by the Royal Air Force. I settled down to enjoy the RAF's catering, described as "First Class Plus", on the two-hour flight to Oslo along with some 30 colleagues from the lobby.

As often happened during Thatcher visits, controversy was never far away. While the British party attended a banquet in the medieval Akershus Castle 1,500 people protesting against British policies on South Africa, Northern Ireland and the environment broke into the castle courtyard. It was the first time the building had been breached in its 800-year history.

At a news conference Thatcher said she had tried long and hard to persuade the Norwegian leader that economic sanctions against South Africa, strongly supported by Oslo, would not end the policy of apartheid. She also disagreed with Norway's recent move to cut crude oil exports to curb over-supply and defend prices, saying her government was opposed to any intervention in free markets. Despite their differences, the visit had been thoroughly enjoyable and the two had got on extremely well, she added

On our return to London we noticed a lot of ambulances and fire engines racing alongside us as we landed at Heathrow. As we disembarked we were told an anonymous caller had warned there was a bomb on board. Nobody seemed particularly concerned.

Back in the UK the annual party conference season, when the political parties announce their programmes and seek to rally their supporters over a three-week period while parliament is in recess, was in full swing. Arriving at the conference centre in Bournemouth, a resort on the south coast, I noticed that a champagne reception was under way hosted by the party's deputy chairman, best-selling author Jeffrey Archer. I once sat next to Archer at a banquet following the 1966 Oxford vs. Cambridge athletics match. Representing Oxford where he was studying for a diploma of education, he had some form as a sprinter, and later represented England in a B-International. However at Cambridge, where I was studying, we had a Nigerian sprinter who was very quick. Archer decided to switch to the 200 metres low hurdles but was beaten anyway by our boy. At the post-match banquet Archer already came with a reputation after raising one million pounds for the charity Oxfam, among other things by inviting the Beatles to visit his college. Clearly a young man in a hurry, he was not interested in me at the banquet, even for small talk. But sensing the possibility of gaining a key source in the country's ruling party, I went ahead at the party conference and button-holed Archer, 46, reminding him of our previous meeting, and, unwisely, that he had been beaten. Dismissing his hurdling effort as a bit of fun, he agreed to meet me in the coming weeks and told me to arrange it through his assistant. I fixed up a date with his young assistant, whose parting advice was: "By the way, he doesn't like being beaten."

Feeling quite excited, I woke up the next morning to be greeted with splash newspaper headlines announcing that Archer had resigned over allegations that he had paid money to a prostitute for her silence. He was quoted as saying he had never had any association with the named call-girl but had made an error of judgment in trying to pay the girl money to avoid a scandal.

The affair did not do any serious harm to the fortunes of the Conservative Party, but it did mean I had lost a potential golden source before I had a chance to use it.

Back in London I decided it was time to find out about the House of Lords, the upper chamber in Britain's bicameral parliament composed mainly of elderly aristocrats whose chief requirement was that their ancestors helped out some English monarch over the past 1,000 or more years. While over the past 30 years the ranks of the 800 or so hereditary peers had been swelled by the creation of around 400 life peers for their services to the community and politics, this did little to dispel the idea of a ruling class with a birth-right to govern. With limited powers, to amend and revise but not reject government bills coming up from the fully elected House of Commons, the question facing any newcomer to the scene was "Why is it there"? Even those working within the lords admitted the system was sometimes bizarre. Nobody really knew in advance how many lords would be attending a debate, or what the majority political persuasion would be. A hard core of lords attended regularly, others a few times a year, some never. If all eligible peers attended at the same time, the system would collapse, prompting one 19th century lord to comment: "We should be grateful to those who grace the meetings of this House by their absence."

The leader of the Liberal Party peers in the lords, Baroness Seear, wrote in the House of Commons magazine: "If we were starting from scratch, no one in his right mind would invent the second chamber in precisely its present form."

And yet, according to Conservative chief whip Lord Denham, the system somehow worked. "We usually manage to get an approximate balance from the ranks of the very regulars, occasionals and very occasionals."

The government had not lost a major vote in the Commons since it came to power in 1979. In the Lords it had been defeated over 100 times in the same period, stalling the passage of bills.

Back in the commons Thatcher appeared to have made another poor judgement call as a major political storm broke over her government's efforts to block publication of the memoirs of a former secret agent. An ailing 71-year-old former member of Britain's counter-espionage service MI5, Peter Wright, was trying to publish in Australia, where he was living in retirement. His main allegations were that senior MI5 agents were involved in a plot to undermine Harold Wilson's Labour government in 1974 and other unauthorised "dirty tricks". The British government, accusing Wright of breaching the Official Secrets Act, feared publication would damage British national security and the confidence of other friendly intelligence services and sent the country's top civil servant to argue the case in a Sydney court.

Wright's legal team led by a rising young lawyer called Malcolm Turnbull soon had the visitors on the run as he revealed that similar allegations had been made in a previous published book by a journalist based almost entirely on information supplied by Wright. The British case was thrown out by the New South Wales court. Turnbull went on to become Prime Minister of Australia 30 years later.

The row did not appear to have seriously damaged the government's standings, and with polls showing support for the Conservatives growing and elections on the horizon, Thatcher went for an ambitious move.

# 22. THATCHER GOES TO MOSCOW

Two years previously the country had been visited by the Soviet Union's deputy leader Mikhail Gorbachev, a technocrat identified by Britain's Moscow embassy as a man to watch. He was the first top Soviet official to visit the country in 28 years, and his eight-day visit included five hours of talks, described as "very friendly" with the British leader. The topics included arms control, the Middle East and Afghanistan, but avoided human rights issues. After the talks Thatcher told the BBC: "I like Mr Gorbachev. We can do business together."

The visit was widely interpreted as signalling a thaw in relations between the Soviet Union and the West. And the warm welcome given to Gorbachev by Thatcher, one of the dominant European leaders of the time, was also seen by many as a factor in ensuring his rise to the top job after succeeding Konstantin Chernenko in 1985. Gorbachev wasted no time in setting out wide-ranging reforms of the Soviet system, including "perestroika" (restructuring) to decentralise economic decision-making and improve efficiency and "glasnost" (openness) allowing more freedom of speech and press. Whatever the extent of his gratitude to Thatcher, Gorbachev wasted no time in extending an invitation to the British leader, dubbed the "Iron Lady" in East Europe, to visit the Soviet Union. When it happened two years later it was the first official visit by a British PM for 12 years and came only 18 months after both countries were engaged in the mass expulsion of diplomats over the defection of the KGB's London chief Oleg Gordievsky.

On March 29 1987, we of the lobby found ourselves on board the VC-10 for a five-day visit that with each hour looked more and more like a Conservative Party election campaign video. While Gorbachev got five hours with Thatcher on his visit, this time the leaders met on five separate occasions, including a whole day of talks, while the British PM was given numerous opportunities to meet ordinary people, all filmed, a visit to the

Bolshoi Ballet and a 45-minute interview with Soviet TV broadcast live and uncut to the nation. French Premier Jacques Chirac, visiting Moscow two months later, saw Gorbachev only briefly when he unexpectedly attended a dinner in his honour.

On the four-hour flight to Moscow we were settling in for our gourmet dinners when Foreign Minister Sir Geoffrey Howe emerged from the back of the plane to address us with a finely-honed rundown of British-Soviet relations. We made notes as useful background for later stories but continued eating. An hour later Bernard Ingham appeared to announce the Prime Minister would talk to us, and meal trays and glasses flew aside as laptop computers came out. During a brief talk to us Thatcher made clear the main subject of any talks would likely be arms control, following the recent breakdown of international arms reduction talks in Geneva and a U.S. plan for a space-based defence system that could shoot down ballistic missiles, known as "Star Wars". The plan, which was never put into practice, had drawn the Soviet Union into a frenzied arms race it could ill afford.

Asked whether arms control would be linked to human rights, Thatcher responded: "If a country persists in putting people in prison for their political or religious views, it is something we have to take into account in arms control."

On the first full day of the visit Thatcher attended a church service at the monastery at Zagorsk, near Moscow, the spiritual centre of the Russian Orthodox Church, and was filmed lighting a votive candle "for peace, freedom and justice". Along the way to the city there were frequent stops where Thatcher left the car and was welcomed by friendly, though clearly curious ordinary Russians. After touring a housing complex she visited the local supermarket and bought cheese, bread and canned fish, commenting: "I should have bought my shopping bag, they had such lovely things inside."

Asked by a foreign journalist if her visit was part of her election campaign, Thatcher bristled. "If you mean in the context of party politics at home, no. I'm here to represent my country on a historic mission, and I would ask you to take it that way, and to enlarge your view of what it is about."

In the evening Gorbachev and his wife Raisa invited the British party to a performance of Tchaikovsky's Swan Lake at Moscow's famed Bolshoi Ballet. As the press watched from a gallery, a local Russian journalist gasped in surprise, saying that the "cygnets", four dancers in attendance to the main star, were all prima ballerinas. "I have never seen that before," he said.

On her last evening Thatcher gave one of the most extraordinary interviews ever heard in a communist state by ordinary people. Questioned by three senior journalists from the official media, they appeared nervous that it was all going out live. When they accused the West of risking a nuclear catastrophe, Thatcher retorted that the Soviet Union had more nuclear weapons than any other country in the world, "and you say there is a risk of an accident?" When they reiterated Soviet complaints about Star Wars, she said: "We know you are working on a laser-based defence system, but we're not complaining." On chemical weapons, she said the UK had given theirs up, the U.S. had some but had not modernised them, while the Soviet Union had large up-to-date stocks, "and that gives us great cause for concern". There was no real attempt by her interlocutors to rebut any of these charges.

Thatcher did have some kind words for her hosts, saying how much she had enjoyed the welcome she had received "and I hope to see quite a lot of you in the United Kingdom".

On the flight home the British party was invited to stop over in Georgia, the birth country of reformist foreign minister Eduard Shevardnadze, and, coincidentally, of former Soviet dictator Joseph Stalin. In an after-dinner speech Thatcher noted that England and Georgia shared the same patron saint, St. George, whose red cross on white background emblem featured on both national flags. She also praised Georgians as the natural entrepreneurs of the Soviet Union.

Back in Britain all eyes were focussed on the forthcoming elections. In early May, with opinion polls showing the Conservatives with a comfortable lead over Labour and the centrist Liberal Democrat/Social Democrat Alliance, she chose June 11.  An opinion poll conducted for Independent Television gave the Conservatives 44 per cent of the vote, an 11-point lead over Labour, which would leave them with an overall majority of 90 seats in the Commons.

There was a slight panic 10 days later when one poll showed the Conservatives' lead slashed to three percentage points, which would deprive Thatcher of an overall majority, while two others were in line with previous figures. This immediately revived speculation earlier in the year when the Conservatives were struggling in the polls that the country might have its first coalition government since World War Two. To the average Briton, coalitions were essentially foreign, the result of too many parties leading to short-lived and chaotic governments. Thatcher echoed a widely held view earlier in the year when she commented in a radio phone-in programme: "Coalitions break up pretty quickly, because they frequently tend to duck the difficult questions."

A growing body of supporters for coalitions pointed out regularly that West Germany, the economic powerhouse of the European Community, had run itself by coalitions since the Federal Republic come into being in 1949, with impressive results.

On election day itself all Conservative worries were banished as the party lost 21 seats but still registered a landslide overall majority of 102 seats. It had campaigned on a programme of lower taxes, a strong economy, with unemployment down and inflation at its lowest level for 20 years, and a strong defence. Thatcher became the first British Prime Minister since the Earl of Liverpool in 1820 to lead a party to three successive general election victories.

As I was settling into post-election reporting Reuters announced internally that they were looking for a new Chief Correspondent, Austria and Eastern Europe, based in Vienna. I had barely had a year in my post, but with my background, and a sense that Gorbachev's arrival on the scene was starting to have an effect in the region, I put myself forward.

I got the job, and was soon heading back to Vienna, boosted by the faint hope that I might still be around for the beginning of the end of Communism in East Europe. As it happened, I was there for the beginning, middle, end and aftermath.

# 23. THE EAST BLOC CRACKS

The Vienna office had swelled from the tight little operation I remembered from the early 80s. There were now five reporters including myself, and rooms full of sales and technical staff as the more reformist East Bloc countries were demanding access to our financial services. Our reporting also took on a new dimension with the addition of a photo service, following the takeover of UPI's overseas operations three years earlier. For the first time Reuters correspondents had to think pictures when planning a story. At the same time our photographers, highly experienced and drawn from all over the East bloc, offered an extra pair of eyes and ears when on an assignment without a reporter. On many occasions we found ourselves writing a story under someone else's name based on interrogating one of our "snappers".

Before I could start serious work there was the usual problem of housing, and schools. After enrolling our children in the American International School – a British international school had no vacancies as UN families had priority – we looked for suitable accommodation close to it. My predecessor's flat, a bachelor pad in the heart of the inner city, was not suitable. We found a perfect property overlooking vineyards and the Vienna woods, within walking distance of the school, but it was still under construction, so we spent a month in a single room in a small hotel.

Before the journalists' team had a chance to check out the situation in the East Bloc we had to focus, unusually, on two major stories dealing exclusively with Austria, and a part of their past that many would have preferred to forget.

In February 1988, an international historical commission issued its report on whether Austrian President Kurt Waldheim had been involved in war crimes during his service with Hitler's army. Waldheim, a two-time United Nations Secretary-General, had failed to mention much of his wartime service in a recently published autobiography. The commission found that he had known about and in some cases eased the way for war crimes in the Balkans, but it left open the question of his personal guilt. At one point a Jewish member of the commission had scornfully rejected Waldheim's claim, as a Nazi intelligence officer based in Salonika, Greece, to have been unaware of the deportation of the city's 50,000-strong Jewish community, the largest in Greece.

Waldheim was quoted by a Vienna newspaper a few days after the commission's findings as saying: "Yes I knew, but what could I do. I had to either continue to serve or be executed."

While the country was wrestling with this controversy, a month later it faced another, the 50th anniversary of its annexation by Austrian-born Adolf Hitler. The event produced much soul-searching as there was plenty of eyewitness and other evidence that the "Anschluss" (annexation) had been welcomed by a large section of the Austrian population.

"The Anschluss was no rape, it was a love affair, a marriage made in heaven," the leader of the World Jewish Congress, Edgar Bronfman, wrote in the New York Times.

Most of the Austrian papers chose to ignore the anniversary.

For many commentators both inside and outside Austria the Waldheim controversy, coinciding with the Anschluss anniversary, reflected not just the past of one man but of the whole country, and whether its people had come to terms with it.

The London Independent newspaper put it thus. "A man who likes to forget his wartime past at the head of a people now confronted with their own."

Some commentators saw a major problem in the decision of the victorious allies after the war to declare Austria the first victim of Naziism. For many historians and sociologists the Western Allies' decision, aimed at releasing Austria from Soviet control and aligning it with the West, encouraged Austrians to sweep their wartime past under the table. The purge of Naziism was not pursued as vigorously in Austria as it was in post-war Germany.

Turning our attention to East Europe, there were few signs at the beginning of 1988 that Gorbachev's call for perestroika and glasnost was having much effect in the region. In Czechoslovakia, Charter 77 human rights activists continued to be hounded by police. In Poland, regarded as more open than most, the Solidarity union was still outlawed after being banned under martial law, though it continued to operate underground. In Romania workers who rioted over food shortages the previous November were rounded up and the ringleaders jailed. In East Germany the authorities had recently cracked down on a small but active peace and human rights movement sheltering under the umbrella of the Protestant Church. In Bulgaria Zhivkov appeared to initially support Gorbachev's reforms but quickly showed his true colours when a group of intellectuals set up a Club for the Support of Perestroika and Glasnost, he arrested its leaders and threw them out of the party.

Even in Hungary, which ran a relatively liberal system and had introduced free-market reforms to its economy, anyone refusing military service still faced up to three years in jail.

But cracks were beginning to appear in the foundations of the communist system that had held the region in an iron grip for four decades, in some countries at least. Led by Poland and Hungary there were tentative moves to introduce political reforms, though initially they fell short of a total overthrow of the system. In other countries there was growing pressure from an increasingly disenchanted and angry public.

While Gorbachev's rise to power and reforms were destined to play a major role, other influences were at play, particularly the access by ordinary people to information from abroad through satellite television. Across the Soviet bloc satellite dishes of all shapes and sizes were sprouting from roof-tops as information-hungry East Europeans took advantage of "television without frontiers".

"We don't know where it comes from of what will be on, but it's wonderful to have," said a 30-year-old Prague teacher, one of thousands in the city to receive Western satellite programmes. The dishes were smuggled in from the West piece by piece or improvised from locally available parts. In East Germany, residents in apartment blocks clubbed together to buy them.

Solidarity leader Lech Walesa had a dish. "The monopolistic system cannot win, as there is no way the communists can stop people from learning about the rest of the world – and people will learn mainly from the satellites," he had said.

While a few years previously communist governments would have cracked down ruthlessly on any alternative sources of information, most of them now appeared resigned to satellites.

"There is no point trying to ban something when there is no easy way to enforce it," an East German party official said. As early as 1972 the Soviet Union had urged the United Nations to introduce an international convention on controlling satellite broadcasting, without success.

Communist authorities throughout the region were also starting to face growing public anger over increasing pollution, mainly from heavy industrial development and low-quality fuels, that was scarring the countryside and threatening the health of millions of people. In Czechoslovakia people were refusing to live in North Bohemia, a key industrial and mining area rated the most polluted in Europe producing 40% of the country's electricity and 75% of its coal. According to official figures up to 20 times the permissible amount of sulphur dioxide was being released into the air over Prague. A Polish study comparing two groups of children in heavily populated Silesia and rural north-east Poland showed the country children two to three years ahead of those in the industrial belt in physical and mental development. In East Germany, bordering both these countries, statistics on pollution were classified, and the Protestant church press was warned to curb their critical reporting on environmental issues.

East Bloc authorities, after ignoring the problem for years in their rush to overtake the West, and after treating environmentalists as dissidents, were starting to take notice as people took to the streets.

Colin McIntyre

In one country, Bulgaria, long regarded as Moscow's staunchest ally, the environment emerged as the basis of the country's first dissident movement and played a major part in the collapse of communism two years later. At the end of 1987 demonstrations by mothers and children broke out in the city of Rousse in protest against the pollution from a Romanian chemical plant across the river Danube. Another protest drew a crowd of around 6,000. Neither event was reported by Bulgarian media but they became the subject of a film by Bulgarian director Yuri Zhirov called "Breathe". The film became a hit, prompting the creation of what became the country's first dissident movement and a major force in the country.

Meanwhile the first real moves towards serious political reform in the East Bloc were initially led by Hungary in May 1988 when Janos Kadar, who had headed the Communist Party after succeeding Imre Nagy following his ill-fated revolt in 1956, was replaced by Prime Minister Karoly Grosz. At the same time 40% of the party's central committee were replaced by younger, more liberal members. Grosz declared his support for radical economic and political reforms but ruled out the immediate prospect of a multi-party system. In September the opposition Hungarian Democratic Forum, a loose group of nationally minded intellectuals who were looking for a "third way" between capitalism and communism, called for major political reforms leading to multi-party rule.

These moves followed a Soviet declaration in March, contained in a joint statement following a meeting with the Yugoslav Communist Party, to respect the right of all communist parties to choose their own paths.

"Proceeding from the conviction that no one has a monopoly over the truth, the two sides do not have the pretensions of imposing their concepts of social development on anyone."

The declaration was taken by many as a clear renunciation by Moscow of the Brezhnev doctrine binding communist states to intervene in other ones if their system was threatened.

These developments persuaded Reuters to open a bureau in Budapest for the first time since the 1950s. A young member of the Vienna bureau, David Lewis, was appointed Budapest bureau chief and we set about looking for a local correspondent and an office.

After putting a job advertisement in English in the Hungarian Communist Party daily, we were swamped by applications. As we were weeding them out a young Hungarian journalist with the national news agency MTI, Emil Varadi, took a train to Vienna, walked into our office and offered his services, underlining his familiarity with news agency journalism. We were impressed, but decided to have a look at the others, booking a hotel room in Budapest for two days for interviews. In the end we decided on Varadi, whose English was perfect after years in international schools, and reckoned his access to MTI would be useful.

For the office we rented a modest apartment in central Budapest handily placed for covering parliament, and around the corner from central Europe's first McDonalds, opened in April 1988, and an Adidas store which had record queues outside its doors. We opened the bureau with a formal reception attended by government officials and leading journalists. Reporting for the national press for MTI was a young woman, now not quite so young but instantly recognisable as my assistant during that football match in 1968. It was also attended by our current part-time "stringer" Charlie Coutts, an elderly Scottish communist who worked for Hungarian radio's English-language service and had provided routine, non-political news, particularly on sport, for decades when little of note was happening in Hungary. Kadar had maintained a low profile for his country, following Moscow's orders faithfully while quietly introducing economic and other reforms. Charlie had never made a secret of his communist beliefs, which had moderated over the years, and never tried to influence our reporting.

Reuters European Editor delivered a speech in which he failed to make a single mention of Charlie's contribution over the years, which I had laid out in a briefing paper to him. As the speech ended I felt a movement behind me, and Charlie had walked out, and a number of Hungarian colleagues, particularly those at the radio, shared his disappointment. A few months later I organised a small party for him and his colleagues and presented him with a state-of-the-art short-wave radio – he was a keen radio ham – which he accepted eagerly.

Poland was also in the forefront of reform moves when a series of crippling nationwide strikes in the Spring of 1988 prompted the government to open secret talks with the outlawed Solidarity union. A second wave of strikes in the summer came as a surprise to the government and Solidarity leaders, as it was organised by local activists unaware that talks between the two sides were going on. At the end of the year Walesa established a Solidarity Citizens' Committee, a semi-legal organisation of the democratic opposition which paved the way for ground-breaking Round Table Talks the following year.

In Czechoslovakia, there was little sign of movement in the government as public discontent was growing over the lack of civil rights and the stagnant economy. But in March thousands of mainly elderly Catholics holding candles demonstrated in the Slovak capital Bratislava calling for religious freedom and human rights. The protest, the largest mass demonstration against communist rule since 1969, was organised by dissident Catholics and Slovak emigres. It was put down by police using water cannon and dogs, witnessed by Western journalists including myself who made the 80 kilometres journey to the Slovak capital across the Danube from Vienna. The police response to the peaceful demonstration, which went ahead after official permission for it was refused, caused an outcry in the West, particularly as it coincided with a follow-up meeting of the European Security Conference in Vienna discussing ways to build confidence between East and West. It also caused some unrest within the Czechoslovak government, prompting the culture minister to resign a few months later.

While the action seemed to confirm Czechoslovakia's place among countries firmly opposed to Gorbachev's reforms, alongside Romania, recent moves in Hungary and Poland had persuaded Reuters to reopen its Prague bureau closed in 1982. On one of my trips to the city, I dropped by some local journalists who told me they were aware Reuters was looking for a new local correspondent and knew of a possible candidate who was both well qualified and interested. I called a number they gave me and arranged to meet him at one of the many bars in Prague's Old Town before heading back to Vienna. As we sat talking politely I complimented him on his English, and he replied he had spent some time in Canada. Something clicked and I said "don't I know you", and he asked the same question. It was Michael Žantovský, my student friend of 20 years previously, who was working as a translator of modern American and British writers, including playwright Woody Allen, and was close to dissident intellectuals around Havel. I explained that he would not have an easy time in his new role, but he accepted the job and I returned to Vienna.

Before returning to Vienna I had an interview with the foreign editor of the communist party daily Rude Pravo, Milan Jelinek, seeking to learn whether the Prague government were thinking of adopting some of the reforms of their neighbours. His response, firm and unsmiling, was basically no, expressed in jargon straight out of the communist handbook.

"I won't talk to people who openly state their aim is to change the social system in my country," he said.

"I see no reason to talk to a very limited group of people who I know have no support in the country. We are talking of about 50 people, and there are some strange characters among them."

As we headed out I asked my official translator allocated to me by the foreign ministry, presumably after serious vetting, what she thought of his response. "I never heard such a load of horse-shit," she said in a loud voice as I bundled her out of the building.

Just over two years later those 50 people were running the country.

We also decided to establish a full-time local correspondent in Sofia and were helped by our London-based sports editor who had just attended a major international sports event in Sofia and had been impressed by a rival news organisation's local assistant. On my next visit to Sofia I made contact with Nick Antonov, a university graduate working as a driver for the editor of a national sports daily. With the permission of the Bulgarian foreign ministry press department Nick began sending us regular pieces about sport, but as the political situation developed he began sending other reports as well. His English was quite basic, but he had an acute understanding of local politics and excellent contacts. Working with Vienna correspondent Meriel Beattie, a bright Oxford graduate who had come on a regular one-year training assignment but performed so well she was kept on, they formed a formidable team. As the political crisis deepened, leading to the overthrow of Zhivkov in 1989, the state-owned Bulgarian media increasingly used Reuters and other Western agencies for their domestic coverage as they found themselves in unfamiliar territory. At the end of 1989, Nick was voted Bulgarian journalist of the year.

In Romania the economic and political situations were still bleak as Ceausescu insisted on pushing ahead with his plan to pay off the country's debts as quickly as possible, by exporting anything valuable for foreign currency.

In November 1987 reports emerged of a major workers' protest in Brasov, an ancient city in Transylvania which had a significant minority of ethnic Germans dating back centuries. Their number was decreasing rapidly as the West German government was buying them out for hard currency desperately sought by the regime. As an accredited correspondent to Romania I managed to get a visa and headed to Bucharest dressed in what I hoped were downmarket clothes that would not make me stand out, a choice that was not difficult for me to make. Arriving in Bucharest, the city was in a deep freeze, with uncleared snow on the roads and pavements and temperatures inside public buildings limited to $10^\circ$ Celsius. Children were skating on the pavements, with ice-skates, as I made my way to the station and caught the first train to Brasov, one of Romania's largest cities and a major industrial centre.

The town, like the rest of the country, was freezing, with one resident saying: "No danger of burning yourself on the radiators. They just heat enough to stop the pipes freezing up". In the famous 14th-century Black Church, religious centre for the German minority, Paster Matthias Pelger faced the prospect of cancelling a Christmas concert because it was too cold inside.

"It is not the singers I'm worried about, but the violinists can't play if it gets any colder."

Walking through the town I sought out townspeople, but most were reluctant to talk. A middle-aged woman, speaking German, said I was clearly from the West because of my clothes, and raced away. As she turned the corner, however, she called back: "At least someone has the guts to do something." Eventually I met an elderly man who said he was on the verge of leaving for Germany under the buy-out scheme and told me what had happened.

On November 15 some 200 workers of the Red Flag industrial plant marched through the city in their overalls protesting over wage and job cuts. Starting with economic demands such as "give us bread", they soon switched to "down with Ceausescu", "down with the Communist Party". As the marchers moved to the centre they were joined by other workers from a large tractor plant and other citizens, swelling the crowd to over 15,000. Reaching the main square they broke into the party headquarters and brought out books, papers and portraits of Ceausescu, which were set alight, as well as food from its well-stocked larder intended to celebrate victory in local elections, a foregone conclusion, including oranges, an item ordinary Romanians said they never saw.

Securitate police moved in quickly and forcibly broke up the demonstration, arresting some 300 people. Not a word of the protest, the biggest since the Jiu Valley miners' strike in 1977, appeared in any Romanian media.

Colin McIntyre

A further example of the regime's refusal to acknowledge popular discontent over its hard-line policies came a few months later when it was reported to have started implementing its policy of "systematisation". This plan for rural resettlement, which Ceausescu brought back from his visits to China and North Korea, basically involved eliminating villages of under 1,000 inhabitants, deemed "irrational", and moving inhabitants to "agro-industrial complexes" housed in modern blocks with shared kitchens. According to Western diplomatic and emigré sources the policy was deeply unpopular, among other reasons because it barred villagers from cultivating private plots which provided most of their food.

The policy had been on the table for several years but there was no hard evidence it was being implemented. However reports had begun to appear in the Western press, mainly based on sources in Hungary in touch with the two million-strong ethnic minority in Transylvania, that some villages had already disappeared. Relations between Romania and Hungary had been deteriorating for years over Bucharest's refusal to recognise the country's largest minority as a separate ethnic group. They came to a head when thousands of Hungarians marched to the Romanian embassy in Budapest protesting against the reported destruction of villages in Transylvania.

I decided it was time to have a look, and managed to get a Romanian visa, no longer granted automatically as the government was reacting to the growing negative reporting of the country by clamping down on visits. Booking into the Hotel Bucuresti, widely assumed to be run by the Securitate, I ordered a car for the next day without revealing my planned destination.

The next morning my driver arrived, with "spook" written all over his crumpled face. We set off in a battered Peugeot through snow-covered landscape on icy roads, with bald tyres, headed for Transylvania. As cars and lorries slid around, and into each other, the driver showed uncanny skill in negotiating the hills, and avoiding collisions. Not far out of town he started looking from left to right, then commented, in broken English, "but there used to be a village here". It was, as far as was known by Bucharest-based diplomats at the time, the only known case of a village being destroyed. It was believed to have been chosen because it lay on the road between Bucharest and a lakeside villa often used by the Ceausescus and had been levelled after he complained of seeing no progress in systematisation. We headed into Transylvania, stopping off to visit one of the 150 fortified churches in the region dating back to the 13th to 15th centuries, practically untouched in the absence of tourism. As we entered the mainly ethnic Hungarian city of Târgu Mureş, the driver suddenly announced "my mother lives here, I can get some potatoes", to my surprise and delight, anticipating that he might share some of his fellow-Hungarians' antipathy towards the government. But his shoulders sagged as he added that he had nothing to give her in exchange. I quietly dropped two packets of American-made Kent cigarettes onto the seat next to him, and his shoulders sprang back. With basic consumer goods in short supply or unavailable in the country and money largely worthless, foreign cigarettes had long since become the currency for getting things done. Romanians were particularly attached to menthol-flavoured Kent with filter, as these were produced locally in pre-war days. I had given up smoking in 1975 but made sure I always carried Kents in Romania.

We were now firm friends as he led us to a group of remote villages that had been listed in Western press reports as having been already destroyed. We were unable to drive right up to the villages as the narrow lane leading to them was impassable due to the heavy snow. However we met a group of elderly villagers at the end of the trail who assured us they were still standing, but were expected to be pulled down any day, and described how angry people were over the plan. The driver happily translated all this information, including personal attacks against Ceausescu and the party. Back in Târgu Mureş we drove to a restaurant where he ordered a huge meal with three sorts of meat and a carafe of good wine for me and left to see his mother. He returned an hour later, grinned as he lifted the boot to show several bags of potatoes, and we drove back to Bucharest.

My next trip to Romania six months later ended with me being thrown out of the country. Six months after that, on Christmas day, 1989, the Ceausescus died in a hail of bullets from a firing squad.

That came at the end of a year that saw the collapse of communism in Europe as some governments in the region moved gradually but steadily towards reform while others held out and were overtaken by events. Although the signs were there, the speed of developments took everyone by surprise.

# 24. 1989, REVOLUTION YEAR

The year began with early moves from pace-setting Hungary as its parliament approved a law in January on the right to demonstrate, to free speech and to set up political parties free of Communist Part control. The following month the party's central committee agreed to support the country's transfer to a multi-party system. At the same time it ruled that the 1956 anti-communist uprising crushed by Soviet tanks, which was officially declared a counter-revolution, had begun as a popular revolt. In March Hungary joined Western nations in co-sponsoring a U.N. resolution to investigate Romania's human rights abuses against its minority, the first time a Soviet Bloc country had asked for an investigation into another. Later in the same month it eased restrictions on media ownership, ending four decades of communist monopoly control.

In July three opposition candidates won seats in parliament in by-elections, the country's first non-communist MPs since 1947.

A more spectacular move came in June when Hungarian Foreign Minister Gyula Horn and his Austrian counterpart Alois Mock met at the Hungarian border town of Sopron to cut a symbolic hole in the "Iron Curtain". Wielding giant wire-clippers, the two cut a hole large enough to step through the two-metre high barbed wire barrier.

Mock said the fence was an anachronism and its partial removal symbolised the hope that the barrier would be torn down across Europe and that an end to the continent's division was in sight. However Hungarian police continued patrolling the border.

Meanwhile Poland was also pressing ahead with reforms as the Round Table Talks ended with an agreement under which Solidarity, which had been banned for the past seven years, re-entered Polish life. Lech Walesa told the assembly: "We came to the Round Table from prison under the truncheons of ZOMO riot police". The agreement also included curbs on the power of the Communist Party and wide-ranging changes to parliament, with the creation of a new 100-member Senate and the right of independent parties to contest elections against the communists.

In June the country held parliamentary elections in which Solidarity won all freely contested seats in the Sejm lower house, with some reserved for communist deputies, and all the seats in the Senate.

Although the elections were only partly free, they made Poland the first country in East Europe in which democratically elected representatives gained real power and showed the way for other East Bloc countries to follow within the next few months.

In Czechoslovakia there was a brief outburst of public anger in January when dissidents organised a week of demonstrations to mark the 20th anniversary of the self-immolation of Jan Palach. On the first evening 5,000 people turned out to demonstrate on the spot at the end of Prague's Wenceslas Square where he had died. Several were violently detained by riot police and some of the organisers were jailed.

There was another demonstration on August 21 when some 2,000 people turned out in the city centre to mark the anniversary of the Warsaw Pact invasion, some shouting "freedom, freedom" and "long live Hungary", a reference to the political reforms next door that their own country rejected. A small group of Hungarians took part brandishing a banner proclaiming "The Bolsheviks came with tanks, we come with flowers," which was immediately destroyed by plain clothes police. But the protest, like the Palach demonstration and one the following October to mark the anniversary of the founding of Czechoslovakia in 1918, failed to draw enough people to generate real momentum.

In Romania, things were going from bad to worse as Ceausescu faced growing isolation, under attack abroad from both East and West and at home from former top party officials.

In March a resolution to the U.N. Human Rights Commission demanding an investigation into alleged human rights abuses by Romania against its Hungarian minority was co-sponsored by independent groups in Czechoslovakia and Poland. In another major departure from traditional

East bloc solidarity formerly staunch allies the Soviet Union, East Germany and Bulgaria either abstained or did not take part in the vote. French President Francois Mitterrand had told diplomats at a new year's reception he had no intention of visiting a regime he described as "anachronistic and wounding to the human conscience". A meeting of European Community foreign ministers heard Britain's Geoffrey Howe cite "universal astonishment about the way Romania behaves towards its citizens".

Ceausescu's most serious challenge came from within as six former Romanian Communist Party officials, including a former foreign minister, former deputy prime minister and former ambassador to Washington and the U.N. signed an open letter accusing him of violating human rights accords, ignoring constitutional guarantees and mismanaging the economy.

"At a time when the very idea of socialism, for which we have fought, is discredited by your policy, and when our country is being isolated in Europe, we have decided to speak up," the letter said.

Thinking it was time to visit Romania I applied for a visa but was told none were being issued for journalists. Fortunately a British parliamentary delegation was due to visit the country and I managed to attach myself to it, citing Reuters' close links with the UK. In fact these were now tenuous at best after our British and Commonwealth media owners had sold out in a public offering in 1984.

I arrived in May and while doing the rounds of Western embassies learned that there was growing concern among diplomats and their families after the wife of a senior West German diplomat was beaten up by a uniformed policeman in downtown Bucharest in broad daylight. Diplomats said the Bonn government had sought to hush up the incident, worried that it might endanger its ethnic German repatriation programme and were concerned about the safety of their families.

I waited a day to try to collect any further information and filed the story back to London, suspecting my trip might be a short one, and attended an England-Romania rugby international in the afternoon, won by the visitors 58-3. I cheered every one of the England tries, to the discomfort of my obvious Securitate shadow sitting a few seats away. As expected I got a knock on the door of my hotel room that evening and was told to leave the country at the earliest opportunity the next day. At the airport, after my visa was cancelled with a large "persona non grata" stamp, I demanded to be put on an indirect Lufthansa flight to Vienna via Zagreb rather than the direct one with the Romanian airline Tarom, which I had learned to avoid. When the official at the counter asked why I was making such a roundabout trip, I replied "anything to avoid Tarom". He was clearly struggling to stop laughing and I heard a similar response from the queue behind me. What little was left of public support was clearly ebbing away.

# 25. IRON CURTAIN BREACHED

In August a significant event took place on the Austrian-Hungarian border at a "Pan-European Picnic" organised by Hungarian and Austrian groups. It was held under the patronage of Otto von Habsburg, the son of the last Austro-Hungarian emperor and a member of the European Parliament, and Imre Poszgay, a reformist senior official in the Hungarian Communist Party. It was planned as a peaceful symbolic event to demonstrate Hungary's new freedoms under Glasnost, and to promote friendship between East and West. The idea was to open a gate in a small stretch of the border near Sopron for three hours to allow people on both sides to exchange greetings.

The event took place on a dusty track next to the border where groups had gathered on both sides, witnessed by Meriel. The border guards appeared relaxed as they flirted with the prettier of the Hungarian girls. But not long after a gate of wood and barbed wire was opened groups of East German tourists arrived, having picked up rumours that the border was porous and something was going on, and rushed through the gap as the Hungarian guards stood aside. "They simply turned around when they saw the people coming," a West German man said after giving a lift to three escapees, one crying with relief.

The East Germans were mainly young, some with children, with just the clothes they were wearing. "We were East Germans, but not anymore," one said.

"They just marched through," an Austrian border guard told journalists. Around 600 succeeding in getting across before the gate was closed again as planned, and Hungarian guards continued to police the border. It was the largest single exodus of East Germans to the West since the Berlin Wall went up.

Most of the East Germans had been camping at a site in Sopron. "The camp site is full, but the tents are empty," one of them said.

The head of the Hungarian police unit, Lieutenant-Colonel Arpad Bella, was quoted later as saying he had only a few seconds to decide on his course of action in the absence of orders from above and decided he "did not want to be a mass murderer". All indications suggested those orders were "do not intervene".

Hungarian guards continued to patrol the border and arrested hundreds of East Germans trying to cross to Austria, cancelling their visas. But with ordinary wire mesh replacing barbed wire on some sections of the border, thousands more of their fellow-countrymen poured into Hungary looking for escape. Many of those whose visas had been cancelled occupied the West German embassy in Budapest, camping in the grounds. Others waited in makeshift camps in and around Budapest and at Lake Balaton.

As the news spread several hundred East Germans climbed into the West German embassy in Prague, while smaller numbers did the same in Warsaw and East Berlin.

Hungary, struggling to deal with the refugee influx but reluctant to repudiate a bilateral agreement with East Germany barring them from allowing their citizens to go to a third country, planned a one-time operation to allow 5,000 to go to the West. However Deputy Foreign Minister Ferenc Somogyi told journalists it should not set a precedent for other would-be emigres.

"Hungary does not want to become a springboard to the West for East Europeans," he told parliament.

As Hungary urged Bonn and East Berlin to settle the matter between them, the government finally decided enough was enough.

On the night of September 11 Hungarian radio announced: "Interior Minister Istvan Horvath instructed the police and border guards to let East German citizens leave Hungary with East German travel documents. The border guards are instructed to let them through at any border point."

At the stroke of midnight the barrier at the main crossing at Hegyeshalom swung up and a battered orange Trabant led a procession of cars across to Nickelsdorf on the Austrian side after a cursory glance at their identity documents by smiling Hungarian guards. Some East Germans could not wait for border guards to raise the barrier and hurled themselves under it on the stroke of midnight into Austria and a new life in the West.

While most of the emigres were overjoyed, and many celebrated with champagne, some had mixed emotions. "It's a great feeling but also a sad one," said Dieter Hoffman from Dresden. "Whatever things were like there, it's still home. My parents are there. That's where I grew up."

Another man carried aloft a message to East German leader Erich Honecker, whose regime had refused to consider the reforms being enacted in some of its neighbours. "Give up Honecker, aren't 100,000 refugees enough?"

The East German government issued a statement describing the exodus as "organised trade in humans".

On the Austrian side Red Cross officials handed out food, maps for the 320-kilometre journey to Passau, West Germany, and the equivalent of £30 for petrol to get them there. Over the next few days some 14,000 East Germans had left for the West, and a couple of months later the figure was closer to 50,000.

# 26. THE WALL COMES DOWN

Meanwhile East Germans were continuing to climb into the fence surrounding the West German embassy in Prague, which had a large garden, and by the middle of September over 10,000 people were camped inside the mission or outside in large tents. I was visiting Prague at the time organising new premises for our bureau and talked to some of the refugees through the garden fence. Some had recently learned of the luxury life-styles senior East German officials had been leading while the rest of country struggled with austerity, and their anger burst through.

Under pressure from Bonn Czechoslovakia's new hard-line leader Miloš Jakeš, who had taken over from Husak in 1987, finally agreed to allow them to travel to West Germany in sealed trains.

Announcing the decision to the masses in the garden from a balcony of the embassy, West German Foreign Minister Hans-Dietrich Genscher said: "Fellow countrymen, we have come to you to share that news that as of today your departure to the Federal Republic of Germany is now possible." The last part of the statement was drowned out by the wild cheering of the campers.

Between October 1 and 4 the refugees left Prague by train in three waves, passing through Dresden on the way to East Berlin. After they passed the track was littered with torn-up passports and identity documents. The refugees left behind some 1,600 East German made Trabants and Soviet built Ladas littering the streets surrounding the embassy. The East German government sent in 70 drivers to bring them back, cars being as always in short supply at home, but many had already been cannibalised by local car owners.

When the first train passed through Dresden there were major riots as crowds rushed the station in the belief that it would be stopping to take on more passengers. Police intervened with water-cannon and clubs, and dozens of people were injured. The clash was widely seen as the first real sign of revolt among the East German population, though opposition to the government had been growing under the surface for some time.

The centre of the opposition movement was not the capital East Berlin, but Leipzig in the state of Saxony, once a major cultural centre and the home city of Johannes Sebastian Bach. Its role in the collapse of the wall and the end of communist rule, which only became widely known after the event, eventually earned it the title "hero city" among East Germans.

The opposition in the city had begun 10 years previously as a peace movement targeting NATO plans to install Pershing medium-range nuclear missiles in Europe in response to a Soviet nuclear build-up. It was centred around the city's historic St Nicholas church where Bach performed several of his cantatas, including the St John Passion, for the first time. Every Monday a few people would gather and march "for peace" around the area. The backing of the Protestant Church offered some protection, and the marches were initially supported by the government as they were directed against the West. But as popular discontent grew over the government's refusal to address the sort of reforms initiated by Gorbachev and followed by some neighbouring countries, the marchers' demands became more political and their numbers increased. The ranks of the protesters were swelled by East Germans who had applied to emigrate to the West and had lost their jobs and education prospects while waiting for a decision.

Things changed dramatically in May when volunteers monitoring the vote count in local elections, a right embedded in law but never previously exercised, revealed they had been manipulated to get a 99 per cent result for candidates. When word got out protests mounted, and the government put pressure on the Protestant Church to curb the marches.

The number of marchers doubled in early September after a protest by several thousand demanding political reforms was broken up by police in full view of West German TV crews covering the annual East-West trade fair in the city, whose reports were watched by East Germans. Tension reached a peak later in the month when police closed streets surrounding the church and stopped people coming to the Monday meetings, making several arrests.

On Monday October 9, word went out that the police were drafting in 8,000 extra officers, enough to control a crowd of 20,000, and there were fears that the government was planning a Tiananmen Square response, recalling the Chinese government's decision the previous June to send in tanks to crush a students' protest in the centre of Beijing. Within hours 70,000 people, a sixth of Leipzig's population, had jammed the streets outside the church and beyond. Trams and buses ground to a halt as more and more people joined in, shouting "No violence" and "We are the people". Some also shouted "We are staying here", a response to the government's decision to close all the country's borders to stop further emigration. Police looked on but did nothing.

Commenting later on what became known as "the miracle of Leipzig", one of the organisers, Rainer Eppelmann, said: "They were ready to crack down on 30,000, but 30,000 didn't show up. There were 70,000."

The situation was coming to a head as the next Monday 150,000 joined the march, and the following week it was 200,000. On November 4 half a million people demonstrated in East Berlin's central Alexanderplatz.

As the government's crisis grew it called a press conference on November 9 to announce the decisions of an emergency meeting of the Communist Party's Central Committee the previous day tasked with regaining control and restoring order. Towards the end of the briefing an Italian journalist asked politburo member Günter Schabowski if there were any changes in the restrictions on travel. Flustered, he looked at his notes and read out: "Private travel can now be applied for without prerequisites." As stunned journalists clamoured for more details, he replied that as far as he was aware it was effective immediately. It later transpired that the announcement had been planned for the following day, along with details of how to apply for visas. As East German media hesitated while seeking clarification West German radio and TV seized eagerly on the news and their reports were picked up and spread quickly through East Berlin. Thousands of people gathered at the main border crossing point to West Berlin, and the border guards, confronted by huge crowds but with no orders, eventually opened the barriers.

On the 25th anniversary of the event, the policeman who gave the order to open the border said he had spent hours trying to get guidance from his superiors as 20,000 people waited at the crossing clamouring to get out. In an interview with Reuters in Berlin, by then reunified, Lieutenant-Colonel Harald Jaeger said that after being told by his commanders to sort it out for himself, he ordered the 46 armed guards at the Bornholmer Street crossing to lift the barrier.

"My world was collapsing and I felt like I was left alone by my party and my military commanders," he said. "I was on the one hand hugely disappointed but also relieved that it had ended peacefully. It could have been a different outcome."

As soon as the news broke I was ordered to fly into Berlin the next day and went straight to the Wall to watch as a tall West Berlin policeman greeted each crossing group with "You are very welcome". Once across most people headed straight for the nearest bank where on presentation of their identity document each of them received 100 West German marks, about £30 at the time.

On the following Monday I was told to head for Leipzig in time for the service at the St Nicholas Church and the "peace march" that normally followed. In the confusion at the office, and my fading memory of East Berlin's geography, I was sent to the wrong station. With time running out and Leipzig 190 kilometres from the capital, I hailed the first city taxi I could see and told the driver "I'm going to make you a happy man" as I offered to pay the likely fare of 200 marks all in West German currency. After almost fainting for joy he took off. Along the way he was stopped for speeding but grinned nonchalantly as he was fined 10 East German marks. With the black market rate currently running at between 5 and 10 East marks for every West mark, he was looking to receive upwards of 1,000 marks in local currency.

I arrived as they were about to close the doors of the packed church and went in to hear the sermon which gave thanks for a peaceful conclusion to the growing protests here and elsewhere and joined several thousand people on a march around the streets. In an interview with Pastor Arndt Haubold he recalled how the Monday marches "for peace and social renewal" had been attended by no more than 10 people when they began in 1979. The previous Monday the total was 200,000.

"We wanted more justice, more truth, more freedom of expression and freedom to travel," he said, seated in the sacristy of the magnificent 800-year-old church. "But we were a tiny voice, and no one listened to us." As the numbers grew "they told us that they would freeze church-state relations and warned us that we would be held responsible for any violence," Haubold said, adding: "But we have always stressed that we want no violence."

A local journalist said the slogans of the marchers had changed. "They were calling for free travel. Now they are calling for free elections."

As I remained in Leipzig interviewing local officials word came through from Reuters that a student had been killed when police had broken up a student demonstration in Prague on Friday, November 17. Knowing that our Vienna staffer charged with covering Czechoslovakia, a young American called Michael Wise, was away visiting his family in the US, I took a train to East Berlin, crossed to West Berlin, flew to Munich and drove to Prague in a hired car, arriving at the weekend. It turned out that the student had not died during a brutal attack by police. Our bureau had received the news from a senior dissident spokesman, had confirmed it with a second source but that turned out to have heard it from the original one.

The demonstration was organised by the official Socialist Union of Youth to mark the 50th anniversary of the Nazi storming of Prague university in which nine students were killed and was approved by the party authorities. Some 15,000 students marched through the centre of the city shouting "we are not carrying weapons", but as they approached the central Wenceslas Square they were confronted by riot police who waded in with clubs, injuring some 600 people, including an American woman reporter from the Chicago Tribune.

The attack on a peaceful demonstration, seen as a panic move by a regime rattled by the previous week's events across the border in East Germany, sent shock waves through the city. Many of the students had parents holding senior positions in business, the professions and the arts. The following day students in Prague went on strike and called for a general stoppage across the country on November 27. On the Sunday Havel met with senior members of Charter 77 and other dissident groups and announced the formation of a Civic Forum, as a mass popular movement for reform. The group called for the dismissal of officials responsible for the violence against the students, an independent investigation into the incident and the release of all political prisoners.

The following day Žantovský and I sat in our temporary office in the Yalta Hotel near the top of Wenceslas Square to await developments. As we watched, the crowd began streaming in and slowly moved up the square, and within a few hours had swollen to 200,000, calling for free elections and a general strike. Shouting "It's the end, Miloš", and "Jakeš out", they jangled their keys, symbolising the unlocking of doors in what became the defining soundtrack of the "Velvet Revolution". There were no signs of police, a strong indication that the government had decided further resistance to reforms was useless. The demonstration was followed five days later by another on the huge Letna plain overlooking the city, once the site of the world's largest statue of Stalin, which drew 500,000 people. On November 27 a two-hour general strike across the country went ahead which was reported to have been supported by 75% of the population.

On November 29, just 12 days after the student demonstration crushed by police that marked the start of the Velvet Revolution, the parliament declared an end to one-party rule and the communist system that had ruled the country for 41 years. It was, one commentator remarked, an example of "the power of the powerless", the title of an essay written by Havel in 1978 which was circulated in secret, translated into several languages, and became a manifesto of dissent in Czechoslovakia, Poland and other communist countries. In December Havel was appointed president.

Meanwhile changes elsewhere in the East Bloc were coming thick and fast, threatening to overload the Vienna bureau. On November 10, the day after the Wall came down, Todor Zhivkov was forced to resign by senior members of the Bulgarian Communist Party over his refusal to recognise current problems and deal with public protests. The last straw was his decision to order the CSS to beat up members of the independent environmental group Eco-Glasnost invited to attend an international European Security Conference in Sofia called by reform-leaning Bulgarian Foreign Minister Petar Mladenov. Zhivkov also ordered some 30 other opposition activists to be driven into the countryside during the conference and forced to walk back to Sofia. Both events provoked international outrage.

The following month the party's central committee called for free elections and asked parliament to change the constitution to end the party's leading role. In January the party's 46-year hold on power ended.

# 27. CEAUSESCU FALLS

In Romania, trouble for the Ceausescu regime sprang from a most unlikely source. In Timisoara, Romania's second largest city close to the Hungarian border, Father László Tőkés of the Hungarian Reformed Church announced to his congregation one morning in December that he had been ordered by city officials to move to another parish. Ethnic Hungarian churches had long complained of harassment by local communist authorities.

On the day of the planned eviction on December 15 members of his congregation set up a permanent vigil around his church in the city centre. By the end of the day their numbers had swelled to over 1,000 and growing as they were joined by people from other ethnic groups and religions. The following day officials led by the mayor pleaded with them to disperse, promising to revoke the eviction order, but were met with jeers and calls for "freedom". A day later police arrived and there were clashes across the city, but the revolt appeared to be spreading.

Ceausescu was in Teheran at the time on a pre-planned visit with his wife. When word reached him about the situation in Timisoara he was reported to have been furious, shouting "Why didn't they shoot?", and issued instructions for live ammunition to be used. The security forces in Timisoara duly opened fire on demonstrators, killing dozens and wounding two American and a Yugoslav journalist and an Italian photographer. Years later the official death toll in the Timisoara revolt was put at 93, but many more died as it quickly spread across the country. It was the only one of the anti-communist uprisings in East Europe where blood was spilled.

Reporting of the events in Timisoara had come mainly from Hungarian media getting information from their ethnic kin in the region and monitoring local radio and television. Reuters had no permanent presence in Romania, and some of the country's borders had been closed.

Our reports from Budapest, where I was covering the first session of the partly democratic Hungarian parliament, were based on Hungarian radio and the Yugoslav news agency Tanjug which could tap into a significant ethnic Serbian minority in Romania..

Apart from Tanjug, which was always able to report more freely under Yugoslavia's looser brand of communism, official news agencies of the Warsaw Pact states all had permanent bureaus in Bucharest. Their correspondents, free of communist controls that had hitherto limited their reporting to routine domestic events and bilateral news, now threw themselves into reporting the unfolding drama across Romania with relish, skill and flair. Reports from Poland's PAP, Hungary's MTI, Bulgaria's BTA, East Germany's ADN and the Soviet Union's TASS, including some vivid eye-witness material, were picked up in our Vienna office or in their home countries.

With events moving at breath-taking speed Ceausescu flew back from Teheran and gave a speech from the balcony of the central committee building in a bid to calm the situation and restore order. As he began speaking jeers and whistles could be heard clearly during his televised address, and he stopped, unsure how to proceed in what was uncharted territory for an absolute dictator.

As Ceausescu was making his televised address we set up a monitoring operation in the Budapest bureau with native speakers covering Romanian television, which could be picked up. As the crowd became more unruly soldiers joined the demonstration and the Ceausescus, faced with a mass revolt, took off by helicopter from the roof of the building. Landing on a main road after the pilot reportedly refused to fly any further for fear of being shot down, the small party commandeered a car from a local doctor. He dropped them off at a town up the road, where they took over another car and headed to Târgoviște, the former royal capital of Wallachia some 50 kilometres from Bucharest. Here they were locked in an office and handed over to soldiers from a local garrison.

As we were reporting the main developments from Budapest I got a call from Michael Žantovský from Prague saying he needed to speak to me urgently. Replying that this was not the ideal time for a talk, as I was filing urgent stories both from the Hungarian parliament and Romania, he announced he would, regrettably, have to quit. As I remained speechless, he explained that Havel had asked him to be his official spokesman, and there was little I could say apart from warmly congratulating him. After serving as Havel's spokesman he was appointed Czech ambassador to the USA, after the country has split from Slovakia, and then to Israel and finally the UK.

Our first direct report from revolutionary Bucharest came from Johnny Krčmař, who had left Czechoslovakia legally a few years earlier and was now based in Vienna. He flew into the capital in a private two-seater plane on the day Ceausescu was trying to flee from the roof. Arriving just before the airport was closed, and with fighting going on in the streets, Johnny was eventually escorted by soldiers to the Austrian embassy in the capital. There he charmed the ambassador, a woman, into personally punching out his hand-written report on the embassy telex. Local security regulations, even in such extraordinary times, barred non-embassy personnel from touching the keys. Still pinned down by street fighting, he called a local journalist we had been using as a sports stringer, Radu Timofte, who braved the shooting to ferry him to the Hotel Intercontinental in downtown Bucharest. As he was walking in he bumped into a local journalist who was leaving and who asked if he needed a translator, and suddenly we had an office and a local Bucharest correspondent.

Johnny was joined a couple of days later by Richard Balmforth, who had done some reporting of Romania in the past, and drove with another journalist from Belgrade to Bucharest, stopping off in Timisoara on Christmas Eve. Sniper fire was still going on in the city and a young Romanian invited them to spend the night in his parents' apartment, saying it was too dangerous outside. Richard reported the father removing a heavy obstacle from behind the door, clutching an axe behind his back as he let them in, before sharing the family's festive dinner with the guests.

Richard arrived in Bucharest on Christmas Day, a few hours after Romanian TV revealed the last few hours of the Ceausescus' lives. At 4 p.m. on Christmas day the couple were taken to a military base near Târgoviște and executed by firing squad after what could only be described as a Stalinist-type show trial by a hastily convened tribunal. Hundreds of soldiers volunteered to be part of the execution squad.

No hard evidence of the charges was offered by the prosecution, and the couple were given no right of appeal, as mandated by law. Facing several charges including genocide, corruption and embezzlement, their trial lasted barely an hour. They were not allowed to choose a defence lawyer, and one of them allocated to them, Nicu Teodorescu, eventually joined the prosecution. In an interview a few days later with the London Times Teodorescu said he had tried to persuade the couple their only chance of avoiding execution was to plead insanity.

"They felt deeply insulted, unable or unwilling to grasp their only lifeline," he was quoted as saying. "They rejected my help after that." Teodorescu, one of Romania's top lawyers, told the newspaper Ceausescu showed "absolutely nothing but contempt when the tribunal delivered its verdict, telling the prosecutor: 'When this is all over I'll have you put on trial'. We all laughed".

"Ceausescu was convinced all along that his Securitate would rescue him."

The speed of the trial and execution inevitably gave rise to speculation that what was hailed as a popular uprising had been organised, at least to some extent, by disenchanted senior members of the old regime. One of the organisers of the trial, Defence Minister Victor Stânculescu, was quoted later as saying a quick trial was needed into order to ensure the army supported the newly created National Salvation

Front. One of its leaders Petre Roman told French television they had acted quickly on rumours that loyalists planned to rescue the couple.

In the absence of firm news on developments paranoia had swept Bucharest as rumours and counter-rumours circulated that Ceausescu was staging a comeback backed by the Securitate. One commonly accepted rumour was that Ceausescu's forces had been reinforced by a specially trained unit of "Libyan eunuchs" parachuted into the country. The rumours were laid to rest when Romanian television showed the bloodied bodies of the couple, struck by 120 bullets according to later official reports. The hotel staff, many of whom were widely believed to belong to the Securitate, stared in disbelief as the images were flashed on the screen.

With the Reuters team boosted by a small army of reporters flown in from different parts of Europe they fanned out across Romania shining a torch on a country where for four decades travel without a secret police shadow had been virtually impossible. In Bucharest the revolutionary National Salvation Front appeared to be establishing their grip on law and order, although violence and shooting continued well into the New Year. Though a final death toll during the revolution was hard to pin down a widely accepted estimate was between 800 and 1,200, including the uprising in Timisoara.

In the capital Romanian flags with the communist hammer and sickle emblem torn out of the middle were flown from official buildings. The headquarters of the Securitate where extreme loyalists had tried to hold out was gutted and charred. Throughout the city candles commemorating victims of the shooting flickered in windows and shop fronts. At Ceausescu's 40-room palace in a luxury compound of a dozen houses for his ministers, generals and friends in north Bucharest the doors were opened to reveal a treasure trove of paintings, valuable ornaments and gilded furniture. The bathrooms were decorated with Italian tiles and gold-plated taps, and even the nuclear bunker was lined with marble.

"It is almost too hard to comprehend," Major Stancu Valentin told journalists viewing the mansion. "I hope one day this place will be turned into a museum of madness."

Outside the capital our reporters wrote about the plight of women, particularly those seeking an abortion. In a bid to boost the population Ceausescu had banned contraception and ruled that terminations were illegal for women with less than five children. There were cases of women recovering consciousness from an illegal abortion to find a Securitate agent at their bedside waiting to interview and charge them.

I arrived in Bucharest a week after Ceausescu's death to check on our operation. As I handed across my passport at the airport, with its large "barred from the country" stamp from my last visit, I got a huge grin and a handshake from the border official.

# 28. ALBANIA JOINS THE FUN

Romania became the last member of the Warsaw Pact defence alliance to throw off communism and start along the rocky path towards multi-party rule. But there remained one country in Europe still sticking firmly to the communist system, in its most extreme form. Albania, which withdrew from the Warsaw Pact in 1968 in protest over its invasion of Czechoslovakia, was under communist rule for longer than any other country outside the Soviet Union. In November 1944 communist partisans liberated the country from German occupation and set up a provisional government headed by Enver Hoxha, who ruled unchallenged for the next 41 years.

Hoxha died in 1985 and was replaced by Ramiz Alia, who showed no early signs of loosening the country's ideological straitjacket. Mr Bejo from the Albanian embassy was still making his regular visits to the Vienna bureau, typically dropping a copy of a long Alia speech on the desk with a comment like "bottom of page 27". Presumably after reading our reports on Albania for years, he had a good eye for spotting a story. As events in neighbouring countries threatened to change the political landscape Alia started to gradually introduce some limited reforms. One of them, in May 1990, lifted the country's 23-year ban on practising religion. The same month U.N. Secretary General Javier Perez de Cuellar made a visit to Albania which provided the first opportunity for some time to get another first-hand look at the country.

By this time I had a new deputy, Paul Holmes, who joined a small group of foreign journalists accompanying de Cuellar during his visit. Each member of the group was assigned a local reporter as a "guide" to keep an eye on them. When the guide reported there was no crime in Albania Paul asked why there were bars on ground-floor apartments. "It's a tradition here," came the response. After hearing of isolated protests in some parts of the country Paul, an Italian speaker, headed off with a

British colleague who had driven in by car and managed to stand up some of the reports. After a couple of days they were spotted by police having committed three infringements: being in a restricted area without a permit, having a private car, which was illegal, and having a beard (Paul), also illegal. I would also have fared badly as left-handedness was also banned, at least in the 1970s. Before leaving the country Paul was able to meet a number of contacts, two of them local journalists who proved to be invaluable when events came to a head at the end of the year.

Two months later Albania was in the news again when thousands of Albanians stormed foreign embassies seeking asylum and emigration to the West. Diplomats contacted by phone from Vienna reported that over 3,000 burst into the West German embassy after one group crashed a truck through the wall surrounding it. Hundreds of others occupied the Greek, Italian, Czech and French missions. Four jumped into the Cuban mission but were thrown back by embassy staff. After the Albanian government rejected demands for food and tents for the refugees, saying "either take them out or given them up", they were evacuated to Italy and other countries by boat and plane. As the majority were taken by bus to the coast villagers lined the streets to wave goodbye, and some refugees were reported to have thrown their watches and money from the windows.

In December Paul was working late in Vienna when he got a call from one of the journalists he had met In May who told him the Communist Party central committee had agreed to legalise the formation of political parties, signalling the end of the one-party system that had ruled for over four decades. Reluctant to send such a key story based on one source he called Tirana and eventually got through to the other journalist, Ilir Ikonomi, fluent in English and Chinese who worked for Radio Tirana and was about to announce the decision in his next news bulletin. Paul sent out the story which beat Radio Tirana, the state news agency ATA and the rest of the world.

"The plenum is of the opinion that the creation of independent political organisations is to the good of the further democratisation of the life of the country and pluralism", the statement said.

The historic announcement followed a major protest by students at Tirana university that began over living conditions but quickly turned political as thousands chanted "reforms" and "no dictatorship". The students founded the Democratic Party, the country's first non-communist political organisation which went on to contest free elections the following year.

Ilir Ikonomi went on to become Reuters first resident correspondent in Albania.

Albania hit the headlines again in January 1997 when a popular revolt which turned into a virtual civil war broke out after a series of pyramid investment schemes, some supported by the government, collapsed. Many were so-called ponzi schemes operated by criminal gangs in which early investors were paid with money from later ones, without any other investments being made. With interest rates offered at between 10% and 25%, some two-thirds of the population put a total of $1.5 billion into the schemes before they folded, with an average loss of $400 per person in a country with an average monthly wage of $80.

I flew into Tirana in March, having moved back to London in 1991, to join two other Reuter correspondents flown in earlier from London as the revolt broke out in the south of the country over investment losses and allegations of corruption in President Sali Berisha's government. Military barracks were stormed and arsenals ransacked as army conscripts melted away, leaving every civilian armed with at least one automatic weapon and plenty of ammunition. As the revolt spread north and eventually reached the capital, foreign nationals including some journalists were evacuated by air, sea and even overland, braving roads controlled by armed bandits and other criminals free to roam. Our small group of remaining journalists was holed up in the Austrian-run Rogner Hotel in Tirana waiting to see how long it would take people outside to work out that foreign correspondents usually carried plenty of cash and expensive camera equipment. The barman in the hotel had an AK-47 which he occasionally brandished. The British Ambassador was staying at the hotel accompanied by a soldier of the SAS special forces carrying a large holdall, but they were soon evacuated. As tension mounted a tank clattered along the street next to the hotel, prompting one excitable British journalist to race to a phone and shout "hold the front page, we have a coup".

The Reuters office in Tirana had managed to set up a very effective communications system bypassing the expensive hotel switchboard by bringing a telephone line directly from the office a few blocks away through a window and connecting it to one of our room telephones. It was popular with relatives and friends of the office staff who lined up to call family members abroad for free.

The next morning the office manager arrived to advise that a minister in the newly created all-party National Salvation government was staying at the hotel, as a member of the royalist party funded by Albania's exiled Crown Prince Leka and had some important news. Invited for breakfast he told me the government had decided to offer volunteers $100 dollars and issue them a weapon if they would go out into the streets and stop the fighting. The idea was ridiculed by some of the journalists, but it appeared to bring at least a temporary lessening of the street violence and we were able to go out to interview people. While the firing in the streets had subsided there was still danger from falling bullets as Albanians continued to fire off their newly-acquired weapons into the air, either in anger or celebration, it was hard to tell. The nights were the worst, known as "lead nights". As several people had been killed by falling bullets those interviewed in the streets usually insisted on holding the conversation under cover.

One thing that emerged from these conversations was that while public anger was fired mainly by losses from the ponzi schemes and government corruption, a key reason for the disappearance of the army from the streets was that they had not been paid for months.

The crisis stumbled on for several weeks until the middle of April when a 7,000-strong international military force led by Italy, backed by a U.N. Security council resolution, was sent in to restore order, particularly to apprehend criminals and collect looted weapons. By then I was back in London.

# 29. FREE ELECTIONS

Within months of throwing off the shackles of communism East Bloc countries rushed to put multi-party politics into practice in the first free elections for over four decades, with a large section of their populations able to remember how it was the last time. In some countries like Hungary and Poland, the poll was a straight protest against the communists, and they fared badly even though they helped bring in the reforms that led to their eclipse. In others voters chose parties of former communists, renamed, as there had been no proper opposition under their harsh rule and no time for alternative parties to form.

First up was Poland, which had jumped the gun by holding partly-free elections in June 1989. Since the Communist Party had given up its monopoly of power in April the opposition Solidarity movement won all 161 contested seats in the 460-seat Sejm lower house, the rest being allocated to the communists. Solidarity also won all but one of the seats in the fully contested Senate. With this popular mandate Tadeusz Mazowiecki was chosen prime minister in August, the first non-communist government leader in the East Bloc. Poland's first fully democratic elections were held in June 1991. With Solidarity's influence on the wane the political scene was fragmented as 29 parties gained seats in the Sejm, none of them communist, and 22 in the senate, giving no party a decisive majority.

Elections in East Germany were held on 18 March 1990, just months after the collapse of the communist regime, following a hastily organised campaign by newly formed political parties. For the country's 16 million population these were their first contested elections since 1933, the dying days of the Weimar Republic that followed World War One. In that poll, held amid a campaign of violence and intimidation against opposition groups, the Nazis emerged the strongest party with 288 of the 647 seats, but lacked an overall majority as the Social Democrats gained 120 and the

Communists 81. A few months later the Nazis got the government to ban political parties and took full control.

The 1990 elections were dominated by one overriding topic, the reunification of Germany and how quickly it should happen. The election was won convincingly with 48% of the vote by the conservative Alliance for Germany, dominated by an East German version of West Germany's ruling Christian Democratic Party, which was pushing for quick reunification. The Social Democratic Party, backed by West Germany's main opposition, which favoured a more gradual process of reunification, gained 21.9%. The former communist Socialist Unity Party, contesting the first free elections in its history, did surprisingly well in coming third with 16.4%.

The Alliance won despite the chairman of one of its three coalition members, Democratic Awakening, being unmasked as a former Stasi informer a few days before the election. The small right-wing party was formed shortly after the collapse of communism by active church groups and faded into obscurity shortly after the election, in which it gained less than 1% of the vote. Its main claim to fame was that its spokesperson was Angela Merkel, a clergyman's daughter who was born in West Germany but moved to the East as an infant. She went on to become united Germany's third longest-serving chancellor, and a dominant political figure of the 28-nation European Community.

I was asked to travel to Leipzig, the crucible of the East German revolution, to report the election and how the situation was developing in the brief transition from communism to democracy. Attending a polling station in the historic centre of Leipzig, I met an elderly woman who had taken part in the last contested election in 1933. She remembered the event quite clearly, including the weather at the time, but was unable to recall exactly how she had voted. When I dictated my story through to our Berlin bureau I learned that similar memory lapses had been reported from other parts of East Germany.

The elections coincided with the twice-yearly Leipzig International Trade Fair, traditionally the largest event in the region for bringing East and West businesses together. With the prospect of the East German economy bursting open Western firms rushed to Leipzig to discuss buyouts or joint ventures. There was particular interest in Karl Zeiss Jena, one of the world's oldest optical companies founded in 1846, and one of the few East German companies able to compete in a global market. Meanwhile West German car giants Volkswagen and Opel, a subsidiary of US company General Motors, circled around the snappily-named VEB IFA-Kombinat PersonenKraftwagen, makers of the Wartburg and Trabant. There was little chance however that those two models would survive. In a desperate attempt to clear existing Trabant stock the car, loved and hated in equal measure, had been re-invented as a mini-jeep "Trabant Tramp" with the roof cut off, a bikini-clad model lounging in the back and the current hit song "All Around the World" blaring from loud-speakers.

While I was in Leipzig I took the opportunity to visit East Germany's best-known political cabaret the Pfeffermühle (Peppermill) to see how they were coping with the new realities.

"We try to be topical, but we simply can't keep up with what is happening in this country," complained Dieter Richter in an interview, adding that during last November's mass demonstrations in the city they had to update a sketch three times in the same week as police changed from being oppressors to protectors. It was a far cry from the dark days of communist rule when the pace of change was so glacial that the cabaret used to sometimes use the same material unchanged for two or three years. "The only reason we changed it was when we got bored with it," he said.

Richter said their cabaret was always allowed a little more freedom than its rivals in Berlin, partly because the annual Leipzig Fair drew Western audiences.

"They wanted to give the impression there was cultural freedom in East Germany. But every sketch was vetted beforehand by a four-man committee of party officials."

Barred from attacking the Communist Party, he said: "We were allowed to attack lazy workers and poor morale because the party felt they weren't responsible for that. But of course they were."

As for the future, Richter said some of his colleagues felt they no longer had a role. "In the communist years we could offer people a little encouragement when they could come out of our show saying 'at least we can laugh about our problems'."

But he predicted there would be plenty of new problems to be addressed – social disruption caused by the hasty introduction of a market economy, the rise of right-wing extremism, and the process of reunification.

The next post-revolution country to go to the polls was Hungary, where the transition from communism to democracy, among the smoothest in the East Bloc, was described as "system change" rather than revolution. The election on 25 March 1990 was the first free poll in the country since 1945, when it was under Soviet occupation. That election was won overwhelmingly by the independent Smallholders' Party but the communists, who came third, gradually eased themselves to power.

The 1990 election saw the conservative-nationalist Hungarian Democratic Forum emerge as the largest party with 24.7% of the vote, ahead of the more liberal and internationalist Alliance of Free Democrats. The Hungarian Socialist Party, the former communists, suffered a crushing defeat, winning only 10% of the vote.

One of the more interesting results was that of Fidesz, established in 1988 as an underground student movement opposed to communist rule, co-founded by a young law graduate called Viktor Orban. The party, which had an upper age limit of 35 for membership in the early days, produced some of the most arresting campaign posters. One showed the widely mocked picture of Honecker and Brezhnev kissing on the lips alongside another with an attractive couple embracing in a park above the comment "Which do you prefer?"

Fidesz finished only sixth in the election, with less than 5% of the vote and only one seat. However just eight years later the party led by Orban, which he had moved dramatically to the right over the years, won its first election. In 2010 the party came back to power after a landslide victory that set Orban on a right-wing, homophobic and anti-immigration path putting it at odds with most EU leaders.

Next in line with elections was Romania, on May 20, which saw the National Salvation Front formed by senior members of the old Communist Party that took power immediately after its collapse romp home with 85% of the vote. With little time to campaign and no history of anti-communist opposition newly formed parties struggled to compete, particularly as they were largely denied access to mass media, particularly television. The US government which monitored the poll expressed concern about organised violence and campaign irregularities, but pronounced the election, the first proper one since 1937, free and fair.

A month later it was Czechoslovakia's turn, and unsurprisingly Czech and Slovak branches of a movement led by President Havel gained majorities in both houses of parliament with 46% of the vote on a 96.2% turnout. The communists won 13.6%, seen by some as a surprisingly good result in view of the party's recent standing in the country. However commentators pointed out that the communists had polled 35% in 1946, the last fully free elections, making them the strongest party in parliament.

A year later Albania, which had come from extreme Stalinist rule to the foothills of democracy in just two years, held its first multi-party elections since 1923, barely three months after the government allowed the creation of opposition parties.

Meriel drove in from the Montenegran capital Titograd and was joined three days later by Paul Holmes and a photographer bearing a satellite phone, very much new technology at the time, in the knowledge that Albanian communications were rudimentary and likely to be swamped by visiting foreign media. The phone was a success, but at huge cost in transmission fees. The satellite phones available at the time were carried in two huge suitcases, one just for the dish which unfolded when removed. In the era before digital cameras our photographer had to develop their pictures in the hotel bathroom, then send them by sat-phone using a drum transmitter that took 15 minutes to send each black and white picture, and 45 minutes for a colour photo. Any break in the line meant having to repeat the process.

Not long after their arrival a key part of the phone, the removable handset, was stolen from their hotel room, witnessed by our team who gave chase. They spent an hour at a police station talking about football, and the handset was returned later that afternoon.

The next time I used a sat-phone, during the Kosovo war in 1999, the latest version was the size of a normal lap-top computer, with the screen serving as the dish. Five years later, on an assignment to Baghdad, I could almost get the latest version into my pocket.

A few days before the elections on Easter Sunday, March 31, Albanian priest Simon Jubani was preparing to celebrate the resurrection not only of Christ but of democratic and religious hope in his country. Jubani's Easter mass in the northern city of Shkoder was to be the first time in 23 years that Albania's estimated 250,000 Roman Catholics could openly celebrate the religious ceremony without the terror of persecution and prison.

"On Sunday I will tell my followers that just as Christ vanquished his opponents and was resurrected, so we will triumph over the communist dictatorship and live in happiness," Jubani said in the small side-street bungalow which was his home after 26 years in communist jails.

"Christ was dead and buried but he rose again," Jubani said. "Now we are burying communism -- but nobody is crying at the funeral."

The elections came a month after anti-communists tore down a statue of Hoxha in Tirana. A total of 11 political parties and organisations

203

were formed at a gallop to run against the Party of Labour, the communist party that ruled unchallenged for nearly 50 years. But with no time to organise and campaign, particularly in the remote villages where most of Albania's 3.3 million population live, they faced an uphill struggle. The PLA won 162 of the 250 seats in parliament, with the urban-based Democratic Party, formed only four months previously, second with 65 seats. The poll also saw a humiliating defeat for President Alia and Foreign Minister Muhamet Kapllani, both losing urban seats.

The Democrats blamed their result on the lack of time and facilities available to the party to penetrate the countryside. They also faced PLA claims that if they won power they would privatise land holdings and restore them to pre-war landlords.

"We didn't lose on elections day, we lost in the campaign," Democratic Party President Gramoz Pashko said.

International observers who watched voting said there were a number of irregularities and the communists had enjoyed better facilities, but overall the elections had run smoothly.

"A positive thing has happened here in that pluralism has been legitimised," said Thomas Melia from the U.S. National Democratic Institute. "But to say that democracy has been achieved with this election would be a naive overstatement."

News of the PLA victory sparked protests in some parts of the country, with four people killed in clashes with police in the town of Shkodra.

The last Warsaw Pact member to go to the polls was Bulgaria, in October 1991, its first free elections since 1931. With opposition groups allowed for the first time under a new constitution approved just three months earlier a total of 39 parties rushed to fill the void. The poll produced a narrow victory for the Union of Democratic Forces, a grouping of organisations opposed to communist rule, with 34.4% on a turnout of 84%. The Socialist Party, the former communists, ran them close with 33.1

per cent of the vote, not surprising in a country long regarded as the Soviet Union's closest ally with no background of organised opposition.

They did even better in the next election in 1994 when the Democratic Left, with the Socialist Party at its core, won a narrow overall majority with 125 of the 240 seats, and Socialist Party leader Zhan Videnov became Prime Minister.

# 30. GOODBYE IVAN

As the newly enfranchised citizens of the East Bloc were casting their first proper ballots in four decades, there was a new sound across the region, of frantic packing as half a million Soviet troops deployed to underline Moscow's control were starting to pull out. The Soviet Union had around 500,000 troops stationed in its former communist allies, some 370,000 of them in East Germany. Maverick Romania refused to allow them, Albania quit the Warsaw Pact and no troops were needed in Bulgaria, Moscow's most trusted ally.

As the troops loaded their tanks and bags onto rail cars under pressure from newly democratic nations, they were finding it was easier to send in troops than to get them out again. The once all-powerful Soviet army was faced with some unfamiliar adversaries – lawsuits, claims for damages and angry local environmental groups. And the boys faced an uncertain future back home as the government acknowledged their country faced a chronic housing shortage.

In contrast to some other military pull-outs elsewhere in the world, where well-paid foreign troops helped the local economy and were often made welcome, the departure of the Soviet troops could not come fast enough for their former allies. Particularly as there were reports of departing troops selling weapons to eke out meagre pocket-money. Deliberately shielded from the local population, and paid a pittance, Soviet soldiers were tolerated in sullen silence by ordinary people who saw them as oppressors. Fraternising with the opposite sex appeared to have been almost non-existent. Whereas US troops often succeeded in turning a girl's head with a Hershey Bar or a pair of nylon stockings, a packet of Russian cigarettes never had the same appeal.

In Hungary, the Soviet Army was involved in an acrimonious row with the new government over Soviet claims for compensation for what it was leaving behind – not a cent, in Budapest's view. As the first of the 65,000 troops of the force sent in to crush the 1956 anti-communist uprising began pulling out early in 1990 the Soviet side lodged a claim for 40 billion Hungarian forints (around £300 million at the time) for its investment in 6,000 buildings and locations. Hungary replied it would pay compensation only for investments made with its consent – some 2,000 sites came under this category – but added that after deducting the cost of medical treatment and rent, the figure payable was zero. A Hungarian defence spokesman said the departure of the Soviet forces would hit some local people working at the bases, but this would be more than compensated by the return of an estimated 100 billion forints (£750 million) worth of assets, including 15,000 desperately needed apartments. After the Soviets threatened to leave behind guards at evacuated camps if Budapest refused to pay, they were accused by a parliamentary committee of methods "verging on blackmail".

In Czechoslovakia, like Hungary, the new government wasted no time in giving marching orders to the 75,000 troops sent in to snuff out the 1968 Prague Spring. At the garrison town of Frenstat, south-east of Prague, the first of the 1,250 Soviet tanks were loaded onto a special train along with personal belongings, including Czechoslovak-made bicycles and household appliances. A brass band played the socialist anthem the "Internationale", but few of the local population turned out to watch.

"It's better for them and better for us that they are going," a young factory worker commented.

A local government official said that for Czechoslovaks the Soviet troops represented "empty shelves in shops, polluted water, occasional fights in bars and a reminder that we are not free."

The new Czechoslovak government had threatened to present a huge bill to Moscow for polluting water reserves and other environmental damage it claimed the occupying army had caused. Some estimates put the damage claims as high as 2 billion crowns (£50 million). As the first troops were leaving the Interior Ministry confirmed local press reports about sales of weapons by soviet soldiers, saying an organised network was operating in Czechoslovakia. In one case a schoolboy gave his digital watch in exchange for a live hand grenade. Other reports mentioned weapons being dumped by departing troops into rubbish bins, gardens and parks. One man complained of finding a machine-gun ammunition belt filled with live cartridges in his front garden.

In Poland a planned pull-out of 50,000 was delayed while Warsaw sought a final guarantee of its post-war border with East Germany, fixed under the 1945 Potsdam Agreement which ceded large sections of German territory to Poland. For Poles the presence of the troops, brought in when the Red Army liberated Poland from the Nazis in World War Two, was a constant reminder that communism was imposed on the country and maintained by force. When the pull-out finally began in April 1991 it was greeted with jubilation by the government and press.

"Law, freedom and democracy have won", said President Walesa. "Gone", one newspaper headline proclaimed. "Soviets go home!" said another.

Soviet soldiers were publicly accused by officials of everything from theft, unsanitary personal habits, wrecking their apartments to illegal hunting. In the southwestern city of Legnica, site of the biggest concentration of Soviet troops in Poland, residents had complained about water contamination by army latrines and leakages from an underground fuel tank – although this had its benefits by supplying the neighbourhood with free petrol. Elsewhere in Poland local pressure forced the Soviets to remove supersonic planes from an airfield close to a town and promise to stop night flights near inhabited areas.

By far the biggest pull-out was from East Germany, where the huge task of bringing out 370,000 men and their equipment meant the evacuation, begun in 1990, took nearly four years even at a rate equivalent to five train loads a day. The West German government had avoided pressing for a speedy withdrawal for fear of causing Moscow to dig in its heels against German unification, which eventually took place in October 1990. To ensure the troops' departure the Bonn government also agreed to pay over £3 billion to the Russians to build homes in the Soviet Union, meet officers' salaries and help teach new skills to the departing soldiers. As the troops left they took everything with them, doors, windows, pipes, bathroom equipment, electricity cables, even gutters from the roof.

Apart from the troops, the Soviets moved out 4,200 tanks, 8,200 armoured personnel carriers, 3,600 artillery pieces and 1.350 planes and helicopters, after Soviet officers pledged not to leave a single cartridge behind. Some of the tanks had been used to crush the 1953 workers' revolt.

In a testimony to the professionalism of the Soviet forces, over 700,000 tonnes of munitions and high explosives were taken out without a single mishap.

At one of the largest Soviet bases at Wünsdorf, known locally as "Little Moscow", some 75,000 Soviet men, women and children lived on a site covering 75 square kilometres located 40 kilometres from Berlin. The base had been used 50 years previously by the Nazi High Command to plan, of all things, the invasion of the Soviet Union.

While all of this was going on, trouble was brewing in the Balkans, a notoriously volatile part of Europe, and we had to direct our attentions south to Yugoslavia.

# 31. YUGOSLAVIA

Yugoslavia, "South Slav land" in the Serbo-Croat language, was a federation formed from the collapse of the Austro-Hungarian empire after World War One. It was made up of Serbia, Croatia, Bosnia-Herzegovina, Macedonia, Slovenia, Montenegro, and two autonomous provinces within Serbia, Kosovo, with a huge ethnic Albanian majority, and Vojvodina, with a large Hungarian minority. It constituted the first union of South Slavic peoples as a sovereign state after centuries in which the region was divided between the Ottoman Empire and Austro-Hungary.

After the monarchy was abolished in 1945 it came under communist control a year later headed by Josip Broz Tito, who ruled the country as a dictator until his death in 1980. After he split with the Soviet Union in 1948 he introduced a "middle way" economic system mixing the socialist and market-driven models, encouraged foreign investment and allowed people to work abroad for much-needed hard currency, and the country enjoyed some prosperity. He also made a point of treating the various nationalities in the federation on equal terms.

After his death in 1980 the country was run by a rotating presidency of member states which lasted for several years. However economic problems, increasing calls from Kosovo to be treated as a full republic and rising nationalism among member states as they watched East Bloc neighbours challenge Moscow's supremacy put increasing pressure on the system.

Things came to a head in 1987 when an ambitious ultra-nationalist Serbian communist official called Slobodan Milošević seized his opportunity to overturn the political consensus laid down by Tito by turning one of Yugoslavia's national groups against another. Milošević, whose ultimate dream was to create a Greater Serbia out of ethnic Serb minorities in the other republics, was addressing a crowd of nationalist Serbs in Kosovo protesting against the 1974 constitution giving the province a leading role in the federation. As truncheon-wielding police started to attack the demonstrators Milošević told the adoring crowd "Nobody should dare to beat you again." Learning of his words Yugoslav President Ivan Stambolić, his former mentor, declared it was "the end of Yugoslavia", shortly before being deposed and being replaced a year later by his former protégé. Milošević's declaration sent a tremor through the other republics and served to accelerate moves already under way to break from the federation.

First to go was Slovenia, closely followed by Croatia, after the two countries coordinated some of their moves in the run-up to their breakaway. A mountainous country of two million people bordering Austria and Italy, as well as Hungary, Slovenia was always different from the rest of Yugoslavia, looking and trading West rather than East and speaking its own language. Crucially, it did not have a significant ethnic Serb minority as in Croatia and Bosnia which led to bloody conflicts in pursuit of Greater Serbia. The beginnings of opposition in Slovenia emerged in the early 1980s with the foundation of the alternative journal Nova Revija, a move widely regarded as the opening shot in the gradual process of the country's democratisation process. In 1987 Slovenian workers went on strike calling for independent trade unions and political pluralism, and a few months later the Slovenian Peasants' Party was founded, the first openly non-communist political organisation in Yugoslavia.

All of this was being covered by our fully staffed Belgrade bureau, leaving Vienna to get on with the fast-moving events elsewhere in East Europe. But we became directly involved in 1991 when Slovenia declared its independence on June 25 and the Yugoslav Peoples' Army (JNA) mobilized its forces to quell the revolt, and what become known as the 10-Day War broke out. We needed to send reinforcements to the Slovenian capital Ljubljana and Belgrade, to join others flown in from elsewhere organised from London.

It was a classic David and Goliath contest, with the heavily armed and armoured JNA pitted against what amounted to a Home Guard, a Territorial Defence Unit that existed in each Yugoslav republic as part of an overall strategy in case of attack from outside. Belgrade, responding to early moves towards independence across the federation, had ordered all territorial defence units to be disarmed and their commands brought under central control. Slovenia ignored the order, transferring its territorial defence forces into new units under local command. The strategy was to avoid direct confrontation with the JNA and concentrate on guerrilla warfare, picking off the heavy armour in the mountains. To help them accomplish this the Slovenian High Command went shopping for Western-made light missile systems to be used against tanks and helicopters.

With the JNA clearly wrong-footed by the strength of Slovenian resistance the briefest of wars formally ended on July 7 with the Brioni Accord. Under this Slovenia and Croatia agreed to delay their independence by three months, and the JNA would withdraw all its forces by October. Ljubljana insisted that the JNA leave behind much of its heavy armour, which was later deployed locally or sold to other republics.

Despite some fierce fighting casualties were relatively light, with 44 JNA dead and 146 wounded, as well as 31 tanks, 22 armoured personnel carriers and six helicopters lost, and 19 dead and 182 wounded on the Slovenian side. While they were clearly outgunned the Slovenes had a moral advantage as they were fighting for self-determination against an army made up of conscripts from all the republics, including Slovenia, most of which were already on the path of independence. There were many cases of desertion from the JNA, particularly by Slovenes, who were forced to fight against their own people. We reported cases of members of the same family fighting on opposite sides of the war. The pilot of the first JNA helicopter shot down and killed in the opening stage of the war was Slovene.

Croatia was the next country to break away, but its uncoupling from Yugoslavia was a much messier and bloodier affair, largely due to the presence of a significant Serb minority of 580,000, or 12% of the population. Encouraged by Serbia the minority had declared a separate Serb state in Croatia as an autonomous part of Yugoslavia. Tension built during 1990 and broke out into fighting the following year between Croatian security forces, Serb militias and the Yugoslav army. The savagery of some of the fighting was partly fuelled by historic grievances, many stemming from World War Two when most of Croatia was a Nazi puppet state led by the notorious Ustashe. This was a fascist ultranationalist organisation that killed thousands of Serbs who formed the bulk of Tito's communist partisans fighting and ultimately defeating the Axis powers, with the help of the Soviet army. One of the darkest episodes of the war was the murder of an estimated 100,000, mainly Serbs, at the Jasenovac concentration camp run by the Ustashe. The episode, along with many like it, was a forbidden topic under Tito's policy of trying to maintain harmony among the various republics, simmering under the surface until it finally burst out.

One of the bloodiest battles of the Croatian-Serb war was the siege of Vukovar, a Baroque and once-prosperous Croatian town on the river Danube with Serbs making up around one third of its population. It was virtually destroyed during an 87-day siege by the Yugoslav army and Serb paramilitaries. An estimated 12,000 artillery shells and rockets a day were hurled at the town, which was defended by 1,500 diehard Croatian militiamen and civilian volunteers. Croatian casualties were put at over 900 dead and nearly 800 wounded. It was the fiercest and most protracted battle seen in Europe since 1945. It ended with one of the worst atrocities of the war when some 300 patients were removed from Vukovar hospital by the JNA under international protection but were then handed over to Serb paramilitary militias, massacred and buried in mass graves. At least 20,000 inhabitants were forced to leave the town in what later became known as ethnic cleansing, a word associated with the

Yugoslav War, the process of removing one or more ethnic groups by force to establish a homogeneous population. The process was carried out during the wars in Croatia and later Bosnia and Kosovo mainly by Serb paramilitary groups, the most notorious of which was the Serb Volunteer Guard, also known as the White Tigers. They were set up in 1990 by ultra-nationalist fans of the all-Serb Red Star Belgrade football team. It was led throughout the Yugoslav wars by Željko Ražnatović, known as "Arkan", one of the leading organised crime bosses in the Balkans who had been on Interpol's most wanted list since the 1970s and 80s for robberies and murders committed in several European countries.

When I visited Vukovar on the first anniversary of the end of the siege some 70 per cent of the houses were destroyed, leaving a ghostly nightmare of shattered buildings and rubble-strewn streets recalling pictures of Dresden after the Allied raid in 1945. But people were living among the ruins, after one third of the original population of 50,000 had returned to the wreckage.

"You have to be mad to live here," said Lepa Jovic, 33, in her leaking one-story house. "But where would be go?" Without electricity, running water or heating, the family slept fully dressed, in coats.

The Jovics depended for their existence on Red Cross food parcels, a barter system involving goods and services -- and a friend, a giant Serbian militiaman who wore battle fatigues with a red ribbon dangling from one epaulette. "We used them for identification during the battle," he explained as he swigged home-made spirit in Jovic's smoke-filled kitchen. "Since both sides were wearing the same uniform, Yugoslav army issue, we had to know who we were shooting.".

Town council leader Milorad Visic, a doctor, said work to clear and rebuild the town was hampered by lack of funds or equipment. What they had done was clear all the houses of explosives, with the help of army engineers, and mark every building with a colour code. Blue was for historic buildings to be rebuilt exactly as they were, red for total demolition, yellow for repairable, green meant habitable after some repairs.

"Unfortunately many of the buildings have since deteriorated further, so many of the greens and yellows should now be marked red," Visic said.

Vukovar was just one of many atrocities committed during the Croatian war of independence, which ended in 1995 after Croatian forces overran the Serb enclaves and forced some 300,000 inhabitants to move to Serbia. An estimated 20,000 people, combatants and civilians, were killed during the fighting.

While the siege was going on Croatia declared its independence from Yugoslavia. Despite serious reservations about the move in Western Europe, because of the ongoing problem with the Serb minority, West Germany recognised Croatian independence two months later. Other European countries, which reluctantly joined Germany, were also concerned that Bosnia-Herzegovina, a republic with an ethnic mix divided between Bosnian Muslims, known as Bosniaks, Serbs and Croats would quickly follow suit, opening the possibility of a new nightmare of conflict.

Their fears were fully justified when the republic declared its independence in March, 1992, the Serb minority that represented 30% of the population and controlled 46 % of territory declared a separate Srpska Republic and a third Yugoslav war broke out.

At this point Reuters decided that in view of the changing role of the Vienna bureau, with former East Bloc states going their own way as independent countries, it was time to pull me back to London to the World Desk. Within a few months I was on the road again heading for Belgrade, where a sort of regional desk had been created to handle reports from the various parts of former Yugoslavia. It was a journey I would make every couple of months for the next eight years as the breakup of Yugoslavia went through its phases.

By the time I first arrived at the beginning of 1992 the Socialist Federation of Yugoslavia had been reduced to the Yugoslav Federation consisting only of Serbia and Montenegro, since Macedonia had since joined the other republics in opting for independence. Milošević 's dream of forging a Greater Serbia had left the country almost landlocked with his arch-rival Croatia controlling 5,800 kilometres of Adriatic coastline and 1,200 islands, enabling it to become one of Europe's top holiday destinations within a few years. Serbia was left with access to the sea via Montenegro's small coastline until that disappeared when the tiny country of 600,000 inhabitants declared its independence in 2006.

# 32. BOSNIA

The three-year Bosnian War broke out as local Serbs backed by the remnants of the Yugoslav army and hard-line paramilitary groups headed by Arkan's Volunteer Guard went on the rampage to claim any territory with a significant Serb population. But within that war another bloody conflict erupted as Bosnian Croats in Herzegovina, who began it fighting alongside the Bosniaks against the Serbs, turned on their former allies and declared a separate state of Herzeg-Bosna. At the height of the Bosnian conflict up to seven military forces were engaged in fighting, often each other – Bosniak, Srpska Republic and Herzeg-Bosna regulars, backed by Yugoslav and Croatian army units, Serb paramilitaries and, in one area, forces of a self-declared Autonomous Province of Western Bosnia led by a Bosnian businessman opposed to the new government. Trying to make sense of all this was a daily nightmare for any journalists covering the war.

But for outsiders the main conflict, and the one that seized the world's attention, was over the capital Sarajevo. A beacon of multiculturism as naked nationalism swept through Yugoslavia, it was sometimes called the Jerusalem of Europe, one of very few major cities with a mosque, Roman Catholic church, Orthodox church and synagogue in the same neighbourhood. Its population, including outlying suburbs, was 520,00, of whom 49% were Bosniaks, 30% Serb, 10% Yugoslav, indicating mixed ethnicity, and 6% Croat.

At the beginning of April Bosnian Serb forces backed by the Yugoslav army attacked Sarajevo as the Srpska Republic sought to expand its territory by taking over some majority Bosniak areas. Facing an army of 70,000 troops, they were initially beaten back, and decided on a different strategy. Throwing a blockade around the city they proceeded to bombard it from 200 reinforced positions and bunkers in the surrounding hills, opening a siege that lasted 1,425 days, the longest of a capital city in the modern history of warfare. It was three times longer than the battle of

Stalingrad, and a year longer than that of Leningrad. Nearly 14,000 people died during the siege, including 5,400 civilians.

With the city under constant fire from artillery and sniper fire, the risks for journalists covering the conflict were considerable. Housed in the Holiday Inn hotel within range of Serb positions, foreign journalists dodged bullets in nearby "Sniper Alley" when venturing out in armoured vehicles wearing helmets and bullet-proof vests. Reuters rotated in a number of correspondents, but one was there for the duration, an American called Kurt Schork with an interesting background. After winning a Rhodes Scholarship to Oxford University, at the same time as former U.S. President Bill Clinton, he worked as a property developer and a senior official in the New York underground before deciding, aged 43, to become a foreign correspondent. After operating as a freelance from Kurdistan in the Gulf War he was picked up by Reuters and sent first to Afghanistan and then to Sarajevo. He operated on an unusual contract which amounted to full-time freelance, an arrangement that suited both him and Reuters editorial management.

We handled reports coming out of Sarajevo from Belgrade, including from Schork, who soon showed himself to be a fearless war reporter with an eye for colourful and dramatic features. One famous story that will always be associated with him became known as Sarajevo's Romeo and Juliet, about a young couple, a Serb and a Bosniak who were killed by a sniper while trying to flee the city. Their bodies lay together on a bridge in no-man's-land for eight days before they could be recovered.

His story, which went around the world, began:

*SARAJEVO, May 23, 1993 - Two lovers lie dead on the banks of Sarajevo's Miljacka river, locked in a final embrace. For four days they have sprawled near Vrbana bridge in a wasteland of shell-blasted rubble, downed tree branches and dangling power lines. So dangerous is the area no one has dared recover their bodies.*

*Bosko Brckic and Admira Ismic, both 25, were shot dead trying to escape the besieged Bosnian capital for Serbia. Sweethearts since high school, he was a Serb and she was a Moslem.*

*"They were shot at the same time, but he fell instantly and she was still alive," recounts Dino, a soldier who saw the couple trying to cross from government territory to rebel Serb positions.*

*"She crawled over and hugged him and they died like that, in each other's arms."*

Schork went on to report on a number of conflicts in the world, including Kosovo, where I met up with him again, and Chechnya, and was widely regarded as one of the best in the business. His luck ran out in 2000 covering the civil war in Sierra Leone when his car ran into a group of young fighters, probably high on glue, and he was killed, along with a Spanish cameraman. Following his wishes he was cremated and half his ashes were buried next to the star-crossed lovers in Sarajevo, where a street was named after him. The other half went next to his mother's grave in Washington D.C.

His family and friends with backing from Reuters decided to create a fund in his name offering annual financial awards to freelance journalists, local correspondents and "fixers" who provide the eyes and ears for foreign correspondents, particularly those covering hostile environments, often with little recognition and at great risk to themselves.

Meanwhile there was no let-up in the ferocity of the war as Bosnian Serbs directed their attacks against U.N. peacekeepers. NATO responded in July 1995 with air strikes against Serb installations but were forced to halt them temporarily after Serbs seized dozens of peacekeepers and used them as human shields, chaining them to gates and bridges near ammunition dumps and other strategic targets.

Serbian television showed one captive peacekeeper speaking haltingly of the air strikes as "crimes against humanity", but his statement appeared to have been coerced. The other captured peacekeepers stood impassively.

A transcript of a radio transmission from one of the captive monitors to U.N. headquarters in Sarajevo was released to Western news agencies.

"Be advised that it is extremely tense here right now," the unidentified monitor reported. "There is a crowd of civilians. One person loaded his pistol and was trying to kill us. I've been beaten already. We are now handcuffed inside the car. We've been advised that the next bomb that falls, we'll be killed."

A few minutes later, the transmission was interrupted by a Bosnian Serb soldier, speaking in English, who said "Three U.N. observers are now at the site of the warehouse. Any more bombing, they'll be the first to go. Understood?"

Watching all this in the Belgrade office, the tension was palpable. Although the large majority of the local staff were not ultra-nationalist Serbs, or did not show it, a couple of the young camera staff clearly were, and cheered when the TV showed the chained peacekeepers. This did not help the atmosphere in the office where one of the main translators was half Bosniak and half Croat. She regularly had problems calling our local staff in Pale, the headquarters of the Bosnian Serb civil and military administration just outside Sarajevo, because of her Muslim first name, Amra. A female member of our TV unit was a Croat but was protected as the partner of the head of the unit, a giant Serb. Tragically she was killed in a freak accident when a man accidentally let off a pistol in a crowded Belgrade bar, the bullet hit a wall and broke up and a minute splinter entered her heart, killing her instantly.

While the standoff with the captured peacekeepers was going on, a much worse atrocity took place as Serb forces overran the majority Bosniak town of Srebrenica, which had been declared a U.N. safe area after it was besieged for three years. Its pre-war population of 9,000, 75% of them Bosniaks, had been swollen to around 40,000 with refugees fleeing from surrounding areas being "ethnically cleansed". Some 160 lightly armed Dutch peacekeepers were forced to stand by as hundreds of heavily armed Serb troops entered Srebrenica after a Dutch call for air strikes was refused. The Dutch later echoed complaints by other U.N. units that the peacekeepers lacked a strong enough mandate to take on heavily armed and hostile forces who had no intention of suing for peace. The Dutch handed over several thousand Bosniaks sheltering in their base in exchange for 14 Dutch peacekeepers who had been taken hostage.

After the Serbs separated the men from women and children they slaughtered around 8,000 men, the largest mass killing in Europe since the Second World War. When the fighting was over an international criminal tribunal convicted a number of senior Bosnian Serb army officials of various crimes associated with genocide in Srebrenica. Army commander General Ratko Mladić, who became known as the "Butcher of Bosnia", and President Radovan Karadžić were sentenced to life imprisonment. Mladić evaded justice for 12 years, sheltered by Serbian security officials and later his family. Karadžić, a trained psychiatrist, managed to stay free for 16 years working under an alias at a private clinic in Belgrade specialising in alternative medicine and psychology.

The Bosnian War came to a head in August 1995 after Serb artillery in the hills struck an open market in Sarajevo, killing 37 people, and NATO launched a new round of air strikes in retaliation. A few days later Bosnian, Croatian and Yugoslav foreign ministers met in Geneva to discuss a Western peace plan to create a single sovereign Bosnian state but split into Bosnian-Herzegovina and Srpska Federations. In November delegations of all warring states flew to Dayton, Ohio in the United States and signed an agreement to end the third, though not the last of the Yugoslav wars, with Kosovo still to come. The talks were held at an air force base outside the city, deliberately chosen for security and to take the delegates out of their comfort zones and away from regular contact with the media.

As part of the agreement a new international Implementation Force (IFOR) to relieve the U.N. peacekeepers was quickly assembled, bringing together over 50,000 troops from 32 countries including non-NATO member Russia. As the forces headed for Bosnia by road, train and plane in December 1995 the main armoured division rolled across Croatia until it arrived at the Sava river on the border with Bosnia. With the only useable bridge destroyed in the early days of the war NATO engineers were faced with the task of putting together a pontoon bridge over the 300-metre wide river capable of taking 7,000 vehicles including M-1 Abrams main battle tanks, each one weighing 60 tonnes. Work was going smoothly until the river, swollen by weeks of snow and rain, burst its banks and forced the extension of the bridge by another third. After a delay of over two weeks the juggernaut began to cross as the local people watched in awe on local television.

Our local staff in Belgrade reported that the successful crossing, particularly under such adverse weather conditions, had a profound affect in Serbian households, bringing home for many a realisation that their armed forces were not remotely in the same league.

As the wars were going on in Croatia and Bosnia the situation in rump Yugoslavia was deteriorating fast, particularly after the U.N. slapped economic sanctions against Serbia and Montenegro. This was partly a response to the bombardment of the medieval Croatian coastal town of Dubrovnik, a UNESCO World Heritage Site with no military connections, which caused international outrage.

The imposition of sanctions, which cut off supplies of many essentials, had the almost inevitable effect of creating a new class of gangsters growing rich by breaking them. With truckloads of petrol and other valuable goods representing huge profits underpaid local customs and border officials were an easy touch for the criminals. Within a few months Belgrade was full of young men in sharp suits and dark glasses driving Western limousines with tinted windows, accompanied by pneumatic women dripping with jewellery.

Inflation, which had been the highest in the region, rocketed to world record levels as Milošević plundered the budget to pay for his wars and police. During the country's hyperinflation between 1992 and 1994 per capita income fell by 50%, unemployment hit 24% and monthly inflation rose to 313 million per cent, dwarfing the figure during Germany's Weimar Republic after World War One.

During this period the National Bank issued 33 different banknotes, 24 in 1993 alone, as the national mint at Topcider on a hill overlooking Belgrade was working around the clock. The last note in the series was for 500 billion dinars (500,000,000,000), which was worth less than the ink it took to print it by the time it went into circulation. I have one of the notes, snapped up in the few hours it was available before sanity prevailed and a former International Monetary Fund official ordered the dinar pegged to the West German mark. During hyperinflation restaurant prices rose between the time you ordered your meal and when you came to pay. In shops prices were changed three times a day in a desperate effort to keep ahead of the numbers.

The hyperinflation had a devastating effect on ordinary people. Most of the Reuters staff received at least part of their salary in hard currency, but most others were forced to dig into their savings. Many people, on receiving their weekly or monthly pay in dinars, went straight to their nearest black market money changer on the street, converted the whole amount into German marks or US dollars in small denominations and gradually exchanged them for dinars to keep themselves afloat until the next payday.

Some of the more enterprising citizens resorted to low-level smuggling, particularly clothes bought abroad. One of the favourite destinations was Istanbul, travelling on a local version of the famed Orient Express, where decent quality clothes could be bought relatively cheaply and sold at a profit back home. Regular travellers learned how to avoid the attentions of customs officials, including by wearing all the clothes, and how much to pay them if caught.

The Serbian media soon came under the control of the ruling Socialist Party as Milošević used it to inflame ethnic tensions and draw attention away from economic and political problems. In 1991 the government introduced a new law which resulted in the dismissal of the entire managements of state TV and radio and opened the way to the sacking of any journalists refusing to promote the official message of hate and fear towards other Yugoslav peoples. The government concentrated on controlling TV and radio, the only information source available to the vast majority of the population. There were a few independent publications but after hyperinflation struck it was reckoned that only 8% of the population could afford to buy a daily newspaper.

One of the few sources for independent news in Serbia was provided by the B-92 TV and radio station, founded in 1989 with support from George Soros's Open Society Foundation and USAID. It quickly gained a loyal, mainly youthful audience with its mixture of news, quality music and irreverent jibes at politicians of all colours. An early slogan was "Don't believe anyone – including us". The station, which was shut down four times under Milošević's rule, used to introduce the main morning news with recorded remarks of government and opposition leaders interspersed with the sound of a flushing toilet.

With the wars in Slovenia, Croatia and Bosnia settled, the Serbian government turned its attention to the one area left for "cleansing" and incorporation into an ethnically pure Greater Serbia, Kosovo.

# 33. KOSOVO

The starting point of Serbia-Kosovo relations goes back 1,300 years, when ethnic Serbs migrated to the central Balkans, then parts of the Roman and Byzantine empires. Kosovo became the centre of a Serbian empire and the site of Orthodox monasteries and churches, dozens of which had been destroyed during the ethnic troubles of the past few decades.

To this day Serbs still regard Kosovo as the cradle of their national culture, even though few chose to live there. Over the years Serb emigration and a high birth-rate among its ethnic Albanian majority saw the Serb population dwindle to 10% by the 1980s. Amid growing demands that the autonomous province be granted the status of a full republic, like other members of the federation, Kosovo Albanian students staged a series of protests in 1981 which were put down by the police.

Tension in the province mounted after Milošević revoked Kosovo's autonomy in 1989 and a Democratic League of Kosovo (LDK) was formed dedicated to gaining independence through peaceful means. It set up what became a parallel state with its own education and health systems as Albanians boycotted the official authorities.

In 1995 the Kosovo Liberation Army (KLA) made its appearance aiming to achieve independence through armed struggle and ultimately union with neighbouring Albania. It quickly gathered support from inside and outside the country after the LDK's softly-softly approach brought no let-up to official harassment and the Dayton Agreement ending the Bosnian War offered nothing for Kosovo. From outside came money from the Albanian diaspora in the USA and Europe and a mass of weapons from Albania left over from the 1997 popular revolt.

Fighting between the KLA and Serb regulars and paramilitaries broke out in 1998 and exploded into all-out warfare in March after a Serbian special anti-terrorism unit killed two brothers belonging to the KLA along with 60 members of their family.

The fighting increased in intensity and savagery through the decade and reached a pinnacle in January 1999 with the mass killing of 45 Albanians in the tiny Kosovo village of Raĉak, widely condemned as a massacre of innocent civilians. The Serbian government insisted the victims were active KLA members killed in fighting with its security forces, and a joint Yugoslav-Belarusian team appeared to confirm that. However a Finnish team brought in by the European Union concluded that the victims were unarmed civilians and called the killings a crime against humanity. The outside world was outraged and there were growing calls for military intervention by NATO.

I was called to the Kosovo capital Pristina shortly after the Raĉak killings to join a Reuters team of journalists, photographers, camera operators, video producers and translators billeted in a former brothel on the outskirts of the city. In freezing weather we went out in mixed groups, in two Land-rovers, one armoured, clutching our Serbian army press accreditation in one pocket and our KLA one in the other, hoping not to mix them up when it came to the numerous checkpoints and roadblocks across the country. This was a potentially serious issue when it involved a Serbian cameramen or Albanian translator/fixer, for both sides were capable of ordering out and taking away members of the rival ethnic group. By now journalists in the field were armed with mobile and satellite phones.

Our journalist team included Kurt Schork, who had been in Kosovo for several months teamed up with his old Reuters travelling companion from Bosnia, Greek photographer Yannis Behrakis who went on to win a stack of international awards, including a Pulitzer Prize, for his coverage of conflict zones and natural disasters across the world.

The situation in Pristina was relatively quiet, although there were occasional bomb attacks on cafés and bars. I celebrated my birthday in a restaurant on the top floor of one of the tallest buildings in town, for security, with the Reuters staff and a few other journalists.

The aftermath of the Račak killings developed into a grisly game of pass the parcel as the bodies were shunted between the village and Pristina in refrigerated trucks after the families called for a mass burial outside the village. The Serb authorities, mindful of the bad publicity this was likely to provoke, insisted they be buried in batches over three days. International peace monitors accusing both sides of using the bodies for political ends.

After a few days of standoff agreement was finally reached for a mass burial on a hill overlooking Račak, deserted apart from one old man who looked after horses and other animals. Serbian security forces had set up positions within range of the burial site but had been contacted by peacekeepers and pledged not to intervene. The burial went ahead without major incident, although at one point a KLA fighter in full uniform pushed his way through the crowd but was asked to leave by international monitors. Hundreds of people joined in to carry the dead across the muddy hillside to the freshly dug graves, an unbroken line of coffins draped with the red Albanian flag with double-headed eagle, and each with a single red rose taped to the lid.

To add another layer of misery and horror to the events in Račak, the massacre and subsequent funeral took place within sight and sound of a mental hospital, causing further anxiety to its troubled inmates. And in an ironic response to the ethnic hatred raging outside its perimeter fence, both the staff and inmates came from all over Yugoslavia, a nostalgic throw-back to the days of ethnic harmony in the country. Built just after the end of World War Two, the asylum housed 350 inmates. They and many of the 100-odd staff included Croats, Bosnians and Macedonians, as well as ethnic Albanians, Serbs and Montenegrins.

"There is no nationalism here, we are from all over Yugoslavia," the institution's director Vesna Stamenkovic said. "Neither staff nor patients differentiate between each other's origins."

"I am proud of this institution because in spite of all our problems we have kept above this nationalism poison."

"Inside here we are punished only by God. Outside it is worse, for there men punish one another."

While the funeral was going on Kurt was heading to Rambouillet, in France, after the KLA agreed to attend talks with a Yugoslav delegation on a peace plan drawn up by the NATO Contact Group for the Balkans that included Russia. Much to everyone's surprise he showed up in the Kosovo office two days later, before the talks had really started. He explained that he had written a background piece trying to set the meeting in context, recalling that it was a short distance geographically from Rambouillet to Versailles outside Paris, but a huge jump historically. The Versailles and Paris accords at the end of World War I established a new European order including a Serb-Croat-Slovene state that became Yugoslavia. It was a fine piece running to about 800 words. The Reuters Paris bureau chief, a newly appointed young journalist from the financial sector apparently unaware of Kurt's unusual status, read the piece, declared features must be no longer than 500 words and ordered him to cut it. The edict appeared to be part of a perennial battle between Reuters finance department editors wanting short snappy pieces for their business clients and general news journalists who sought more space for important and complex stories.

Kurt announced he would return immediately to his hotel, sent the piece uncut to London via his personal satellite phone, and flew straight back to Kosovo. He arrived in Pristina, the piece was issued by London amid wide praise, and nothing further was said.

The peace plan called for NATO to administer Kosovo as an autonomous province within Yugoslavia, backed by 30,000 NATO troops to maintain order and unhindered right of passage for all NATO troops across Yugoslavia, including Kosovo. The plan was doomed from the start as the Kosovo side insisted on full independence and the Serbs fiercely opposed an international role in the governance of Kosovo, particularly the presence of NATO troops on its territory. There was a widespread view, expressed among others by former U.S. Secretary of State Henry Kissinger, that the plan was designed to fail.

The agreement was signed on March 18, 1999, by the U.S., British and Albanian delegations, while the Serbian and Russian teams refused. Two days later monitors from the Organisation for Security and Cooperation in Europe (OSCE) were withdrawn from Kosovo for their safety in anticipation of a NATO decision to bomb Serbia, boosted by continued public outrage over the Račak killings. Two days after that, March 24th, NATO planes began attacking Serbian positions in Kosovo and the rest of Serbia including eventually the capital Belgrade, in a campaign that lasted 11 weeks. It was the first NATO military action without specific approval from the U.N. Security Council.

On the evening of the 24th Serbian radio and TV announced:

"Attention, attention, this is an air raid. Turn off the electricity, turn off the gas. Open your windows, put the blinds down, draw the curtains. Take your essentials and go to the nearest shelter."

The Serb military responded immediately by going on a rampage of killing, wholesale destruction of villages and forcible expulsion of their inhabitants at gunpoint. Albanian civilians were often used as human shields to escort military convoys across the territory, while in some areas Serbs used local health centres as protective cover for military attacks. An estimated 7,000 to 9,000 Kosovo Albanians were killed and some 800,000 fled to neighbouring Albania and Macedonia, while a further 500,000 were internally displaced within Kosovo, meaning some 90% of Kosovo Albanians had to leave their homes.

The NATO bombing started by attacking military targets, but after the Serbs showed no signs of ending their brutal campaign it switched to strategic targets such as transport links, particularly bridges. Some of these caused major civilian casualties, such as one when NATO missiles fired from U.S. aircraft hit a train on a railway bridge crossing a river near Grdelica, south of Belgrade, killing an estimated 20 civilians. An attack on a crowd of Albanian refugees on a road in Kosovo by aircraft mistaking it for a military convoy killed over 70 people. After reporters visited the scene and established the victims were civilians, many with tractors, NATO apologised.

Serbia's second city Novi Sad was the target for some of the heaviest strikes of the campaign as oil refineries, roads and telecommunication relay stations deemed to be key military installations were knocked out. The three bridges across the river Danube linking the two halves of the city were destroyed, forcing inhabitants to put together a temporary pontoon bridge made of barges, which was then pushed across by three small boats.

*East Germans burst through the border during the Paneuropean picnic. Tamas Lobenwein, Paneuropean '89 Picnic Foundation*

*East Germans duck under border barrier before guards could open it. Reuters, Laszlo Balogh*

*Abandoned East German Trabants left in Prague streets after owners flee to West*

*Palace of the People, Bucharest. HP gruesen, goodfreephotos*

*East and West Berliners join each other on the Wall after it opened*
*(9 November 1989). creative Commons Attribution*

*Opposition poster for 1990 Hungarian elections.*
*Text reads - "which would you prefer"*

*Funeral of 45 Kosovo Albanians in Raĉak village killed by Serbs.*
*Yannis Behrakis, Reuters*

*Serbs floated across Danube after NATO destroys Novi Sad bridges. Darko Dozet*

# 34. BELGRADE HIT

On April 3 1999, 11 days into the campaign, cruise missiles fired from U.S. and British vessels in the Adriatic slammed without warning into targets in downtown Belgrade, including the Yugoslav and Serbian interior ministries and the police headquarters. A NATO statement said the attack was directed "at the core of the regime's ability to conduct the campaign against the Kosovar Albanians". A NATO general described it as "going after the head of the snake".

The following day Belgrade residents emerged in a daze, some crying, others voicing their outrage against NATO. Many Serbs vented their anger at Western embassies. An American flag was hoisted outside the U.S. embassy with the stars replaced by swastikas. At the Canadian mission glass doors were smashed and "The Quebec Republic" smeared on the walls, an oblique reference to the independence aspirations of Kosovo Albanians.

Yugoslav Deputy Prime Minister Vuk Drašković compared the attack to the three-day air raid on Belgrade by Nazi forces in 1941 leading to their takeover of the city.

"Downtown Belgrade is in flames," he told CNN television. "They're pushing Europe very close to European war, to disaster of our mankind. Please give peace a chance."

Reuters was scrambling to send another journalist to Belgrade to support our hard-pressed correspondent, but the Yugoslav authorities were refusing visas for citizens of NATO countries. I was in London, having just been granted British citizenship, after finally meeting the requirement of spending seven consecutive years in the UK – 44 years after first arriving in Britain – but I kept my Australian nationality and passport. I applied for a two-week visa, the Yugoslav consular department concluded that Australia was not part of "Operation Noble Anvil" (the Serbs called it "Merciful Angel", a prime case of 'lost in translation'), and the following day I was on a plane to Budapest, where I was picked up by the office driver from Belgrade, 380 kilometres away.

It was a strange feeling driving through the Yugoslav countryside watching NATO jets screaming overhead on the way to bombing their targets. The idea of war going on in Europe at the end of the 20th century was difficult to grasp. It was even more surreal arriving in Belgrade, where at first glance life was going on as normal. NATO bomb damage was confined to a few targets, struck repeatedly by missiles but leaving other buildings largely intact, but the attacks on the city were continuing, mostly at night. The six bridges linking the city across the Sava River were still standing after civilians, mindful of what had happened in Navi Sad, came out in their thousands and occupied them. Many of the citizens, including children, wore tee-shirts emblazoned with a target motif and the words "I am a target".

By the time I arrived in the country public anger had subsided somewhat, replaced by a feeling of hurt and disappointment that the World War Two Allied powers had turned on one of their staunchest wartime supporters. With the government controlling the air waves and most of the written media, the bulk of the Serbian population were unaware of the full extent of Serbian military and police activity in Kosovo, and the international reaction to it. Even among the most educated there was a feeling that Serbia was being unduly punished for carrying out legitimate actions.

This sense of deep sorrow over the current NATO action came out clearly in talking to Zivorad Mihailovic, a former partisan who guided downed allied pilots out of Yugoslavia and worked with Winston Churchill's son Randolph during World War Two.

"Of course I'm disappointed," the 79-year-old journalist and writer said in an interview. "We rescued them, and their successors are now paying us back," looking angrily up into the sky as air-raid sirens sounded warning of impending air strikes.

Asked for his thoughts on having German planes once again in the skies over Yugoslavia, he replied: "It's awful. But I would not like to be in a German pilot's boots when he is shot down. Come to think of it, I wouldn't like to be in an American or British pilot's boots. They're all the same now."

Of Randolph Churchill, who was parachuted into Yugoslavia in 1944 as an intelligence officer, he said: "He impressed all of us because although he walked with a stick, he never bent or ducked when there was shooting. He had plenty of guts."

Mihailovic was contemptuous of NATO's tactics of high-level bombing raids and strikes by long-distance guided missiles, citing an old Serbian saying "they fight like whores."

"They don't have the guts to fight a proper war. You can't see them and they are dropping bombs on you. Let's look each other in the eye and have a proper battle, hand-to-hand, and see who wins and who loses," said Mihailovic, who was wounded twice during the war.

"This is the Nazis' way of fighting. They thought they could bomb, bomb, bomb, and then come in with ground troops. And they also used to use other nationals to do their fighting - just as the Americans are doing now."

I had a discussion with a group of doctors in Belgrade's main hospital where I had gone to report on civilian injuries from the bombing. They made a direct comparison with their actions and the UK government's military intervention in Northern Ireland against Irish nationalist guerrillas fighting to reunify the province with the Irish Republic. My attempts to point out the major differences between the two cases fell on deaf ears. Some of the doctors, particularly the older ones, felt that the wartime allies should have supported the Chetniks, a Yugoslav royalist, nationalist guerrilla force rather than the communist partisans under Tito. History records that the allies had supported both groups at the beginning of the war but switched to the partisans as the Chetniks began collaborating with the Nazis and were reluctant to kill their soldiers, fearing reprisals. Winston Churchill was reported as opting for the partisans "because they kill more Germans".

Foreign reporters were directed to an international press centre set up in the Serbian army headquarters in downtown Belgrade. On the roof of the building Reuters had set up a system linked to a satellite enabling us to send out not just our own photos and video material, but those of other news organisations, at a price. Television correspondents voicing their reports on the roof made a habit of positioning themselves within view of one of Belgrade's key bridges linking the two parts of the city in anticipation that one day NATO's patience would run out and they would destroy it, live on camera.

In the first really controversial attack by NATO – the whole campaign was seen by many outside as illegal and disproportionate – the Serbian state radio and TV building was hit by a single missile on April 23, killing 16 members of staff. Less than 24 hours after the attack the radio returned to the air broadcasting from a secret location. The word around Belgrade was that the broadcaster had been warned of an imminent strike, but Milošević, regarding the station as crucial to his propaganda campaign, had insisted staff stay at their places. According to sources in Belgrade senior editors at the station were forced to go around with bodyguards for weeks after the attack for fear of reprisals by family members of the victims. Reports that there had been a warning were confirmed later by a top NATO general who said a question had been planted at an international news conference whose reply indicated an attack was imminent.

Meanwhile NATO were stepping up their attacks on Serbia's infrastructure, hitting power plants with sophisticated bombs releasing carbon filaments that short-circuited the system without causing lasting damage. The plants were up and running several days later, but the effect on civilian morale was huge as up to 70% of power at a time was knocked out, according to our local staff.

Helping to keep up morale was a unique internet site set up by volunteers to inform anxious Yugoslavs and the outside world when and where the next NATO bombs were landing and which areas were affected by power cuts and other shortages. In what was possibly the first organised use of social media during a war, www.belgrade.com was set up at the start of the bombing by a handful of dedicated computer buffs working 18 hours a day. It was receiving an astonishing nine million "hits", the number of times it was accessed, every day. When electricity went down across Serbia after NATO knocked out the power stations, beograd.com brought in a generator to run the computers and was soon back in business.

"We set up the site when the air strikes began, giving the e-mail addresses of all the local radio stations in Yugoslavia so that people could call and find out how their relatives were faring," said 43-year-old computer graphics designer Nenad Cosic.

"It was basically to provide a service, as the telephone lines were completely overloaded," he added. "We had no idea it would grow into this."

As he was speaking a message flashed across his screen. "A few minutes ago the vampires flew over Skopje (Macedonia) towards you. I hope they don't return - shoot them down."

A few minutes later, another message landed from Novi Sad. "It's quiet tonight, but very tense, we're waiting for them. I just heard something - is it thunder or is it NATO?"

Some attacks, particularly those involving conventional bombs as opposed to the smart missiles landing on Belgrade, were first picked up by countries outside the bombing zone like the Czech Republic and Slovakia as the bombers passed overhead. "They're on their way - good luck," was one such message.

The site also carried pictures and sound. When cruise missiles struck army headquarters in central Belgrade a resident living across the road had a microphone hanging out of his window, and the recording went on the website.

"It had a big impact. An American guy wrote in that it was the most terrifying sound he had ever heard and brought home to him what it must be like to be in Belgrade," Cosic said.

One attack during the night of May 7 proved to be the most controversial of all, leaving a relatively small death toll but a huge political headache for NATO, particularly the Americans. Late at night the city was rocked by a huge explosion, and I joined other reporters rushing to the scene, following the sirens of ambulances and police. The target turned out to be the Chinese embassy, a white marble and blue mirrored glass building located some distance from downtown Belgrade, flying the Chinese flag. From the front, in pitch darkness, the damage appeared to be slight. But on further inspection from the rear it was clear that one part of the complex had been completely destroyed. Two Chinese officials with bloodied faces emerged from the building and announced that three Chinese journalists had been killed and 20 staff injured in the attack. The embassy was one of the few in Belgrade that included living quarters for some staff members.

As the Chinese government voiced its outrage and students attacked the US embassy in Beijing, Washington announced it was a mistake. The director of the US Central Intelligence Agency told a congressional committee the bombing, the only one organised and directed by his agency, was using the wrong coordinates for a Yugoslav military target in the same street. That turned out to be the Federal directorate for Supply and Procurement, which coordinated weapons imports and exports. Meanwhile rumours circulated in Belgrade that the embassy was being used as a secret communications hub for Yugoslav security forces fighting NATO.

The US explanation was met by widespread scepticism among governments around the world, including some NATO members, and journalists who had seen the results of the raid. The embassy was situated in the middle of a large green open space and was at least 100 metres from the Yugoslav office building. The precision of the attack, leaving the ambassador's Mercedes and four flower pots at the entrance unscathed, suggested that the embassy, particularly the military attaché's office at the rear, was the real target. One NATO source commented later that "far from not knowing the target was an embassy, they must have been given architect's drawings".

When a US congressman emerged from a meeting and blamed the problem on old maps, I felt a response was required. Travelling to the city centre I bought the cheapest Belgrade city map from a local newsagent. The Chinese embassy was clearly marked, with a red Chinese flag for emphasis. I wrote a piece for Reuters basically saying that NATO could have saved themselves a lot of bother – at the time the alliance was seeking to include China in efforts to find a peaceful solution for Kosovo – for the price of just one English pound.

While senior officials continued to deny the embassy had been deliberately targeted some commentators disagreed. Six months after the event the London Sunday Observer claimed it had been singled out because it was being used to relay messages to Arkan's dreaded White Tigers fighting alongside Yugoslav forces in Kosovo. This view was given some support by the fact that on the same night as the embassy attack the nearby Yugoslavia Hotel, where the Tigers were thought to have had a base, was also bombed. I visited the hotel the morning after the embassy bombing and found Arkan outside the damaged hotel denying that his black-uniformed men were using it, and scornfully accusing NATO of another blunder. For a man sought by half the world's police forces, as well as an international war crimes tribunal, he was surprisingly relaxed, speaking excellent English and fashionably dressed in a suit and tie.

With so many potential enemies the past was bound to catch up with him eventually. On January 15 in 2000 he was shot by a junior police officer as he was drinking with colleagues in the lobby of Belgrade's Intercontinental Hotel and died on the way to hospital. Western countries hoping to bring him to justice for his war crimes were outraged. His assassin Dobrosav Gavric fled the scene and found his way eventually to South Africa, where he was fighting efforts to extradited him back to Serbia.

There was another bomb attack on May 7, which turned out to be one of the busiest days in the whole campaign and proved to be another own goal for NATO. Fighter jets of the Royal Netherlands Air Force dropped two containers of cluster bombs over Niš, Serbia's third largest city located 150 miles south-east of Belgrade, aimed at the airport. But when released in the air the bomblets drifted in the wind to the city centre some 3 kms from the target, landing near a hospital, bus depot and market. The explosions killed 14 civilians and injured 20 others and provoked more outrage both at home and abroad. Five days later there was another misdirected attack by the Dutch when cluster bombs landed in a part of Niš some 7 kms from the airport, injuring 11 civilians, some requiring amputation. One man died months later when he picked up an unexploded bomb. After the second incident the Dutch stopped using cluster bombs in the campaign, though other NATO forces continued with them.

There was a curious incident a couple of days after the embassy bombing when I was dining alone in a popular fish restaurant on the Danube. The BBC's correspondent Jacky Rowland was at another table celebrating with her local assistant who was getting married the next day. I was invited to join them and we were having a jolly evening with the wine flowing until a plain-clothes policeman burst into the restaurant and took us to an office where we were interrogated for several hours. It appeared that someone in the restaurant had complained about our behaviour, accusing us of laughing over the deaths of the Chinese journalists. It was an unlikely scenario as the restaurant, Reka, run by two former female journalists of the national news agency Tanjug, was known as a liberal establishment that often played popular Croatian songs which were banned in Serbia. I was ordered to appear at the office handling visas for foreign journalists the next day with my passport, and my Yugoslav visa was cancelled on the spot.

Strolling over to the army press centre I asked the duty officer if it was normal for the police to override the army press office's accreditation. He looked at me, barked "who did this", and on hearing my reply picked up a phone, hurled a stream of invective down the line and told me to go immediately back to the visa office with my passport, and a very sheepish official issued me with a new three-week visa. It was an interesting illustration of the army's power within Milošević's regime.

As the bombing campaign continued Yugoslavs increasingly resorted to black humour as they were forced to deal with disruptions to heating, power and communications, delivered by countries that until recently most of them regarded as friendly.

According to a joke doing the rounds a Japanese and a German were trying to comfort a Serb who was weeping uncontrollably. Assuming he was upset over the destruction of the country's infrastructure the Japanese reminded him that his country recovered from atom-bomb attacks on Hiroshima and Nagasaki and prospered. The German recalled that his country emerged from the ruins of World War Two an economic powerhouse with the help of the Marshall Plan.

"The trouble is," the Serb wailed, "I'm afraid we are going to win."

The strips of sticky tape criss-crossing thousands of windows throughout Serbia and its sister republic Montenegro, in an effort to minimise the effects of flying glass, were known collectively as "Windows 99", a reference to Microsoft's popular computer operating system.

A joke about Serbia's second city Novi Sad, where all three bridges over the Danube were knocked out, was "what's the name of the river flowing over Zezelj Bridge?" As to the quickest way from Belgrade to Novi Sad, some 80 km north of Belgrade, the answer was to take a train to the Montenegrin port of Bar in the south, cross the Adriatic to Bari in Italy, another train to Aviano where a major NATO air base was located "and there's a flight every 30 minutes".

Some jokes referred to what was known as "special purpose" production in some factories making ordinary commercial goods but also known to turn out weapons and ammunition. Some of these concerns had been repeatedly targeted by NATO. One joke had an elderly employee in a vacuum cleaner factory who, after being presented with one of the products as a long service award, said: "I followed the assembly instructions, but each time it came out looking like a Kalashnikov."

The downing of a U.S.-made F-117 stealth fighter early in the conflict, despite claims that the planes could not be seen by ordinary radar, provided a rich vein of humour. "Sorry, I didn't know it was invisible," was one slogan that had been copied onto thousands of badges and tee-shirts worn across the country.

"Only Radovan Karadzic is invisible," another slogan said, referring to the former Bosnian Serb leader who had been charged with war crimes by the U.N. tribunal in the Hague, but was still at large more than three years after the Bosnian war ended. "The stealth fighter needs some Viagra," was yet another variation on a theme.

One slogan seen scribbled on a wall in the Belgrade suburb of Batajnica, which was next to a military airport that had been hammered virtually nightly since the raids began, read: "We are just gypsies here - the airport is a bit further." In contrast, in another town that had not been hit once in several weeks, a sign was spotted reading: "Why haven't you hit us? - we haven't got the plague". Residents reported that it was hit soon afterwards.

As the daily bombing continued, we received word that the animals in Belgrade zoo were behaving strangely, and I went there to interview director Vuk Bojović.

"The noise starts around half an hour before the bombs fall as the animals pick up the sound of approaching planes and missiles," he said, adding: "It's one of the strangest and most disturbing concerts you can hear anywhere."

"It builds up in intensity as the planes approach -- only they can hear them, we can't -- and when the bombs start falling it's like a choir of the insane. Peacocks screaming, wolves howling, dogs barking, chimpanzees rattling their cages."

"I have made a record every hour of each day of when the animals start acting up. One day, when this craziness is over, I'd like to check it with reliable data on when the planes were flying. "Someone could make a scientific study out of it."

Bojović said the zoo had been hard hit by the power and water shortages. "I had 1,000 eggs of rare and endangered species incubating, some of them ready to hatch in a couple of days. They were all ruined. That's 1,000 lives lost."

Meat in the zoo's freezer defrosted and went off, making it suitable only for scavengers like hyenas and vultures. Belgrade people donated meat from their home freezers when the power went down, "but most of it wasn't even fit for animals." The lack of water meant that some animals, particularly the hippos, were literally swimming in their excrement.

Many of the animals aborted their young in the latter stages of pregnancy, while many birds abandoned their nests, leaving eggs to grow cold. Even a snake aborted some 40 foetuses, apparently reacting to the heavy vibration shaking the ground as missiles hit targets nearby.

The worst night was when NATO hit an army headquarters only 600 meters away, with a huge detonation. `The next day we found that some of the animals had killed their young," the director said. "A female tiger killed two of her four three-day-old cubs, and the other two were so badly injured we couldn't save them."

The grimmest spinoff of the war was the sight of armed guards patrolling the zoo.

"They're not there to keep people from harming or stealing the animals," Bojović said. "Their job is to shoot the animals if the zoo gets bombed and some of them try and break out."

I left Belgrade at the end of May and returned to London after Reuters managed to send in a replacement, and three weeks later, after talks on a peace deal involving NATO and Russia, U.N. Secretary General Javier Solana announced the end of the bombing campaign. A day later the KLA, under NATO pressure, agreed to disarm.

According to most estimates some 13,500 people of all nationalities were killed during the Kosovo war, including 8,500 Kosovo Albanian civilians. Nearly 500 Yugoslav civilians died in the bombing campaign in the rest of Yugoslavia.

# 35. OVERTHROW OF MILOŠEVIĆ

Back in Belgrade in August 1999, I attended a football match which developed into an anti-government protest as the democratic opposition was increasing pressure on the man who had led the country to four disastrous wars. Almost inevitably, the match was between the deadliest of rivals, Serbia, still operating as the Republic of Yugoslavia, and now-independent Croatia.

The match, a qualifier for the European Championships, was held on the eve of a major opposition rally calling for Milošević to step down, and the government went out of its way to try to prevent it becoming a warm-up for that event. It was reported to have bought one third of the 70,000 seats in the stadium, Croatian fans were banned from attending and tickets were issued to Yugoslav embassies, football clubs and state institutions in an attempt to keep hooligans away. The authorities were well aware of the explosive potential of football matches involving the two countries. In 1990 a clash between Dinamo Zagreb and Red Star Belgrade, two of the top teams in the Yugoslav league, descended into rioting off the pitch in which 60 people were injured, either stabbed, shot or poisoned by tear-gas. The match, held just one week after Croatia staged its first multi-party elections for almost 50 years won by pro-independence parties, was widely seen as sparking off the bloody four-year Yugoslavia-Croatia war that erupted in 1991.

In a tense atmosphere the latest match ended in a goalless draw. Expectations of possible violence on the pitch came to nothing as the players, many of whom knew each other from playing together in the old Yugoslav team, treated each other mainly with respect. The main input came from the crowd, which started chanting "Slobo go away" and "the rally is tomorrow". I was with a small group of foreign journalists accompanied by a young lady from the foreign ministry press department, who translated the crowd's jibes without any obvious reluctance. The match was marred by a power failure which shut off the floodlights and forced a 40-minute delay.

I led my report for Reuters with: "What threatened to be the ultimate grudge match turned into a protest against the government and descended into farce when the floodlights went out."

The rally the following day, the first major test of the fragmented opposition, drew a crowd of over 100,000 in front of parliament shouting "resign" and "leave, Slobo, leave". Leading opposition figure Vuk Drašković told the crowd: "Serbia is in jail. We are in jail because ...it is led by those who are totally isolated from the world." However the event fell short of expectations, partly because the government had announced the previous day that early elections would be held by the end of the year, a move clearly aimed at undermining the opposition.

That poll failed to materialise, but in July 2000 Milošević announced presidential elections for September, after changing the laws to enable him to run for two consecutive terms if successful.

A month before the elections Ivan Stambulić, a former Serbian president and prime minister and political mentor of Milošević, disappeared while jogging near his home. While the former leader had kept a low profile after falling out with his protégé in 1988, some people had expected him to run against Milošević in the forthcoming poll, and the president was widely seen as being behind the disappearance. Stambulić's bullet-ridden body was discovered three years later, and Milosevic was formally accused of organising the killing in 2005 when he was already in the Hague facing war crimes charges.

What effect the incident had on the elections outcome was unclear, but early in 2000 the 18 different opposition parties formed the Democratic Opposition of Serbia (DOS) and picked Serb nationalist politician Vojislav Koštunica as their candidate for the presidency.

The election took place on September 24, and the opposition coalition announced that Koštunica had gained over 50% of the votes, enough to defeat Milošević in the first round, However the government electoral commission declared that the challenger was short of a majority and there would be a second round of voting.

The commission's figures showed Milošević had polled strongly in Montenegro and Kosovo, despite the vote being largely boycotted in both places. These and other discrepancies in the poll prompted the opposition to accuse the government of election fraud and call for peaceful protests aimed at overthrowing it.

As I tried unsuccessfully to get back to Belgrade, with the Serbian government refusing to issue visas to journalists, the protests began a few days later, starting with coal miners who provided the country with most of its electricity. They reached their height on October 5 when several hundred thousand people from all over Serbia arrived in Belgrade and chanted "He's finished, He's finished" - and he was.

The October 5 protest that succeeded in bringing down Milošević was popularly known as the "Bulldozer Revolution" after one of the protesters used a heavy loading vehicle to charge a building housing Serbian State Television (RTS), which was quickly renamed "New RTS".

Milošević, who a few weeks earlier had offered to resign, but only after his term expired in June 2001, stepped down two days later having finally run out of options. In April 2001 he was detained by police and later transferred to the Hague to stand trial on war crimes at the International Criminal Tribunal for the Former Yugoslavia. He died in his cell in March 2006 a few months before the conclusion of his four-year trial.

His downfall coincided with the end of my assignment in former Yugoslavia, and the end of my time in Reuters. After 34 mainly happy years I took early retirement in 2001, and, wanting to give something back, spent the next 10 years training journalists around the world for the Reuters Foundation.

# EPILOGUE

Looking back over the 40 years covered by this memoir, much has changed, though familiar problems remain.

In Asia, the "Domino Theory", the idea of capitalist states in South-East Asia falling one by one to communism exported by military force from China, fizzled out when Vietnam introduced its own nationalist version after booting out the Americans in 1975 and brought it to neighbouring Cambodia and Laos. By the end of the 20th century Vietnam and Laos were run along one-party Marxist lines, but operating Western-style market economies while Cambodia was a one-party constitutional monarchy. All three countries have joined the Association of South-East Asian Nations (ASEAN), a 10-nation organisation set up to facilitate economic, political, security and military cooperation. It was created in 1967 by five capitalist countries in the region worried by the spread of communism.

All three countries have become popular tourist destinations, particularly Vietnam where the elaborate network of tunnels used by the Viet Cong and North Vietnamese as hiding places and supply centres during their war against the U.S. are a top attraction. And the famous Ho Chi Minh Trail now refers to a string of championship golf courses running parallel to the elusive system of jungle paths from north to south, much bombed by the Americans, used to supply Communist troops during the war.

The former bogeyman China, under its ambitious new ruler Xi Jinping, has turned its attention to much farther afield, seeking to spread its influence not through force but through its massive economic muscle and diplomacy. In 2013 it launched a global infrastructure strategy targeting over 70 countries and economic organisations known as the Belt and Road initiative, recalling the ancient Silk Road trade route linking China with central Asia and the Middle East.

However Beijing has not given up entirely on wielding the stick. Having pledged to maintain Hong Kong's special political status giving it wide-ranging freedoms when it took over the colony from Britain in 1997, it has introduced a new security law cancelling most of them and cracked down hard on demonstrators. Beijing has also stepped up military activity in strategic islands in the South China Sea claimed by several countries, and has increased pressure on Taiwan, which it has long considered part of China.

East Timor was finally recognised as an independent country by the United Nations in 2002, and renamed Timor Leste, from the Portuguese which remains one of the official languages. Relations with Indonesia have warmed considerably since Suharto's military regime has given way to democracy. It is Timor Leste's largest trading partner, and as many of the new countries' students are in higher education in Indonesia as in Dili.

In Europe former Soviet Bloc countries, freed of communism imposed on them by Moscow, eagerly embraced multi-party democracy and market capitalism and joined the European Community and NATO.

Meanwhile the situation in former Yugoslavia is far from clear. The most pro-Western former republics Slovenia and Croatia have joined the EU, in 2004 and 2013 respectively, while the rest are languishing on the waiting list. Macedonia, one of the first republics to break away, had its accession delayed after Greece complained that its name implied territorial ambitions over a Greek province with the same name. After extended negotiations both sides agreed on North Macedonia, and accession talks were started, but were blocked again, this time by Bulgaria over a 2017 joint friendship treaty covering thorny historical issues.

Serbia's application has been stalled by its failure to settle relations with its province Kosovo, whose unilateral declaration of independence has been recognised by most, but not all of EU and NATO countries.

In the Herzeg-Bosna entity of former Bosnia deep divisions remain. Schools are often divided according to ethnicity, with Bosniak and Croatian pupils attending different classes in the same building, with different entrances, and a fence separating play areas. Occupying the other half of the country is an all-Serb entity the Srpska Republic.

There are indications that the younger generation for whom the Yugoslav wars are increasingly becoming history may be able to put the past behind them. When I was doing a training course in Sarajevo the young journalists, from all over former Yugoslavia, learned together and socialised happily together after work.

# Acknowledgments

This memoir was compiled from newspaper cuttings of my stories over the years, and from my fast-fading memory.

I would like to thank two people who encouraged me to write it, my wife Sigi and my old friend from university Allan Dickie.

I would also like to thank a number of former colleagues and friends who supplied advice, corrections, and, in some cases, encouragement that it should reach a wider public. These include Annette von Broecker, Margaret Smart, David Broucher, Peter Humphrey, Chris Parkin, Sophie Dow, Brendan Keenan, Graham Stewart, Michael Žantovský, Stephen and Maria Wilmer, Ann Kennedy, John Rogers, Derek Parr. Special thanks for David Cutler, of Reuters archives, who dug out a few of my old stories not covered by the old Reuters cuttings service, long since disappeared.